PARDONS by the PRESIDENT

Final report of the names of persons
who lived in
Alabama, Virginia, West Virginia, or Georgia,
were engaged in rebellion and pardoned
by the President, Andrew Johnson.

HERITAGE BOOKS, INC.
1986

Published By

HERITAGE BOOKS, INC.
3602 Maureen Lane, Bowie, MD 20715

ISBN: 978-1-55613-025-0

40TH CONGRESS, 2d Session. | HOUSE OF REPRESENTATIVES. | Ex. Doc. No. 16.

PARDONS BY THE PRESIDENT.

MESSAGE

FROM

THE PRESIDENT OF THE UNITED STATES,

TRANSMITTING

Final report of the names of persons engaged in rebellion who have been pardoned by the President.

DECEMBER 4, 1867.—Referred to the Committee on the Judiciary and ordered to be printed.

To the House of Representatives:

I transmit herewith a final report from the Attorney General, additional to reports submitted by him December 31, 1866, March 2, 1867, and July 8, 1867, in reply to a resolution of the House of Representatives of December 10, 1866, requesting a "list of names of all persons engaged in the late rebellion against the United States government who have been pardoned by the President from April 15, 1865, to this date; that said list shall also state the rank of each person who has been so pardoned, if he has been engaged in the military service of the so-called confederate government, and the position, if he shall have held any civil office under said so-called confederate government; and shall also further state whether such person has, at any time prior to April 14, 1861, held any office under the United States government; and if so, what office; together with the reasons for granting such pardons; and also the names of the person or persons at whose solicitation such pardon was granted."

ANDREW JOHNSON.

WASHINGTON, *December* 4, 1867.

ALABAMA.

Name.	Exemption under amnesty proclamation of May 29, 1865.	By whom recommended.	Date of pardon.
William W. Allen	Rebel brigadier general, and worth over $20,000	Governor Parsons	Sept. 12, 1865.
John D. Alexander	Rebel agent of the nitre and mining bureau, and worth over $20,000.	do	Sept. 12, 1865.
D. C. Anderson	Rebel receiver under the sequestration law	Governor Parsons and F. M. Kellogg, late treasury agent	Sept. 9, 1865.
R. T. Abernathy	Proceedings commenced for confiscation	Joseph C. Bradley	May 10, 1866.
William M. Allen	Ex-United States and rebel postmaster	Governor Parsons	Oct. 6, 1865.
William C. Adamson	Rebel postmaster	do	Oct. 13, 1865.
R. J. Allen	do	do	Feb. 21, 1866.
Henry C. Arnold	do	R. Sherman, United States marshal for Rhode Island district	Sept. 8, 1865.
Robert Alexander	do	Governor Parsons	Mar. 2, 1866.
George C. Arrington	do	do	Mar. 15, 1866.
Robert Allen	Rebel postmaster, and worth over $20,000	do	Mar. 2, 1866.
Lewis Alexander	Rebel tax collector	do	Sept. 12, 1865.
George G. Armistead	Worth over $20,000	Governor Patton	June 11, 1866.
W. E. Alexander	do	Governor Parsons	Sept. 20, 1865.
Charles D. Anderson	do	Governor Parsons and Joseph C. Bradley	Sept. 25, 1865.
D. S. Arnold	do	Governor Parsons	Sept. 18, 1865.
Bryant Avery	do	do	Sept. 11, 1865.
C. P. Antomarchi	do	do	Sept. 13, 1865.
Fountain Armstead	do	do	Jan. 29, 1866.
A. Abercombie	do	do	Feb. 21, 1866.
C. T. Abercombie	do	do	Feb. 21, 1866.
Caroline Alston	do	do	Oct. 25, 1865.
Hilliard J. Askew	do	Governor Parsons and W. B. Mordawell	Nov. 13, 1865.
A. W. Arnold	do	Governor Parsons	Oct. 25, 1865.
Benj. Averett	do	do	Dec. 2, 1865.
W. W. Allen	do	do	Sept. 12, 1865.
George E. Allen	do	do	Oct. 18, 1865.
John Atkins	do	do	Feb. 2, 1866.
William Abney	do	do	Dec. 2, 1865.
John Ardis	do	do	Mar. 2, 1866.
Henry Avery, sr.	do	do	Mar. 2, 1866.
Wm. H. Anderson	do	do	Mar. 2, 1866.
William A. Allen	do	do	Sept. 16, 1865.
John T. Abernathy	do	Governor Parsons, D. C. Humphreys, D. P. Lewis, and Joseph C. Bradley	Sept. 15, 1865.
Asa Amason	do	Governor Parsons, William Foy, J. A. Gibbs, D. C. White, L. B. Williamson, jr., A. T. Torbert, J. S. Wilder, R. G. McMahon, R. F. Stuart, H. G. Johnston, Jacinth Jackson, E. H. Watts, and T. R. Kendall.	Oct. 7, 1865.
Elbert Amason	do	Governor Parsons, G. A. Brown, G. B. Mobley, W. V. Hare, W. O. Winston, Amos Travis, A. J. Hodge, E. Allen, George H. Dunlap, H. P. Snow, John A. Winston, A. D. Hall, B. Garner, A. H. Griffin, and William Foy.	Oct. 7, 1865.
Jacob Abraham	do	Governor Parsons	Apr. 4, 1865.
John C. Anderson	do	do	Sept. 12, 1865.
R. H. Adams	do	do	Sept. 12, 1865.

A. F. Alexander	do	do	Sept. 12, 1865.
Talbot Adams	do	Governor Parsons, L. Oliver, B. Garner, T. D. Bell, A. D. Hall, G. B. Mobley, William L. Wilkinson, W. E. Chambliss, Evan Allen, William H. Gill, William D. Stanton, and H. P. Snow.	Sept. 12, 1865.
John Allison	do	Governor Parsons	Nov. 6, 1865.
Felix L. Ashley	do	do	Sept. 12, 1865.
J. T. Andrew	do	do	Sept. 12, 1865.
H. H. Allen	do	do	May 19, 1866.
John G. Allen	do	do	Oct. 12, 1865.
Samuel L. Arrington	do	do	—— —, 1865.
William Acklen	do	do	Sept. 29, 1865.
Joseph C. Bradley	Member of the rebel State legislature, and tax collector.	By order of the President	June 17, 1865.
N. H. Brown	Rebel cotton agent, and worth over $20,000	Governor Parsons	Oct. 6, 1865.
M. H. Bloodgood	Rebel agent to England, and worth over $20,000	Major General Butterfield	Sept. 21, 1865.
W. G. Browning	Agent of rebel nitre and mining bureau, and worth over $20,000.	Governor Parsons	Oct. 12, 1865.
Jos. L. Browning	do	do	Oct. 12, 1865.
Jonathan Bliss	Rebel receiver, and worth over $20,000	do	Mar. 2, 1866.
James Bond	Commissioner of rebel States	do	Sept. 8, 1865.
Lloyd Bowers	Ex-United States and rebel postmaster	do	Dec. 2, 1865.
David M. Bush	do	do	Sept. 29, 1865.
Henry W. Box	do	do	Nov. 2, 1865.
Allen Barber	Rebel postmaster	do	Oct. 2, 1865.
H. W. Bowers	do	do	Oct. 2, 1865.
Wm. H. Bennett	do	Governor Patton	Aug. 13, 1865.
Thomas E. Branscomb	do	Governor Parsons	Oct. 4, 1865.
E. M. Burton	do	do	Sept. 8, 1865.
Hugh Black	do	do	Jan. 4, 1866.
John W. Boswell	do	do	Oct. 21, 1865.
John F. Beason	Rebel mail contractor	do	Oct. 21, 1865.
Jasper N. Beason	Rebel tax assessor	do	Oct. 21, 1865.
Benj. J. Baldwin	do	do	Sept. 12, 1865.
Lewis B. Brown	do	do	Mar. 2, 1866.
William J. Boone	do	do	Mar. 2, 1866.
W. R. Brown	Rebel tax collector	do	Sept. 26, 1865.
Henry Barnewall	do	do	Sept. 12, 1865.
William Beggs	do	do	Sept. 12, 1865.
P. B. Baldwin	Rebel tax collector, and worth over $20,000	do	Dec. 2, 1865.
Robert A. Baker	do	do	Sept. 11, 1865.
H. W. Bredmax	do	do	Sept. 12, 1865.
J. Beasly	do	do	Oct. 4, 1865.
Alfred Batrie	Clerk in rebel tax department	Attorney General Speed and James Q. Smith	June 13, 1865.
Robert W. Barnard	Violated his oath	Governor Parsons	Sept. 29, 1865.
R. W. Brickell	Proceedings commenced for confiscation, and worth over $20,000.	do	Apr. 30, 1866.
M. A. Baldwin	Worth over $20,000	do	Sept. 12, 1865.
M. Banks	do	do	Sept. 12, 1865.
A. J. Battle	do	do	Sept. 12, 1865.
George B. Bibb	do	do	Sept. 12, 1865.
William S. Barton	do	do	Sept. 12, 1865.
William B. Bell	do	do	Sept. 12, 1865.

Alabama—Continued.

Name.	Exemption under amnesty proclamation of May 29, 1865.	By whom recommended.	Date of pardon.
Alex. R. Bell	Worth over $20,000	Governor Parsons	Sept. 12, 1865.
Edward Blum	do	do	Sept. 12, 1865.
Thomas M. Barnett	do	do	Sept. 12, 1865.
W. P. Bocock	do	do	Sept. 12, 1865.
John S. Bealle	do	do	Sept. 12, 1865.
F. D. Bearse	do	do	Sept. 12, 1865.
William Bell	do	do	Sept. 12, 1865.
Joseph B. Bibb	do	do	Sept. 12, 1865.
C. Battle	do	do	Sept. 12, 1865.
James D. Browder	do	do	Sept. 12, 1865.
G. H. Brown	do	Governor Parsons and Benjamin S. Dartt, major seventh Pennsylvania cavalry, post commander.	Sept. 12, 1865.
George A. Brown	do	Governor Parsons	Sept. 12, 1865.
Robert L. Brown	do	Governor Parsons, J. H. Hendricks, J. N. Suedecor, E. Allen, A. J. Hodge, J. C. Brown, H. G. Johnston, J. P. Hilman, John Phillips, William Huff, W. T. Dimick, and E. R. B. Thomas.	Sept. 12, 1865.
J. C. Browder	do	Governor Parsons	Sept. 12, 1865.
Nathan Bozeman	do	do	Sept. 12, 1865.
William Barnewall, jr	do	do	Sept. 12, 1865.
Thomas B. Brown	do	do	Sept. 12, 1865.
John E. Brown	do	Governor Parsons, A. A. Winston, C. Palmer, J. A. Gibbs, E. H. Watts, R. G. McMahon, George B. Saunders, H. B. Harrison.	Sept. 12, 1865.
J. L. Brown	do	Governor Parsons	Sept. 12, 1865.
G. S. Bunkley	do	do	Sept. 12, 1865.
H. H. Bender	do	do	Mar. 2, 1866.
John Borders	do	do	Mar. 2, 1866.
William A. Battle	do	do	Mar. 2, 1866.
John Brice	do	do	Mar. 2, 1866.
John C. Baker	do	do	Mar. 2, 1866.
Jacob Bruce	do	do	Mar. 2, 1866.
Alameth Byers	do	do	Mar. 2, 1866.
Ervin Blanks	do	do	Mar. 2, 1866.
Mrs. Jane H. Boaz	do	do	Sept. 11, 1865.
F. A. Bates	do	do	Sept. 11, 1865.
Isaac Billingsley	do	do	Sept. 11, 1865.
John Barrow	do	do	Sept. 11, 1865.
Edward A. Blunt	do	do	Sept. 11, 1865.
Mrs. M. S. Bocock	do	do	Sept. 11, 1865.
Alfred Battle	do	do	Sept. 11, 1865.
Mrs. Mary A. Brown	do	do	Sept. 11, 1865.
Cyrus Billingsley	do	do	Sept. 29, 1865.
Robert Boyd	do	do	Sept. 29, 1865.
Joshua H. Beadle	do	do	Sept. 29, 1865.
A. C. Beard	do	do	Sept. 29, 1865.

Henry A. Binford	do	do	Sept. 29, 1865.
Robert Bates	do	do	Sept. 29, 1865.
William H. Bray	do	do	Dec. 2, 1865.
A. R. Barclay	do	do	Dec. 2, 1865.
David W. Bozeman	do	do	Dec. 2, 1865.
John Buchanan	do	Governor Parsons, G. D. Hooper, and A. B. Griffin	Dec. 2, 1865.
Richard Buchanan	do	Governor Parsons	Dec. 2, 1865.
William B. Brannon	do	do	Dec. 2, 1865.
George P. Beirne	do	James M. Wayne, associate justice of the Supreme Court United States	Sept. 8, 1865.
Harriet M. Barnard	do	Attorney General Speed and Joseph C. Bradley	Sept. 2, 1865.
Philip Burt	do	Governor Parsons	Aug. 14, 1865.
O. H. Bymum	do	By order of the President	Nov. 28, 1865.
Milton Brown	do	do	July 21, 1865.
William H. Bullock	do	Governor Parsons	Feb. 2, 1866.
T. B. Bethea	do	do	Aug. 2, 1865.
John Bragg	do	do	Oct. 6, 1865.
R. H. Boykin	do	do	Oct. 31, 1865.
S. T. Boykin	do	do	Oct. 31, 1865.
William W. Boykin	do	do	Oct. 31, 1865.
Frank Boykin	do	do	Oct. 6, 1865.
John C. Boyle	do	Governor Parsons, G. A. Brown, W. V. Hare, Elbert Amason, John A. Winston, M. V. Lacy, E. H. Watts, James Carpenter, H. P. Snow.	Oct. 7, 1865.
John Bowen	do	Governor Parsons	Sept. 26, 1865.
William M. Byrd	do	do	Aug. 11, 1865.
Wilson C. Bibb	do	Gov. Parsons, Joseph C. Bradley, D. C. Humphreys, W. B. Figures, and D. B. Turner.	Sept. 8, 1865.
John D. Barnes	do	Governor Parsons	Nov. 7, 1865.
Burgess Bennett	do	do	Mar. 19, 1866.
Wiley Brownrigg	do	do	April 4, 1866.
H. O. Brewer	do	By order of the President	June 5, 1866.
A. Benners	do	Governor Parsons	Aug. 12, 1865.
A. C. Barton	do	do	Dec. 15, 1865.
H. C. Barton	do	do	Dec. 15, 1865.
James Brock	do	do	Dec. 15, 1865.
John A. M. Battle	do	do	Dec. 18, 1865.
Homer Blackman	do	do	Dec. 29, 1865.
A. M. Barclay	do	Governor Parsons, D. C. Humphreys, Joseph C. Bradley, and C. Womble	Dec. 29, 1865.
B. F. Blount	do	Governor Parsons, F. Bugbee, W. J. Saffold, Thomas O. Glascock, and W. J. Bibb	Sept. 13, 1865.
Nathan L. Brooks	do	Governor Parsons	Sept. 18, 1865.
Wilson M. Bates	do	do	Sept. 8, 1865.
John G. Brown	do	do	Sept. 8, 1865.
Nathan M. Bray	do	do	Sept. 8, 1865.
J. C. Bonner	do	do	Oct. 14, 1865.
James A. Bozeman	do	do	Oct. 14, 1865.
Samuel J. Bolling	do	Governor Parsons and B. F. Porter	Aug. 21, 1865.
William M. Brooks	do	Attorney General Speed	Dec. 22, 1865.
N. D. Barnett	do	Governor Parsons	Aug. 21, 1865.
C. Bellinger	do	do	Oct. 2, 1865.
S. B. Barker	do	do	Oct. 25, 1865.
Eliza Bland	do	do	Oct. 25, 1865.
F. S. Beckton	do	do	Oct. 25, 1865.

Alabama—Continued.

Name.	Exemption under amnesty proclamation of May 29, 1865.	By whom recommended.	Date of pardon.
J. H. Brown	Worth over $20,000	Governor Parsons; Colonel Thomas, George N. Carr, Thomas H. Quail, M. B. Wilson, Jim. R. Collins, S. Elliott, W. B. Stevens, John W. Lacock, W. T. Swift, M. Woods, officers of the 93d Indiana regiment.	Oct. 7, 1865.
Edwin J. Brown	do	Governor Parsons, A. D. Hall, A. H. Griffin, Evan Allen, A. J. Hodge, R. H. Whitfield, John W. Waller, D. C. White, Jack Phillips.	Oct. 7, 1865.
James Boykin	do	Governor Parsons	Oct. 31, 1865.
R. D. Boykin	do	do	Oct. 31, 1865.
C. W. Butt	do	do	Oct. 23, 1865.
T. W. Baker	do	do	Oct. 18, 1865.
Samuel G. Battle	do	do	Oct. 18, 1865.
A. W. Beckwith	do	do	Oct. 26, 1865.
William B. Bowen	do	do	Oct. 26, 1865.
William H. Boswell	do	do	Oct. 21 1865.
B. F. Borom	do	do	Oct. 21, 1865.
H. G. Bradford	do	do	Oct. 21, 1865.
John Brantley	do	do	Oct. 21, 1865.
James C. Burt	do	do	Oct. 21, 1865.
James A. Beasley	do	Governor Parsons and Joseph C. Bradley	Oct. 21, 1865.
William O. Baldwin	do	Governor Parsons	Aug. 19, 1865.
J. Du Bose Bibb	do	do	Aug. 19, 1865.
B. S. Bibb	do	do	Aug. 19, 1865.
Richard B. Baugh	do	Governor Parsons, E. W. Peck, and L. T. Thurston	Nov. 2, 1865.
Daniel H. Bird	do	Governor Parsons and William P. Webb	Nov. 2, 1865.
James M. Bullock	do	Governor Parsons	Nov. 2, 1865.
F. A. Bates	do	Attorney General Speed	Dec. 22, 1865.
William T. Blunt	do	Governor Parsons	Nov. 2, 1865.
Alexander C. Blount	do	do	Feb. 21, 1866.
John M. Burke	do	do	Feb. 20, 1866.
Samuel Brice	do	do	Sept. 18, 1865.
James C. Boyd	do	do	Sept. 29, 1865.
Mrs. M. C. A. Bennett	do	do	Nov. 3, 1865.
George O. Baker	do	do	June 7, 1866.
James H. Clanton	Rebel brigadier general	Lewis E. Parsons, governor of Alabama	Nov. 4, 1865.
F. M. Cockrell	do	do	Mar. 31, 1866.
A. B. Chitheral	Register of rebel treasury	Lewis E. Parsons, governor of Alabama, Hon. Albert Elmore, L. P. Saxon, J. W. Shepherd, clerk supreme court, W. D. Brown, State librarian, Thomas B. Cooper, J. T. Leeper, and R. M. Patton.	Oct. 14, 1866.
Henry Chamberlin	Rebel judge, and worth over $20,000	Governor Parsons, C. P. Gale, J. R. Burgett, R. Yuille, and S. U. Fosdick	Dec. 22, 1866.
W. H. Chambers	Member of rebel legislature	Hon. W. H. Seward, Secretary of State, and R. M. Blatchford	Sept. 8, 1866.
W. E. Clarke	Commissioner to receive subscriptions to rebel loan.	Governor Parsons	Aug. 19, 1866.
Thomas C. Clark	do	do	Dec. 15, 1866.
S. D. Cabaniss	Commissioner to receive subscriptions to rebel loan and worth over $20,000.	Governor Parsons and J. C. Bradley	Sept. 15, 1866.
S. G. Cochran	Rebel commissioner and worth over $20,000	Governor Parsons	Mar. 19, 1866.

J. M. Calhoun	Rebel agent and worth over $20,000	do	Sept. 12, 1866.
John S. Carns	Rebel mail contractor	do	Mar. 2, 1866.
George Cleavland	Rebel contractor and worth over $20,000	do	Jan. 22, 1866.
W. A. Caffey	Ex-United States and rebel postmaster	do	Jan. 22, 1866.
Edward Curtis	do	do	Oct. 12, 1865.
C. M. Cochran	Ex-United States and rebel postmaster and worth over $20,000.	do	Sept. 18, 1865.
G. W. Crymes	Rebel postmaster	do	Oct. 18, 1865.
S. D. Crum	do	do	Oct. 13, 1865.
J. P. Cosper	do	do	Oct. 30, 1865.
J. A. B. Clemmons	do	do	Aug. 21, 1865.
John Crittenden	do	do	Dec. 10, 1866.
E. R. Chandler	do	Governor Parsons and W. M. Griffin	Mar. 2, 1866.
Seabird Cowan	Rebel tax assessor	Governor Parsons	June 11, 1866.
James Chalmers	do	do	Nov. 17, 1865.
G. P. Charlton	do	do	May 22, 1865.
Robert Cunningham	Rebel tax collector	do	Oct. 6, 1865.
J. M. Cheney	do	do	Oct. 6, 1865.
J. W. Crawford	do	do	Mar. 2, 1866.
W. D. Caddill	do	do	Mar. 2, 1866.
R. W. Coltart	Marshal of State of Alabama	Governor Parsons, Joseph C. Bradley, and D. C. Humphreys	Sept. 29, 1865.
John A. Cuthbert	Ex-United States and rebel clerk of district and circuit courts, Mobile.	Governor Parsons	Nov. 2, 1865.
Clement C. Clay	Proceedings instituted for confiscation, and worth over $20,000.	R. M. Patton, governor of Alabama, N. Sargent, and P. M. Dox	Feb. 4, 1866.
John R. Coffey	Proceedings instituted for confiscation, and worth over $20,000.	Joseph C. Bradley	June 8, 1866.
Mrs. C. L. Chapman	Worth over $20,000	Governor Parsons	Mar. 2, 1866.
Francis H. Chamberlin	do	do	Dec. 22, 1865.
Laura E. Cox	do	do	Nov. 1, 1865.
Patrick Calhoun	do	do	Nov. 1, 1865.
W. G. Cain	do	do	April 25, 1866.
Benjamin E. Cobb	do	do	Sept. 18, 1865.
Elisha Calhoun	do	do	Nov. 1, 1865.
William C. Cross	do	do	Oct. 26, 1865.
W. H. Chambers	do	do	Sept. 8, 1865.
Mrs. L. Cheek	do	do	Oct. 13, 1865.
Josiah Collins	do	Gov. Parsons, E. H. Watts, M. D.; G. B. Nobley, A. J. Hodge, E. Allen, G. H. Dunlap, and H. P. Snow.	Oct. 7, 1865.
M. N. Cockrell	do	Governor Parsons	Oct. 7, 1865.
E. H. Caldwell	do	do	Sept. 8, 1865.
J. C. Chamberlain	do	do	Sept. 8, 1865.
J. G. Chappell	do	do	Oct. 4, 1865.
Mrs. Mary Cleveland	do	do	Nov. 1, 1865.
John L. Charles	do	do	Mar. 2, 1866.
Allen W. Coleman	do	do	Sept. 18, 1865.
A. M. Coleman	do	do	Sept. 18, 1865.
William W. Cole	do	do	Sept. 18, 1865.
Sallie T. Carson	do	do	Sept. 29, 1865.
L. B. Cooper	do	do	Feb. 2, 1866.
S. W. Coon	do	do	Feb. 2, 1866.
James A. Curry	do	do	Dec. 22, 1865.

Alabama—Continued.

Name.	Exemption under amnesty proclamation of May 29, 1865.	By whom recommended.	Date of pardon.
Alexander D. Coffee	Worth over $20,000	L. T. Thurston, A. D. Hunt, J. M. Davis, and Russell Houston	June 12, 1865.
J. J. Cox	do	Governor Parsons	Mar. 3, 1865.
T. K. Carson	do	do	Dec. 29, 1865.
John Cocke	do	do	Sept. 8, 1865.
Bryan Croom	do	do	Oct. 18, 1865.
W. H. Coleman	do	do	Sept. 12, 1865.
J. E. Chambers	do	do	Sept. 12, 1865.
R. H. Clements	do	do	Sept. 12, 1865.
J. M. Chapron	do	do	Sept. 12, 1865.
John Collins	do	do	Sept. 12, 1865.
William Cottrell	de	do	Sept. 12, 1865.
Whet. Clark	do	do	Dec. 2, 1865.
Robert Cottrill	do	do	Sept. 12, 1865.
J. F. Carter	do	do	Sept. 12, 1865.
W. R. Calloway	do	do	Sept. 12, 1865.
L. M. Clements	do	do	Sept. 12, 1865.
John Chighizola	do	do	Oct. 21, 1865.
H. W. Clarke	do	do	Oct. 13, 1865.
O. F. Cawthon	do	do	Sept. 12, 1865.
Thos. J. Cannon	do	do	Sept. 8, 1865.
B. J. Coffey	do	do	Mar. 2, 1866.
Samuel Cowan	do	do	Sept. 12, 1865.
Joseph Chapman	do	do	Sept. 12, 1865.
John Cochran	do	do	Sept. 12, 1865.
Platt S. Croom	do	do	Sept. 12, 1865.
A. A. Coleman	do	do	Mar. 26, 1866.
Smith Cullom	do	Hon. James Speed, Attorney General of the United States	Sept. 7, 1865.
T. L. Carson	do	Governor Parsons	Sept. 12, 1865.
M. S. Cassily	do	do	Oct. 25, 1865.
W. T. Coleman	do	do	Dec. 2, 1865.
Hardy Clements	do	do	Oct. 13, 1865.
Marco Carmetich	do	do	Dec. 22, 1865.
J. P. G. Coleman	do	do	Nov. 1, 1865.
Nathan Cook	do	do	Mar. 2, 1866.
Caroline E. Copeland	do	do	Dec. 2, 1865.
Wm. F. Cleveland	do	do	Oct. 6, 1865.
James Crawford	do	do	Sept. 11, 1865.
R. Chapman	do	do	Sept. 12, 1865.
Wm. Cox	do	do	Oct. 31, 1865.
Mrs. M. L. Carter	do	do	Oct. 30, 1865.
Elizabeth W. Clement	do	do	Nov. 2, 1865.
James Carpenter	do	do	Nov. 7, 1865.
Parthenia Crommelin	do	do	Sept. 19, 1865.
J. W. Crenshaw	do	do	Sept. 11, 1865.

J. W. Craig	do	do	Sept. 8, 1865.
T. R. Carter	do	do	Sept. 12, 1865.
J. C. Cade	do	do	Sept. 12, 1865.
W. B. Calhoun	do	do	Oct. 14, 1865.
J. B. Calloway	do	do	Oct. 4, 1865.
Jeremiah Collins	do	do	Oct. 21, 1865.
Thomas Colvin	do	do	Jan. 29, 1866.
Thos. C. Clark	do	do	Sept. 12, 1865.
James B. Clark	do	do	Sept. 12, 1865.
Willy Coleman	do	do	Sept. 12, 1865.
Hugh M. Coffey	do	do	Mar. 2, 1866.
M. W. Creagh	do	do	Mar. 19, 1866.
S. R. Cockrill	do	do	Oct. 24, 1865.
Woodson Cocke	do	do	Sept. 29, 1865.
Miss S. T. Carson	do	do	Sept. 29, 1865.
J. C. Caldwell	do	do	May 24, 1866.
William Cooper	do	do	Mar. 2, 1866.
E. H. Cogburn	do	do	Mar. 2, 1866.
Augustus Carter	do	do	Mar. 2, 1866.
C. E. Collier	do	do	Dec. 15, 1866.
L. L. Cato	do	do	Dec. 2, 1866.
Wm. Curry	do	do	Dec. 29, 1866.
W. A. Coleman	do	do	Mar. 2, 1866.
Andrew Cunningham	do	do	Mar. 2, 1866.
Wm. P. Crooks	do	do	Mar. 2, 1866.
Sam'l W. Crook	do	do	Mar. 2, 1866.
Mrs. M. A. Cantelon	do	do	Sept. 8, 1865.
John M. Crooks	do	do	Mar. 2, 1866.
S. L. Creswell	do	do	Aug. 12, 1865.
James D. Craig	do	do	Sept. 11, 1865.
Jabez Curry	do	do	Sept. 11, 1865.
E. K. Carlisle	do	do	Sept. 11, 1865.
W. G. Croom	do	do	Sept. 11, 1865.
Robert G. Craig	do	do	Sept. 18, 1865.
Nich. Davis	Member of the rebel provincial congress	do	Sept. 22, 1865.
N. H. R. Dawson	Member of the State legislature and worth over $20,000.	do	Sept. 12, 1865.
Z. P. Davis	Receiver of public moneys	do	Oct. 21, 1865.
R. J. Dudley	Rebel bonded agent for the purchase of subsistence for the army.	do	Oct. 14, 1865.
James I. Donnegan	Receiver of subscriptions and worth over $20,000	do	Sept. 22, 1865.
John C. Deas	Purchasing agent and worth over $20,000	do	Jan. 4, 1866.
John H. Dent	Member of advisory board and worth over $20,000	do	Dec. 18, 1865.
Isaiah Dills	Commissioner of rebel district court	Governor Parsons and Major Benjamin S. Dartt	Sept. 29, 1865.
Thos. H. Duskell	Ex-United States and rebel postmaster	Governor Parsons	Mar. 1, 1866.
C. C. Dickinson	do	do	Oct. 13, 1865.
James M. Denson	Rebel postmaster	do	Oct. 14, 1865.
A. M. De Bardlaborn	Rebel tax assessor	do	Mar. 2, 1866.
Hiram H. Doss	do	do	Mar. 2, 1866.
A. C. Davidson	Worth over $20,000	do	Dec. 15, 1865.
James R. Dillard	do	do	Aug. 11, 1865.
Peter Driskell	do	do	Aug. 21, 1865.

Alabama—Continued.

Name.	Exemption under amnesty proclamation of May 29, 1865.	By whom recommended.	Date of pardon.
D. Dew, jr.	Worth over $20,000	Governor Parsons	Aug. 11, 1865.
John R. Drish	do	do	Mar. 17, 1866.
Wm. L. Davis	do	do	Sept. 11, 1865.
John L. De Yampert	do	do	Sept. 11, 1865.
George T. Davis	do	do	Sept. 11, 1865.
George W. Drake	do	do	May 9, 1866.
W. D. Dunn	do	do	Sept. 9, 1865.
J. M. Dillehay	do	do	Sept. 12, 1865.
K. C. Dubose	do	do	Sept. 12, 1865.
John Dudley	do	do	Sept. 12, 1865.
Geo. L. Davidson	do	do	Oct. 18, 1865.
James H. Dubose	do	do	Sept. 12, 1865.
Lewis Durand	do	do	Sept. 12, 1865.
M. H. Daniel	do	do	Dec. 22, 1865.
Gaston Drake	do	do	Sept. 8, 1865.
John Dudley, sr.	do	do	Sept. 12, 1865.
T. W. De Yampert	do	do	Sept. 11, 1865.
Isham Dorsey	do	do	Mar. 2, 1866.
A. H. De Yampert	do	do	Sept. 11, 1865.
Joseph R. Dral	do	do	Oct. 7, 1865.
Otis Dyer	do	Hon. James Speed, Attorney General of the United States	Oct. 26, 1865.
J. H. Doughdrill	do	Governor Parsons	Feb. 21, 1866.
A. C. Davidson	do	do	Oct. 25, 1865.
Lewis R. Davis	do	do	Sept. 18, 1865.
L. O. C. De Yampert	do	do	Sept. 11, 1865.
J. W. S. Donnell	do	do	Oct. 2, 1865.
John H. Drake	do	do	Mar. 2, 1866.
Benj. B. Davis	do	do	Dec. 29, 1866.
David Deshler	do	do	Dec. 18, 1866.
A. G. Due	do	do	Aug. 2, 1866.
E. B. Delong	do	Governor Parsons and J. C. Bradley	Jan. 29, 1866.
C. W. Dorrance	do	Governor Parsons	Nov. 13, 1865.
B. J. Duncan	do	do	Oct. 24, 1865.
I. C. Dubose	do	do	Oct. 6, 1865.
J. H. Duvall	do	do	Sept. 11, 1865.
Martha C. Davidson	do	do	Dec. 15, 1865.
A. J. Dyas	do	do	Dec. 15, 1865.
James Daniel	do	do	Dec. 15, 1865.
T. W. Dunklin	do	do	Oct. 18, 1865.
James W. Dunklin	do	do	Oct. 18, 1865.
David Deshler	do	do	Dec. 18, 1865.
John W. Durr	do	do	Oct. 18, 1865.
W. C. Darden	do	do	Oct. 14, 1865.

R. B. Dickerson	do	do	Mar. 2, 1866.
Edwin C. Dancy	do	do	Oct. 7, 1865.
J. R. Drake	do	do	Sept. 29, 1865.
Edward Davis	do	do	Oct. 25, 1865.
William Dickson	do	do	Oct. 2, 1865.
Caswell Eades	Ex-United States and rebel postmaster	do	April 4, 1866.
Benj. F. Ellis	do	do	Dec. 15, 1865.
W. H. Eager	Rebel postmaster	do	Sept. 18, 1865.
Isaac Estill	do	do	Oct. 21, 1865.
Jacob Eichelberger	do	do	July 26, 1865.
Reuben Estes	Rebel tax assessor	do	June 11, 1865.
F. A. Effinger	Worth over $20,000	do	Mar. 2, 1866.
Geo. T. Edwards	do	do	Mar. 2, 1866.
Thos. C. English	do	do	Dec. 15, 1865.
F. C. Ewers	do	do	Dec. 21, 1865.
J. W. Echols	do	do	Aug. 21, 1865.
R. Ellyson	do	do	Sept. 12, 1865.
Jonathan Emanuel	do	do	Sept. 12, 1865.
W. G. Edwards	do	do	Sept. 29, 1865.
A. D. Edwards	do	do	Sept. 12, 1865.
Alcuin Easton	do	do	Oct. 21, 1865.
C. B. Elerbe	do	do	Sept. 18, 1865.
James Edwards	do	do	Sept. 29, 1865.
W. B. Edwards	do	do	Sept. 29, 1865.
Thomas East	do	do	Jan. 29, 1866.
Edmond Ellits	do	do	Sept. 29, 1865.
Samuel Elliott	do	do	Sept. 15, 1865.
James G. Evans	do	do	Sept. 11, 1865.
John Englehardt	do	do	Sept. 12, 1865.
R. H. Erwin	do	do	Dec. 21, 1865.
George Erwin	do	do	Sept. 12, 1865.
William Erwin	do	do	Sept. 11, 1865.
Samuel Everhart	do	do	Sept. 12, 1865.
W. H. Forney	Rebel brigadier general	do	July 11, 1866.
Benjamin Fitzpatrick	Resigned his seat in the United States Senate, and worth over $20,000.	Governor Parsons and J. J. Sickles	Aug. 15, 1865.
J. A. Farley	Rebel agent to receive cotton for bonds, and worth over $20,000.	Governor Parsons	Aug. 19, 1865.
S. H. Fowlkes	Rebel depositary	do	Sept. 11, 1865.
J. H. Fitts	do	do	Sept. 12, 1865.
R. C. Fariss	Rebel commissioner of appraisement for State	do	Oct. 21, 1865.
Walter Franklin	Rebel mail contractor	do	Mar. 2, 1866.
William Frolichstein	do	do	Sept. 8, 1865.
J. W. Fulenwider	Rebel route agent	do	Mar. 2, 1865.
G. W. Foster	Ex-United States and rebel postmaster	do	Sept. 12, 1865.
J. W. Figures	Ex-United States and rebel postmaster, and worth over $20,000.	do	Sept. 8, 1865.
B. M. Fluker	Rebel postmaster	do	Oct. 21, 1865.
A. S. Frazier	do	do	Mar. 2, 1866.
J. Y. Ferguson	Rebel tax collector	do	Sept. 26, 1866.
James Forman	Rebel tax collector	do	Mar. 2, 1866.
B. J. Fort	Rebel tax collector, and worth over $20,000	do	Oct. 2, 1865.

Alabama—Continued.

Name.	Exemption under amnesty proclamation of May 29, 1865.	By whom recommended.	Date of pardon.
J. G. Freeney	Worth over $20,000	Governor Parsons	Apr. 25, 1866.
E. R. Flewellen	do	do	Sept. 12, 1865.
William Frazier	do	do	Sept. 8, 1865.
J. P. Fulkes	do	do	Sept. 11, 1865.
William Fowler	do	do	Sept. 12, 1865.
Robert Foster	do	do	Sept. 11, 1865.
Jeremiah Fail	do	do	Sept. 8, 1865.
C. J. Fiquet	do	do	July 18, 1865.
W. G. Farley	do	do	Aug. 21, 1865.
Robert Fearn	do	Governor Parsons and E. Skilheiner	Nov. 4, 1865.
J. T. Flewellyn	do	Hon. James Speed, Attorney General United States	Aug. 11, 1865.
John Fountaine	do	do	Aug. 11, 1865.
Mrs. M. Ford	do	Governor Parsons	Dec. 23, 1865.
W. F. Fulton	do	do	June 29, 1866.
J. L. Fariss	do	do	Oct. 21, 1865.
W. B. Fariss	do	do	Oct. 21, 1865.
William Flash	do	do	Oct. 21, 1865.
J. S. Felder	do	do	Oct. 21, 1865.
H. Ferguson	do	do	Oct. 18, 1865.
William Foster	do	do	Oct. 18, 1865.
S. J. Flourney	do	do	Dec. 2, 1865.
John Farrier	do	do	Mar. 2, 1866.
I. J. Fennell	do	Governor Parsons and Joseph C. Bradley	Sept. 29, 1865.
Joseph R. Fulmore	do	Governor Parsons	Sept. 8, 1865.
John J. Fackler	do	do	Jan. 4, 1866.
Daniel J. Fox	do	do	Sept. 18, 1865.
G. W. Foster	do	do	Sept. 12, 1865.
S. Festorozzi	do	do	Mar. 2, 1866.
James Fountain	do	do	Nov. 4, 1865.
Fleming Freeman	do	do	Sept. 18, 1865.
A. C. Felder	do	do	Aug. 19, 1865.
P. D. Forniss	do	do	Nov. 1, 1865.
Robert Flournoy	do	do	Apr. 4, 1866.
P. O. Foster	do	do	Mar. 2, 1866.
Davis Foy	do	do	Oct. 7, 1865.
C. K. Foote	do	do	Oct. 6, 1865.
S. A. Fitts	do	do	Sept. 12, 1865.
Dr. R. L. Fearn	do	do	Sept. 12, 1865.
J. C. Foster	do	do	Sept. 12, 1865.
James N. Fletcher	do	do	Sept. 29, 1865.
Robert Ferguson	do	Governor Parsons, J. Hardman, B. B. Fields, C. B. Woods, N. M. Hyatt, M. C. McDonald, G. D. Conner, and J. H. Butt.	Jan. 4, 1866.
James G. Gilchrist	Member of secession convention, and worth over $20,000.	Governor Parsons, I. I. Seibels, and James Birney	Aug. 21, 1865.

Joseph Goetler	Rebel purchasing agent, mail contractor, and worth over $20,000.	Governor Parsons	Mar. 2, 1866.
N. S. Graham	Rebel commissioner to take testimony	do	Aug. 19, 1865.
W. M. Gilmer	Rebel mail contractor, and worth over $20,000	do	Aug. 11, 1865.
J. C. Guild	Ex-United States and rebel postmaster	do	Dec. 2, 1865.
Peyton C. Graves	do	do	Sept. 12, 1865.
John T. Glaze	Rebel postmaster	do	Oct. 21, 1865.
Edward Goode	do	do	Oct. 21, 1865.
S. B. Guthrie	do	Governor Patton	June 11, 1866.
Greenbery Garrett	do	Governor Parsons	Mar. 2, 1866.
D. P. Gunnels	do	Governor Patton	Mar. 2, 1866.
Terroll Gregory	do	Governor Parsons	Mar. 2, 1865.
John A. Glenn	do	do	Mar. 2, 1865.
M. H. Gilbert	Rebel tax assessor	do	Oct. 18, 1865.
Jacob H. Golson	do	Governor Parsons, W. R. Wyatt, J. B. Wilkinson, H. J. Hall, Charles M. Howard, Leonidas Howard, L. M. Whetstone, and L. Pejus.	Oct. 12, 1865.
William Garrett	Rebel tax collector	Governor Parsons	Sept. 12, 1865.
T. C. Greenhill	do	Governor Parsons, R. S. Watkins, Christopher Tompkins, C. Womble, A. Orr, F. S. B. Goodwin, William Skimmer, and I. B. Moore.	Jan. 4, 1866.
Hiram M. Glass	do	Governor Parsons	Oct. 14, 1865.
Matt. Gayle	Rebel agent to receive tax	do	Mar. 2, 1866.
Mrs. Elizabeth H. Gilmer	Worth over $20,000	do	Oct. 12, 1865.
Jones M. Gunn	do	do	Dec. 22, 1865.
Williamson A. Glover	do	do	Sept. 12, 1865.
Benjamin Edwards Grey	do	do	Sept. 12, 1865.
Robert A. Goodloe	do	Governor Parsons and Joseph E. Bradley	Dec. 29, 1865.
Mrs. E. W. Gould	do	Governor Parsons	Mar. 17, 1866.
Churchill Gibson	do	do	Sept. 12, 1865.
B. R. Garland	do	Governor Parsons, R. S. Watkins, William Skrunner, C. Womble	Feb. 2, 1866.
William W. Garth	do	Governor Parsons, Joseph C. Bradley, F. L. Hammond, James S. Clark, D. C. Humphreys, F. W. Sykes, M. Davis, and Benjamin Julley.	Sept. 15, 1865.
H. C. Gowdey	do	Governor Parsons	Feb. 2, 1866.
Mrs. E. F. Grey	do	do	Sept. 29, 1865.
C. A. Gilbert	do	Governor Parsons, G. W. Turleton, William Freeman, M. Waising, G. Horton, and L. Merchant & Co.	Sept. 13, 1865.
Freeman Goode	do	Governor Parsons, James C. Bradley, David P. Lewis, and James S. Clark	Oct. 2, 1865.
G. W. Grant	do	Governor Parsons	Dec. 21, 1865.
Edward Garland	do	do	Dec. 18, 1865.
William B. Gill	do	do	Sept. 13, 1865.
John H. Garner	do	do	Sept. 8, 1865.
Simeon G. Gray	do	do	Apr. 17, 1866.
John B. Garrett	do	do	Sept. 12, 1865.
John T. Gilmer	do	do	Sept. 12, 1865.
James J. Gilmer	do	do	Sept. 12, 1865.
Colin Gardner	do	do	Dec. 8, 1865.
Mrs. E. G. Gilmer	do	do	Sept. 12, 1865.
Benjamin Glover	do	do	Sept. 12, 1865.
A. M. Goodwin	do	do	Oct. 18, 1865.
J. C. Gwin	do	do	Dec. 29, 1865.
Jacob R. Green	do	do	Mar. 2, 1866.
James A. Gladden	do	do	Mar. 2, 1866.
E. A. Glover	do	do	Mar. 2, 1866.

Alabama—Continued.

Name.	Exemption under amnesty proclamation of May 29, 1865.	By whom recommended.	Date of pardon.
J. E. Groce	Worth over $20,000	Governor Parsons	Mar. 2, 1866.
John S. Gliddon	do	do	Oct. 21, 1865.
J. A. Gibbs	do	Governor Parsons, John J. Dillard, E. H. Walls, W. V. Hare, W. V. Lacy, I. C. Bogle, A. A. Winston, R. G. McMahen, B. Garner, S. W. Murley, J. C. H. Jones, T. Ravis, A. W. McMahen, William J. McKerall, C. Parker, William M. Lewis, L. B. Williamson, jr., A. A. Coleman, William Howard, I. W. Pennington, A. J. Hodge, Evan Allen, W. H. Daudridge, R. Davidrau, W. H. Nevill, and T. Jackson.	Sept. 12, 1865.
John A. Gilchrist	do	Governor Parsons, Joseph C. Bradley, M. Davis, and O. H. Bynum	Oct. 2, 1865.
M. J. Gilchrist	do	Governor Parsons, Joseph C. Bradley, M. Davis, and O. H. Bynum	Oct. 2, 1865.
A. F. Given	do	Governor Parsons	Sept. 29, 1e65.
A. M. Godfrey	do	By order of the President	June 5, 1866.
Joseph A. Guy	do	Governor Parsons, and C. Womble, judge	May 10, 1866.
James Guild	do	Governor Parsons	Mar. 2, 1866.
W. B. Gilmer	do	do	Sept. 12, 1865.
M. L. Gilmer	do	do	Sept. 12, 1865.
Archer Griffeth	do	do	Sept. 12, 1865.
P. R. Grattan	do	Governor Parsons, W. Bibb, L. Owen, and William H. Smith	Sept. 12, 1865.
A. C. Gordon	do	Governor Parsons, J. Cochran, H. E. Owens, I. W. Harper, A. L. Gaston, H. R. Shorter, M. C. McDonald, A. Stow, and I. U. N. Philips.	Sept. 12, 1865.
H. Gray	do	Governor Parsons	Sept. 12, 1865.
C. P. Gage	do	Governor Parsons, G. Young, deputy collector, James L. Bliss, and Thomas Kilby Smith, brigadier general.	Sept. 12, 1865.
F. M. Gilmer, jr	do	Governor Parsons	Sept. 12, 1865.
John H. Garner	do	do	Sept. 12, 1865.
Jesse W. Garth, sr	do	Governor Parsons, D. C. Humphreys, Joseph C. Bradley, F. W. Sykes, David P. Lewis, B. Julley, M. Davis, J. S. Clark, F. L. Hammand, and Z. White.	Sept. 15, 1865.
Lorenzo Griffin	do	Governor Parsons	Nov. 1, 1865.
William Gulley	do	Governor R. M. Patton	Dec. 22, 1865.
J. W. Garner	do	Governor Parsons	Sept. 12, 1865.
Mrs. Sarah W. Gowdy	do	do	Feb. 2, 1866.
John Gully	do	do	Dec. 15, 1865.
John Y. Gholson	do	do	Nov. 1, 1865.
James F. Griffin	do	do	Nov. 1, 1865.
T. J. Goldsby	do	do	Nov. 1, 1865.
T. B. Griggs	do	do	Dec. 21, 1865.
George Goldthwait	do	do	Sept. 12, 1865.
I. R. Gates	do	do	Oct. 6, 1865.
J. P. Graham	do	do	Mar. 17, 1866.
G. M. Gamble	do	do	Oct. 31 1865.
A. W. Gordon	do	do	Jan. 6, 1866.
M. W. Garrison	do	Governor Parsons, I. I. Seibels, and B. Fitzpatrick	Oct. 14, 1865.
John J. Grant	do	R. L. Mott, of Columbus, Georgia	Aug. 11, 1865.
A. S. Garner	do	Governor Parsons and Joseph C. Bradley	Feb. 2, 1866.
Isaac Goldsmith	do	Governor Parsons	Sept. 8, 1865.

C. G Gunter	do	do	Oct. 13, 1865.
John H. Gary	do	do	Oct. 6, 1865.
Lardner Gibbon	do	Major General John Gibbon	Oct. 25, 1865.
Mrs. Emma E. Gibbons	do	Governor Parsons	Oct. 25, 1865.
G. T. Gunter	do	do	Oct. 13, 1865.
George F. Glover	do	do	Sept. 12, 1865.
Mrs. E. F. Grey	do	Attorney General of the United States	Sept. 29, 1865.
John C. Graham	do	Levi W. Lawler, N. H. R. Dawson, L. P. Walker, F. A. Woodson, John Cochran, J. L. Pugh, J. D. B. De Bow, and F. W. Sykes.	Sept. 22, 1865.
T. J. Goodwyn	do	Governor Parsons	Oct. 9, 1865.
Lyman Gibbons	do	do	Oct. 25, 1865.
Francis Gordon	do	do	Oct. 4, 1865.
Garland Goode	do	Governor Parsons and Governor Patton	Mar. 15, 1866.
D. O. Grady	do	Governor Parsons	Sept. 29, 1865.
John A. Greer	do	T. H. Newbern and John W. Leftwick	Dec. 17, 1866.
D. W. Goodman	do	Governor Parsons, R. V. Montague, and Brigadier General Thomas Kilby Smith	Sept. 12, 1865.
James Hagan	Rebel brigadier general, and worth over $20,000	Judge Busteed, and ordered by the Attorney General	Jan. 30, 1866.
F. L. Hammond	Member of rebel State senate	J. C. Bradley and Governor Parsons	Oct. 21, 1865.
Thomas A. Hamilton	Rebel prize commissioner, and worth over $20,000	Governor Parsons and Thomas Kilby Smith, brigadier general commanding	Sept. 12, 1865.
J. G. L. Huey	Rebel depositary and financial agent of the treasury department of the Confederate States.	M. H. Cherysler, brevet brigadier general	Oct. 23, 1865.
J. L. Harrell	Chief of financial bureau for rebel post office dep't	Governor Parsons	Sept. 12, 1865.
David Hubbard	Rebel commissioner of Indian affairs	do	Dec. 8, 1865.
P. Hamilton	Rebel commissioner to examine persons held in confinement by military authority.	Governor Parsons, R. V. Montague, and Brigadier General Thomas Kilby Smith	Sept. 9, 1865.
Jonathan Haralson	Rebel surveyor	Governor Parsons, I. Morgan, J. E. Prestridge, and W. H. Fellows	Sept. 18, 1865.
Joseph Hillman	Rebel mail contractor	Attorney General of the United States	Mar. 2, 1866.
W. T. Hatchett	Rebel agent of the produce loan	Governor Parsons	Aug. 19, 1865.
James Hill, jr	Rebel purchasing agent	Governor Patton	Mar. 2, 1866.
J. D. Houser	Rebel agent for the tax-in-kind department	Governor Parsons, M. A. Chisholm, and George W. Stone	Sept. 12, 1865.
John T. Hamilton	Rebel receiver of the tax in kind	Governor Parsons, Charles S. G. Doston, James A. Reynolds, M. D. La Mar, J. L. Alexander, Hurly Brown, Mills Rogers, A. Y. Smith, and B. Fitzpatrick.	Oct. 28, 1865.
John Howard	Ex-United States and rebel postmaster	Governor Parsons	Oct. 18, 1865.
Zimri Henderson	Rebel postmaster	do	Oct. 21, 1865.
A. D. Hall	do	do	Sept. 12, 1865.
William Howell	do	do	Sept. 26, 1865.
George W. Hale	do	Governor Parsons, W. T. May, A. C. Beard, James Critcher, and A. G. Henry	Mar. 2, 1866.
T. K. Harris	do	Governor Parsons	Mar. 2, 1866.
S. F. Hill	do	do	Oct. 16, 1865.
William S. Hutchinson	Rebel postmaster, and worth over $20,000	do	Mar. 9, 1866.
J. B. Hamilton	Rebel tax assessor	Governor Parsons and Judge C. Womble	Feb. 2, 1866.
E. H. Herbert	do	Governor Parsons	Mar. 2, 1866.
W. B. Hall	do	do	Aug. 7, 1865.
John Howze	Rebel tax assessor, and worth over $20,000	do	Sept. 11, 1865.
R. F. Hammond	Rebel tax collector	do	Mar. 2, 1865.
T. C. Hartwell	do	do	Oct. 24, 1865.
George M. Hamner	do	Governor Parsons and A. B. Cooper	Mar. 19, 1866.
T. L. Hudgins	do	do	Aug. 7, 1865.
Thomas H. Hewlett	Left loyal State	Governor Parsons and Joseph C. Bradley	Jan. 4, 1866.
Stephen W. Harris	Property registered as abandoned, and worth over $20,000.	Governor Parsons, David P. Lewis, Joseph C. Bradley, D. C. Humphreys, E. E. Douglass, marshal northern district of Alabama, and I. I. Giers.	Sept. 29, 1865.
Bolling Hall	Worth over $20,000	B. Fitzpatrick, I. I. Seibels, and Governor Parsons	Aug. 7, 1865.

Alabama—Continued.

Name.	Exemption under amnesty proclamation of May 29, 1865.	By whom recommended.	Date of pardon.
Mrs. Harriet C. Harrington	Worth over $20,000	Governor Patton	Apr. 30, 1866.
Joseph H. Howard	do	Governor Parsons, M. A. Chisholm, and James Birney	Sept. 8, 1865.
Joseph R. Hawthorn	do	Governor Parsons	Oct. 4, 1865.
William Hartwell	do	do	Jan. 4, 1866.
David C. Houston	do	do	Dec. 29, 1865.
S. S. Heningham	do	Governor Parsons and Joseph E. Bradley	Sept. 29, 1865.
Edward Hanrick	do	Governor Parsons	Nov. 3, 1865.
C. A. Hester	do	do	Dec. 21, 1865.
William Hora	do	do	Oct. 2, 1865.
Mrs. Dorian Hall	do	do	Oct. 6, 1865.
Benjamin J. Hughes	do	do	Oct. 14, 1865.
John H. Harris	do	do	Sept. 11, 1865.
Robert Hall	do	do	Sept. 12, 1865.
William B. Hall	do	do	Sept. 8, 1865.
Amos Hugnley	do	do	Oct. 14, 1865.
William H. Hays	do	do	Nov. 4, 1865.
Isham H. Hobbs	do	Governor Parsons and M. Davis	Oct. 21, 1865.
John H. Hargrove	do	Governor Parsons	Sept. 12, 1865.
Shaler Hillyer	do	Attorney General Speed	Nov. 6, 1866.
James L. Holt	do	Governor Parsons	Mar. 2 1866.
Thomas H. Herndon	do	do	Oct. 7, 1865.
A. P. Hatch	do	do	Mar. 2, 1866.
Henry A. Hurxthal	do	Attorney General Speed	Nov. 11, 1865.
A. S. Huntington	do	Governor Patton	Mar. 31, 1866.
Alfred Hatch	do	Governor Parsons	Sept. 12, 1865.
H. C. Hart	do	do	Sept. 8, 1865.
Henry Holmes	do	do	Oct. 6, 1865.
F. F. Hemphill	do	do	Sept. 12, 1865.
Williamson Hawkins	do	do	July 6, 1866.
T. I. Hill	do	do	Sept. 12, 1865.
Robert Henton	do	do	Mar. 19, 1866.
H. C. Hatcher	do	do	Sept. 8, 1865.
Thomas Henry	do	Attorney General of the United States	Sept. 29, 1865.
W. M. Holding	do	Governor Parsons, M. Davis, and Joseph C. Bradley	Sept. 29, 1865.
Mrs. Mary L. Hardee	do	Governor Patton	May 17, 1866.
William W. Horton	do	do	Sept. 12, 1865.
George Huguley	do	do	Oct. 14, 1865.
E. A. Holt	do	do	Mar. 2, 1866.
Mrs. M. J. Hunter	do	do	Mar. 2, 1866.
S. Hirshfield	do	Governor Parsons, G. B. Mobley, J. E. Windham, A. D. Hall, W. V. Lacy, E. Allen, William Nevill, jr., E. N. Wrenn, I. W. Fisher, William H. Gill, H. Bennett, J. E. Hart, W. M. Lambeth, L. D. Godfrey, George H. Dunlap, H. P. Snow, D. H. Smith, A. W. McMahen, Caleb Parker, J. S. Roberts, W. G. L. Crawford, A. D. Hutton, Richard Payne, T. A. McDaniel, J. B. Brantley, and Amos Travis.	Oct. 7, 1865.

J. T. Hearne	do	Governor Parsons	Jan. 29, 1866.
Mrs. L. M. Harris	do	Attorney General of the United States	Oct. 4, 1865.
L. J. Hallette	do	Governor Parsons	Nov. 13, 1865.
Albert G. Houghton	do	do	Oct. 10, 1865.
John C. Hodges	do	do	Sept. 13, 1865.
Samuel M. Hill	do	do	Sept. 11, 1865.
Ralph O. Howard	do	do	Nov. 1, 1865.
H. G. Humphries	do	do	Dec. 21, 1865.
Anderson Holmes	do	do	Dec. 21, 1865.
Luther L. Hill	do	do	Sept. 12, 1865.
Edmund Harrison	do	do	Sept. 12, 1865.
R. N. Harris	do	do	Oct. 21, 1865.
Mrs. Ann F. Howard	do	do	Oct. 18, 1865.
M. W. Hannon	do	do	Oct. 12, 1865.
A. S. Hill	do	do	Sept. 12, 1865.
A. L. Haden	do	do	Oct. 18, 1865.
W. F. Harrell	do	do	Oct. 18, 1865.
Edward P. Holcombe	do	do	Oct. 2, 1865.
Barnard H. Hughes	do	Attorney General of the United States	Dec. 22, 1865.
Robert A. Hardaway	do	Governor Parsons	Oct. 10, 1865.
Samuel W. House	do	do	Oct. 2, 1865.
W. B. Haralson	do	do	Sept. 18, 1865.
John Hogue	do	do	Dec. 22, 1865.
Roger A. Heirne	do	do	Dec. 29, 1865.
B. J. Harrison	do	do	Dec. 15, 1865.
I. T. Hargraves	do	do	Dec. 15, 1865.
John S. Hunter	do	Governor Parsons and James Berney	Sept. 12, 1865.
I. L. Harris	do	Hon. Lewis E. Parsons, provisional governor of Alabama	Sept. 16, 1865.
Mrs. Mary E. Hundley	do	do	Oct. 21, 1865.
P. T. Hurt	do	do	Sept. 29, 1865.
Mason Harwell	do	do	Sept. 12, 1865.
Charles Hopkins	do	Newton St. John, B. Tardy, —— Bliss, Milton Brown, and T. Reavis	Oct. 4, 1865.
E. Harrell	do	Governor Parsons	Sept. 12, 1865.
Arthur F. Hopkins	do	do	Oct. 6, 1865.
J. A. C. Horn	do	do	Sept. 29, 1865.
Wm. B. Hamilton	do	do	Oct. 6, 1865.
Mrs. Anna E. Hobbs	do	Governor Parsons and Attorney General of the United States	July 17, 1865.
Mrs. Margaret C. Holmm	do	Governor Parsons	Sept. 11, 1865.
O Haile	do	do	Sept. 18, 1865.
Robe t S. Hatcher	do	do	Sept. 18, 1865.
Robert F. Houston	do	do	Sept. 18, 1865.
Julius Hessee	do	Governor Parsons, R. V. Montague, collector, P. Youngs, deputy collector, and Thomas K. Smith, brigadier general.	Oct. 18, 1865.
M. C. Houston	do	Governor Parsons	Sept. 18, 1865.
John G. Harris	do	do	Sept. 12, 1865.
J. M. Huston	do	Governor Parsons, Hon. R. M. Patton, Joseph C. Bradley, S. C. Posey, and John W. McAlester.	Dec. 29, 1865.
R. W. Hitchcock	do	Governor Parsons	Nov. 2, 1865.
C. C. Huckabee	do	do	Sept. 12, 1865.
A. G. Henry	do	Governor Parsons and Joseph C. Bradley	Sept. 12, 1865.
E. M. Hastings	do	Governor Parsons	Sept. 12, 1865.
Charles Hays	do	Governor Parsons, John A. Winston, Wm. P. Webb, and Colonel D. C. Thomas	Sept. 12, 1865.

Alabama—Continued.

Name.	Exemption under amnesty proclamation of May 29, 1865.	By whom recommended.	Date of pardon.
Albert G. Hudson	Worth over $20,000	Governor Parsons	Sept. 12, 1865.
Mrs. E. C. Harrison	do	do	Sept. 12, 1865.
A. S. Harris	do	Governor Parsons and J. C. Bradley	Jan. 4, 1865.
Joseph Hardie	do	Governor Parsons	Dec. 15, 1865.
W. J. Hearin	do	do	Oct. 21, 1865.
W. I. Holt	do	do	Sept. 12, 1865.
E. C. Hannon	do	do	Sept. 12, 1865.
Samuel Henry	do	Governor Parsons and Jos. C. Bradley	Nov. 1, 1865.
Theodore A. Hall	do	do	Oct. 25, 1865.
Jacques Hausman	do	do	Oct. 23, 1865.
R. W. Hallett	do	do	Nov. 13, 1865.
William Hester	do	do	Dec. 21, 1865.
John T. Hollis	do	do	Oct. 12, 1865.
William Horton	do	Governor Parsons, Abner McMillian, I. C. Bogie, E. H. Watts, C. M. Hutton, Jesse Hill, S. B. M. Harwood, H. G. Johnston, I. N. Snedecor, J. E. Windham, Solon A. Gates, I. W. Pennington, R. F. Stuart, B. Garner, Wm. M. Lewis, W. H. Bush, E. M. Kellogg, I. A. Gibbs, W. E. Rogers, W. H. Steele, Josiah Mius, Wm. E. Morgan, R. M. Carnathan, W. H. Sanders, Robert B. Mabry, G. H. Dunlap, S. R. Cook, D. C. Green, A. McKerrell, Chas M. Roberts, Wm. V. Stanton, I. A. Mooring, and Richard Payne.	Oct. 7, 1865.
Mrs. S. K. Huey	do	Governor Parsons	Sept. 11, 1865.
Donaldson Huff	do	do	Sept. 11, 1865.
F. F. Hill	do	do	Sept. 12, 1865.
Eugene D. Hill	do	do	Sept. 12, 1865.
William B. Hamilton	do	do	Oct. 12, 1865.
Wm. T. Hatchett	do	do	Aug. 19, 1865.
James L. Hutchins	do	Attorney General of the United States	May 4, 1866.
N. I. Huston	do	Governor Parsons	Sept. 15, 1865.
Gray Huckabee	do	do	Sept. 12, 1865.
William Hooks	do	do	Mar. 2, 1866.
Wm. Hendrix	do	do	Sept. 29, 1865.
R. B. Hill	do	do	Mar. 2, 1866.
G. M. Harris	do	Governor Parsons and Jos. C. Bradley	Sept. 29, 1865.
D. T. Halliday	do	Governor Parsons	Mar. 2, 1866.
R. P. Houser	do	Governor Parsons, E. Stoudenmier, W. D. Whitsline, and L. M. Whetstone	Oct. 2, 1865.
Alfred Iverson, sr	Resigned his seat in United States Senate to aid the rebellion.	Attorney General Stanberry and Governor Parsons	Dec. 1, 1865.
Marcus L. Inzer	Rebel postmaster	Governor Parsons	Oct. 21, 1865.
James B. Irvine	Worth over $20,000	Governor Parsons, Russell Houston, S. C. Posey, and John McAlester	Oct. 18, 1865.
James Isbell	do	Governor Parsons	Dec. 15, 1865.
James Irvine	do	Governor Patton	Nov. 23, 1866.
Wm. B. Inge	do	Governor Parsons	Oct. 18, 1865.
Josiah E. Irby	do	do	Sept. 18, 1865.

Jessee A. Ivy	do	do	Sept. 12, 1865.
Malachi Ivey	do	Governor Parsons and Major Dartt, post commandant	Sept. 12, 1865.
B. Ingraham	do	Governor Parsons	Dec. 29, 1865.
Charles P. Irby	do	do	Mar. 3, 1866.
A. J. Ingersoll	do	Governor Parsons and James Q. Smith, U. S. district attorney for northern Alabama	June 28, 1865.
G. D. Johnston	Rebel brigadier general	Governor Parsons, Mrs. J. N. Barnett, and Mrs. Polk, of Tennessee	Nov. 11, 1865.
H. C. Jones	Member of rebel congress	Russell Houston	June 12, 1865.
George C. Johnson	Commissioner of rebel district court	Governor Parsons	Sept. 18, 1865.
J. R. John	Rebel receiver	do	Sept. 12, 1865.
Levi B. Jones	Rebel mail contractor	do	Mar. 2, 1866.
Wm. J. Jordan	Ex-United States and rebel postmaster	do	Oct. 28, 1866.
A. G. Jones	Rebel postmaster	do	Feb. 20, 1866.
Daniel M. James	Rebel tax collector	do	Mar. 2, 1866.
John F. Johnson	Rebel tax agent, and worth over $20,000	do	Sept. 12, 1865.
Fleming Jordan	Worth over $20,000	do	Jan. 4, 1866.
Charles O. Jones	do	do	Dec. 22, 1865.
Joel W. Jones	do	do	Aug. 31, 1865.
Richard Jones	do	do	Oct. 2, 1865.
Wm. B. Jones	do	do	Sept. 20, 1865.
B. R. Jones	do	do	Sept. 29, 1865.
Thomas B. Jones	do	do	Sept. 18, 1865.
Wm. J. Johnston	do	do	Aug. 13, 1866.
F. L. Johnson	do	do	Oct. 21, 1865.
James R. Jones	do	do	Oct. 21, 1865.
James Jacks	do	do	Mar. 2, 1866.
L. F. Johnston	do	do	Dec. 2, 1865.
Allen C. Jones	do	do	Oct. 25, 1865.
Thomas M. Johnston	do	do	Sept. 11, 1865.
B. C. Jones	do	do	Dec. 2, 1865.
Kennon Jones	do	do	Sept. 12, 1865.
Jason G. Jones	do	do	Aug. 19, 1865.
Samuel G. Jones	do	do	Aug. 12, 1865.
Alex. Jarvis	do	Governor Patton	Aug. 13, 1866.
Andrew Jay	do	Governor Parsons	Mar. 19, 1866.
Mrs. G. T. Jones	do	do	Dec. 18, 1865.
Madison Jones	do	do	Sept. 8, 1865.
N. B. Jones	do	do	Sept. 8, 1865.
W. A. Jones	do	do	Sept. 8, 1865.
Mrs. M. K. Jones	do	do	Sept. 8, 1865.
Thomas H. Jones	do	Governor Parsons and David P. Lewis	Sept. 21, 1865.
Thomas J. Judge	do	Governor Parsons	Aug. 21, 1865.
Ira T. Jordan	do	do	Dec. 2, 1865.
Lorenzo James	do	do	Aug. 19, 1865.
Wm. T. Judkins	do	do	Sept. 12, 1865.
T. D. Jones	do	do	Sept. 29, 1865.
Benjamin Jolley	do	R. S. Granger, brevet major general, and Jos. C. Bradley	Sept. 12, 1865.
Israel J. Jones	do	Governor Parsons	Oct. 6, 1867.
T. F. Jewett	do	Governor Parsons, C. C. Langdon, Cyrus Phillips, Charles P. Gage, Henry C. Semple, and William H. Ogbourne.	Oct. 14, 1865.
John H. Johnson	do	Governor Parsons	Sept. 12, 1865.
James H. Judkins, sr	do	do	Sept. 12, 1865.
John C. Judkins, sr	do	do	Sept. 12, 1865.

Alabama—Continued.

Name.	Exemption under amnesty proclamation of May 29, 1865.	By whom recommended.	Date of pardon.
A. S. Jeffries	Worth over $20,000	Governor Parsons	Sept. 12, 1865.
James R. Jones	do	do	Sept. 12, 1865.
W. H. Jemison	do	do	Sept. 12, 1865.
James Jones	do	Governor Parsons and William P. Webb	Sept. 12, 1865.
John M. Jeffries	do	Governor Parsons	Sept. 12, 1865.
Julian T. Johnston	do	do	Sept. 12, 1865.
Thomas Joseph	do	do	Sept. 12, 1865.
Amos Jones	do	do	Sept. 18, 1865.
W. H. Judson	do	do	Dec. 18, 1865.
Wm. M. Jackson	do	Governor Parsons and Russell Houston	Oct. 18, 1865.
Arnold Jolly	do	Governor Parsons	Sept. 13, 1865.
Absalom Jackson	do	do	Aug. 15, 1865.
Robert A. Johnston	do	do	Aug. 21, 1865.
Jere. Johnson	do	do	Oct. 25, 1865.
Junius Jordan	do	Governor Patton	Feb. 21, 1866.
S. M. Jemison	do	Attorney General of the United States	Dec. 29, 1865.
William Knox	Rebel commissioner of the "fifteen million loan," and worth over $20,000.	Governor Parsons	Sept. 12, 1865.
R. B. Kyle	Rebel agent to receive subscriptions to the cotton and produce loan.	do	Sept. 8, 1865.
Francis M. Kirby	Rebel postmaster	do	Mar. 2, 1866.
Robert R. King	do	do	Oct. 21, 1865.
Elias M. Keils	Rebel tax assessor	do	Dec. 29, 1865.
William Kerr	Rebel tax collector	do	Feb. 2, 1866.
J. S. Kennedy	Worth over $20,000	L. T. Thurston, U. S. A.; S. D. Weakley, and A. D. Hunt, of Ky	July 6, 1865.
W. H. Key	do	Governors Patton and Parsons	Feb. 3, 1866.
J. T. Kendall	do	Governor Parsons	Dec. 2, 1865.
F. M. Kirksey	do	do	Aug. 11, 1865.
T. R. Kendall	do	do	May 4, 1866.
Porter King	do	Governor Parsons, J. F. Marsh, colonel commanding United States forces at Marion, Alabama, and Brigadier General McAuther.	June 30, 1865.
James Key	do	Governor Parsons	Feb. 3, 1866.
Jonathan Kirkbride	do	do	Mar. 13, 1866.
E. L. Kimbrough	do	do	Mar. 2, 1866.
David Kennedy	do	do	Dec. 15, 1865.
Robert King	do	Governor Parsons and Joseph C. Bradley	Sept. 15, 1865.
Mrs. E. H. King	do	Governor Parsons	Sept. 12, 1865.
J. B. Knight	do	do	Sept. 12, 1865.
Mrs. E. A. King	do	do	Sept. 12, 1865.
George A. Ketchum	do	do	Sept. 12, 1865.
Jacob Kynard	do	do	Sept. 11, 1865.
W. H. Ketchum	do	do	Sept. 11, 1865.
Mrs. Rhoda B. King	do	do	Sept. 11, 1865.
Philemon King	do	Governor Parsons and Joseph C. Bradley	Sept. 29, 1865.

Russell J. Kelley	do	do	Sept. 29, 1865.
Oswald King	do	do	Sept. 29, 1865.
R. T. Kernachan	do	Governor Parsons, S. C. Posey, R. M. Patton, and John W. McAlester	Oct. 26, 1865.
Mrs. M. M. Kennedy	do	Governor Parsons	Oct. 30, 1865.
John R. Kloan	do	do	Oct. 7, 1865.
William S. Knox	do	do	Oct. 18, 1865.
W. D. King	do	do	Oct. 6, 1865.
F. S. Lyon	Member of rebel congress	do	Aug. 12, 1865.
M. A. Lyon	Rebel treasury and cotton agent	do	Oct. 12, 1865.
Robert W. Lawler	Rebel agent	do	Sept. 12, 1865.
Levi W. Lawler	do	do	Sept. 8, 1865.
George G. Lyon	Rebel commissioner, receiver, and worth over $20,000.	do	Oct. 12, 1865.
Moses W. Lackey	Rebel mail contractor	do	Oct. 21, 1865.
A. D. Simmons	Ex-United States and rebel postmaster	do	Jan. 6, 1866.
Noble R. Ladd	do	S. C. Posey	Apr. 25, 1866.
Henry S. Lee	do	Governor Parsons	Mar. 2, 1866.
L. D. Lusk	Rebel postmaster	do	Mar. 2, 1866.
Samuel D. Lewis	do	do	Dec. 10, 1866.
James M. Lanning	do	do	Oct. 21, 1865.
William P. Lavender	do	do	Oct. 16, 1865.
John Lyon	Rebel tax assessor	do	Oct. 6, 1865.
R. H. Lee	Rebel agent for purchasing cotton, and worth over $20,000.	do	Sept. 11, 1865.
D. R. Lindsay	Petty civil officer	do	Mar. 2, 1866.
Needham Lee	Worth over $20,000	do	Dec. 2, 1865.
W. W. Lumpkin	do	do	Dec. 22, 1865.
William M. Lewis	do	do	Dec. 21, 1865.
James M. Lane	do	By order of the President	Sept. 26, 1865.
John M. Lampley	do	do	June 16, 1865.
William R. Larkin	do	Governor Parsons	Jan. 29, 1866.
John W. Lapsley	do	William R. Marshall, colonel 7th Minnesota volunteers, commanding post	Aug. 14, 1865.
Emanuel Lehman	do	Governor Parsons	Mar. 2, 1866.
John A. Lile	do	do	Mar. 2, 1866.
Robert F. Ligen	do	do	Mar. 2, 1866.
Sterling Lanier	do	do	Aug. 19, 1865.
C. W. Lee	do	do	Aug. 11, 1865.
W. E. Lucas	do	do	Aug. 21, 1865.
Charles S. Lucas	do	do	Aug. 21, 1865.
Nimrod W. Long	do	do	Aug. 15, 1865.
H. R. Lyman	do	do	Oct. 25, 1865.
James W. Lapsley	do	do	Oct. 25, 1865.
T. B. Lipscomb	do	do	Oct. 30, 1865.
Phillip C. Lightfoot	do	do	Oct. 30, 1865.
Mrs. M. A. E. Lipscomb	do	do	Oct. 30, 1865.
T. B. Lee	do	do	Oct. 31, 1865.
J. M. Lee	do	do	Oct. 31, 1865.
Dent Lamar	do	Governor Parsons and B. Fitzpatrick	Oct. 28, 1865.
Mrs. Mattie Lowe	do	Governor Parsons	Oct. 21, 1865.
John T. Lowry	do	do	Oct. 21, 1865.
H. S. Lide	do	Governor Parsons, John Ritter, W. L. McDow, A. D. Hall, M. V. Lacy, A. J. Hodge, E. Allen, M. W. Davis, and J. H. Manly.	Oct. 7, 1865.

Alabama—Continued.

Name.	Exemption under amnesty proclamation of May 29, 1865.	By whom recommended.	Date of pardon.
W. G. Little	Worth over $20,000	Governor Parsons, John H. Hargood, E. H. Watts, Thomas Daniel, L. Oliver, A. D. Hall, M. V. Lacy, M. W. Davis, and John A. Winston.	Oct. 7, 1865.
Henry P. Lee	do	Governor Parsons, L. Owen, and M. A. Chisholm	Oct. 6, 1865.
James M. Lee	do	Governor Parsons	Oct. 6, 1865.
John M. Ladd	do	do	Oct. 6, 1865.
Charles D. Laney	do	do	Sept. 8, 1865.
Nathan Love	do	do	Sept. 18, 1865.
John Lee	do	do	Sept. 11, 1865.
Napoleon Lockett	do	do	Sept. 11, 1865.
William D. Lee	do	do	Sept. 11, 1865.
John H. Lee	do	do	Sept. 11, 1865.
James Lee	do	do	Sept. 11, 1865.
Jesse G. W. Leftwich	do	do	Sept. 11, 1865.
L. B. Lane	do	do	Sept. 11, 1865.
Nathan B. Lane	do	do	Sept. 11, 1865.
J. F. Lewis	do	do	Sept. 12, 1865.
William Little	do	do	Sept. 12, 1865.
Andrew Lyon	do	do	Sept. 12, 1865.
Thomas H. Lake	do	do	Sept. 12, 1865.
William B Lanier	do	do	Sept. 12, 1865.
C. A. Lomax	do	do	Sept. 12, 1865.
Mrs. S. J. Lawler	do	Attorney General Speed	Sept. 12, 1865.
Theophilus Lacy	do	Governor Parsons	Sept. 29, 1865.
W. H. Long	do	do	Sept. 29, 1865.
P. J. Le Vert	do	Governor Parsons and Joseph C. Bradley	Sept. 29, 1865.
William Lesslie	do	do	Sept. 29, 1865.
Burwell C. Lanier	do	Governor Parsons	Sept. 29, 1865.
William Langford	do	do	Sept. 29, 1865.
William Laug	do	do	Oct. 14, 1865.
M. Lehman	do	Governor Parsons, F. Bugbee, E. H. Metcalf, L. Owen, D. A. Benjamin, W. L. Coleman, and M. A. Chisholm.	Sept. 12, 1865.
A. T. Maxwell	Member of the rebel legislature, and worth over $20,000.	Governor Parsons	Sept. 12, 1865.
William S. Miree	do	do	Sept. 29, 1865.
George G. McWharton	Rebel receiver	do	Mar. 17, 1866.
William H. Martin	do	do	Dec. 22, 1865.
J. W. McConnell	Rebel depot agent for the collection of tax in kind	do	Mar. 2, 1866.
Wiley W. Mason	Rebel commissioner	do	Oct. 30, 1865.
John N. Malone	Agent under the rebel confiscation laws	do	Aug. 11, 1865.
John McNab	Rebel sub-agent and worth over $20,000	do	Sept. 8, 1865.
Henry Morgan	Rebel mail contractor	do	Sept. 18, 1865.
Francis M. Mann	do	do	Oct. 10, 1865.
William B. Martin	Rebel mail contractor, and worth over $20,000	do	Jan. 4, 1866.
T. B. McCall	Rebel enrolling officer, and worth over $20,000	M. A. Chisholm and M. J. Saffold	Sept. 29, 1865.

Benjamin T. Moore	Clerk in the rebel district court, and worth over $20,000.	Hon. Joseph C. Bradley	May 17, 1866.
R. C. McLester	Rebel impressing agent, and worth over $20,000	Governor Parsons and E. A. Powell	Oct. 14, 1865.
Daniel McKenzie	Ex-United States and rebel postmaster	Governor Parsons	Oct. 21, 1865.
John Massey	do	do	Mar. 2, 1865.
A. W. McNeal	do	do	Oct. 12, 1865.
E. C. McDonald	do	do	Mar. 2, 1866.
H. A. Manning	Rebel postmaster	do	Oct. 21, 1865.
P. W. McVay	do	do	Nov. 9, 1865.
James Montgomery	do	do	Mar. 2, 1866.
John J. Moore	do	do	Dec. 21, 1865.
A. J. Martin	do	do	Oct. 3, 1865.
S. W. Murley	do	do	Sept. 12, 1865.
Lewis B. Moseley	do	do	Sept. 11, 1865.
J. H. McDonald	Rebel tax assessor	do	Sept. 15, 1865.
T. A. McMurray	do	do	Oct. 13, 1865.
John Moseley	do	do	Sept. 11, 1865.
William J. Mosely	do	do	Sept. 11, 1865.
S. P. McClellan	do	do	Mar. 2, 1865.
R. D. Marshall	Rebel tax collector	do	Dec. 29, 1865.
William C. Martin	do	do	Sept. 12, 1865.
Abram Martin	Rebel chief collector of taxes, and worth over $20,000	do	Oct. 18, 1865.
A. H. Moses	Clerk of the rebel district court	Governor Parsons and M. J. Saffold	Mar. 2, 1866.
John T. Milner	Proceedings instituted for confiscation, and worth over $20,000.	Hon. Lewis E. Parsons, governor of Alabama	Dec. 21, 1865.
Benjamin W. Macklin	Property returned as abandoned, and worth over $20,000.	Governor Parsons	Sept. 12, 1865.
Kate Moore	Worth over $20,000	Honorable Attorney General of the United States	Sept. 29, 1865.
J. C. B. Mitchell	do	W. A. Bilbo and James L. Seward	Aug. 19, 1865.
T. M. Mosely	do	Governor Parsons and Joseph C. Bradley	Jan. 4, 1866.
F. B. Moore	do	A. M. Patton, governor of Alabama	Mar. 17, 1866.
William H. Mitchell	do	Governor Parsons	Nov. 17, 1865.
E. S. McCurdy	do	do	Oct. 28, 1865.
J. G. McGaughey	do	do	Aug. 22, 1866.
Amos R. Manning	do	do	May 11, 1866.
John Merritt	do	do	Oct. 28, 1865.
G. H. B. Mathews	do	do	Oct. 18, 1865.
Thomas B. Kerrall	do	Governor Parsons and A. W. Dillard	Oct. 7, 1865.
William Miller	do	William P. Webb, G. Horton, and J. A. Winston	Nov. 2, 1865.
L. W. Mason	do	Governor Parsons	Mar. 19, 1866.
William A. McAlpine	do	do	Nov. 1, 1866.
William Miller	do	T. Reavis	Oct. 13, 1865.
F. S. McGuier	do	Governor Parsons	Mar. 19, 1866.
E. H. Metcalf	do	do	Sept. 11, 1865.
J. W. McAlester	do	Russell Houston	June 12, 1865.
William Murrah	do	Governor Parsons	Oct. 14, 1865.
C. A. Marston	do	do	Oct. 26, 1866.
Thomas McKnight	do	do	Oct. 10, 1865.
William L. McDow	do	do	May 4, 1866.
Robert Mitchell	do	do	Apr. —, 1866.
Archer McDonnell	do	Governor Parsons and J. C. Bradley	Sept. 29, 1865.
T. S. McCalley	do	do	Sept. 29, 1865.

Alabama—Continued

Name.	Exemption under amnesty proclamation of May 29, 1865.	By whom recommended.	Date of pardon.
Henry Moore	Worth over $20,000	Governor Parsons	Oct. 13, 1865.
Charles P. May	do	do	Oct. 10, 1865.
Daniel T. McCall	do	do	Oct. 12, 1865.
J. G. Martin	do	do	Dec. 21, 1865.
D. L. Moore	do	Governor Parsons and Joseph C. Bradley	Oct. 12, 1865.
Samuel P. L. Marshall	do	Governor Parsons	Dec. 2, 1865.
J. B. Malone	do	do	Oct. 6, 1865.
John W. McQueen	do	do	Nov. 16, 1865.
Samuel Mathews	do	Governor Parsons and J. C. Bradley	Sept. 29, 1865.
J. G. McLendon	do	Governor Parsons	Dec. 2, 1865.
S. J. Murphy	do	do	Oct. 6, 1865.
Luke Mathews	do	Governor Parsons and J. C. Bradley	Sept. 28, 1865.
J. E. Mathews	do	Hon. Lewis E. Parsons, provisional governor of Alabama	Sept. 18, 1865.
Mrs. Georgia Mitchell	do	do	Sept. 18, 1865.
Mrs. Virginia Matthews	do	do	Sept. 18, 1865.
John Mitchell	do	do	Sept. 18, 1865.
James McCormick	do	do	Dec. 2, 1865.
A. McKellar	do	do	Sept. 18, 1865.
Franklin L. Milhous	do	do	Sept. 18, 1865.
John McInnis	do	do	Sept. 18, 1865.
William F. Moneth	do	do	Feb. 20, 1866.
Duncan McCall	do	do	Sept. 12, 1865.
R. H. Molton	do	Hon. Lewis E. Parsons, provisional governor of Alabama, and James Berney	Sept. 8, 1865.
T. J. Molton	do	Governor Parsons	Sept. 8, 1865.
B. H. Micou	do	Governor Parsons, J. J. Sickles, M. J. Bulger, William Rowe, J. G. Bass, G. W. Merritt, H. P. Smith, J. Meddows, Z. Ware, George Morgan, L. Kimbell, R. Walton, B. F. Mormon, J. W. Fleming, B. S. Wise, H. T. Clemmons, H. J. Bryant, R. R. Brewer, William Scott, G. W. Fowler, W. M. Benson, J. J. Cassidy, G. B. Johnson, S. C. Smith, William Paige, J. W. Cannon, Joseph B. McDonald, J. L. Porter, J. M. Phillips, J. N. Norris, J. T. King, Samuel Knox, John Smith, J. Tucker, John Johnson, E. Haight, Robert Johnson, L. C. Bustin, J. H. Polk, D. D. Grant, John Brice, William James, L. McCoy, Henry Lewis, B. Morgan, John Joy, and Joseph Smith.	Aug. 2, 1865.
William M. Marks	do	Governor Parsons	Sept. 12, 1865.
James M. Muldon	do	do	June 6, 1866.
Letitia D. Moore	do	do	Nov. 1, 1865.
J. L. Moultrie	do	do	Mar. 2, 1866.
W. E. Murphy	do	do	Mar. 2, 1866.
G. B. Mobley	do	do	Sept. 2, 1865.
G. B. Mobley	do	do	Sept. 12, 1865.
Josephine McRae	do	do	Sept. 12, 1865.
Mrs. A. J. Moore	do	do	Mar. 2, 1866.
L. S. Mead	do	do	Mar. 2, 1866.
Frank Martin	do	do	Sept. 22, 1865.

W. T. Mathews	do	do	Mar. 2, 1866.
W. B. Mathews	do	do	Aug. 19, 1865.
G. M. Martin	do	do	Sept. 29, 1865.
Alexander McKeithen	do	do	Sept. 12, 1865.
W. H. Moore	do	do	Mar. 15, 1866.
John McGaugh	do	do	Sept. 8, 1865.
C. L. Merriwether	do	de	Sept. 12, 1865.
A. B. Moore	do	do	Mar. 14, 1866.
D. F. McCrary	do	do	Sept. 11, 1865.
A. S. McKay	do	do	Sept. 8, 1865.
Henry Moffet	do	do	Aug. 13, 1866.
James Montgomery	do	do	Mar. 2, 1866.
William Matkins	do	do	Sept. 29, 1865.
B. F. Marshall	do	do	Oct. 2, 1865.
T. B. Maddox	do	do	Oct. 13, 1865.
Moses McLemore	do	do	Oct. 2, 1865.
J. B. Merriwether	do	do	Aug. 19, 1865.
P. W. Milhous	do	do	Sept. 11, 1865.
Daniel McNeil	do	do	Sept. 12, 1865.
D. W. Murrell	do	do	Sept. 12, 1865.
G. W. H. Mingo	do	do	Sept. 12, 1865.
John Morrissette	do	do	Sept. 8, 1865.
G. D. Miller	do	do	Mar. 2, 1866.
John Marrast	do	do	Sept. 8, 1865.
F. T. Mastin	do	do	Sept. 22, 1865.
W. W. Manning	do	do	Sept. 12, 1865.
William J. McKerall	do	do	Sept. 12, 1865.
James McAdory	do	do	Feb. 2, 1865.
T. M. Mathews	do	do	Sept. 12, 1865.
A. C. Mitchell	do	do	Sept. 12, 1865.
A. G. McGehee	do	do	Sept. 12, 1865.
B. Manly	do	do	Sept. 12, 1865.
G. W. Malone	do	do	Feb. 2, 1866.
Samuel H. Moore	de	do	Sept. 7, 1865.
John U. Mollet	do	do	Mar. 2, 1866.
J. W. McDonald	do	do	Sept. 8, 1865.
A. J. McGinney	do	do	Mar. 2, 1866.
A. J. Martin	do	do	Sept. 8, 1865.
Spencer C. Marks	do	do	Aug. 19, 1865.
W. S. McElwain	do	do	Sept. 11, 1865.
William Mallory	do	do	Mar. 2, 1866.
E. P. Morrisett	do	do	Jan. 11, 1866.
D. M. McLean	do	do	Mar. 2, 1866.
D. L. Moore	do	do	Oct. 2, 1865.
R. W. Moore	do	do	Sept. 11, 1865.
Kate Moore	do	do	Sept. 29, 1865.
James Mallory	do	do	Sept. 11, 1865.
N. H. Mundin	do	do	Sept. 11, 1865.
William H. Moore	do	do	Nov. 3, 1865.
John H. Miller	do	do	Sept. 8, 1865.
J. C. B. Mitchell	do	do	Aug. 19, 1865.
S. B. Marks	do	do	Aug. 19, 1865.

Alabama—Continued.

Name.	Exemption under amnesty proclamation of May 29, 1865.	By whom recommended.	Date of pardon.
R. A. McTyer	Worth over $20,000	Hon. Lewis E. Parsons, provisional governor of Alabama	Sept. 8, 1865.
C. L. Mathews	do	do	Aug. 19, 1865.
Thomas McElderry	do	do	Oct. 21, 1865.
W. A. Morris	do	do	Oct. 21, 1865.
J. M. Minter	do	do	Oct. 18, 1865.
John C. McRae	do	do	Dec. 2, 1865.
R. P. McCord	do	do	Oct. 18, 1865.
James Manning	do	do	Oct. 18, 1865.
J. M. McClannahan	do	do	Sept. 12, 1865.
Thomas Merriwether	do	do	Sept. 12, 1865.
W. H. Mitchell	do	do	Nov. 17, 1865.
Washington Moody	do	do	Sept. 11, 1865.
Stephen Miller	do	do	Sept. 11, 1865.
S. W. McKerrall	do	do	Sept. 11, 1865.
G. L. Mastin	do	do	Sept. 22, 1865.
G. H. B. Mathews	do	do	Mar. 13, 1865.
S. Mordeci	do	do	Mar. 13, 1866.
Rebecca Mathews	do	do	Mar. 13, 1866.
C. B. Moore	do	do	Oct. 18, 1865.
A. J. McAllister	do	do	Jan. 29, 1866.
Albert G. Mabrey	do	do	Oct. 18, 1865.
David Mings	do	do	Nov. 9, 1865.
William Miller	do	Hon. Lewis E. Parsons, provisional governor of Alabama, John A. Winston, G. Horton, W. J. Ledyard, G. W. Tarlton, L. Merchant & Co., John M. Hollingsworth, W. Freeman, S. U. Fosdick, J. Y. Thompson, and C. B. Dickinson.	Nov. 2, 1865.
Mrs. Ann McAlpine	do	Governor Parsons	Nov. 2, 1865.
J. W. McMillan	do	do	Oct. 25, 1865.
E. W. Marks	do	do	Oct. 25, 1865.
Willard Miner	do	do	Oct. 25, 1865.
J. W. McGehee	do	do	Oct. 25, 1865.
J. D. McCall	do	do	Oct. 24, 1865.
John L. Malone	do	do	Dec. 21, 1865.
Sarah A. Martin	do	do	Dec. 21, 1865.
Abner McGehee	do	do	Dec. 21, 1865.
Mark A. Wyatt	do	do	Dec. 22, 1865.
Mrs. M. McClung	do	Joseph C. Bradley	Dec. 9, 1865.
Nashville Malone	do	Governor Parsons	Jan. 4, 1865.
W. J. McCally	do	do	Jan. 4, 1865.
Hugh McIlwain	do	do	Sept. 11, 1865.
J. A. McLester	do	do	Dec 21, 1865.
William E. McGehee	do	do	Dec. 22, 1865.
J. R. McDowell	do	do	Dec. 15, 1865.
J. L. Marshall	do	do	Dec. 15, 1865.
John H. Wyatt	do	do	Dec. 22, 1865.

George Mathews	do	do	Aug. 19, 1865.
James Marks	do	do	Aug. 19, 1865.
Leonard Marbury	do	do	Sept. 12, 1865.
James H. Mastin	do	do	Sept. 22, 1865.
James McGehee	do	do	Sept. 12, 1865.
Precilla W. McDowell	do	do	Jan. 4, 1865.
Mrs. Jane D. Massey	do	Governor Perry, of South Carolina	Oct. 2, 1865.
James M. Norwood	Rebel agent to collect commissary stores	Governor Parsons	Nov. 1, 1865.
William H. Nevill	Rebel agent, and worth over $20,000	do	Sept. 12, 1865.
John H. Norment	Ex-United States and rebel postmaster	do	Jan. 4, 1866.
Yancey Noble	Rebel postmaster	do	Jan. 4, 1866.
James M. Nelson	do	do	Oct. 21, 1865.
French Nabors	Rebel tax assessor	do	Oct. 14, 1865.
G. E. Nelson	Worth over $20,000	do	Sept. 12, 1865.
A. S. Nelson	do	do	Sept. 12, 1865.
A. J. Noble	do	do	Sept. 12, 1865.
B. F. Noble	do	Governor Parsons, E. A. Banks, L. Owen, and M. A. Chisholm	Sept. 12, 1865.
Julius Norton	do	Governor Parsons	Dec. 15, 1865.
George W. Neal	do	Governor Parsons, D. C. Humphreys, and Joseph C. Bradley	Dec. 29, 1865.
E. Napier	do	Governor Parsons	Aug. 4, 1865.
F. G. Norman	do	do	Feb. 2, 1866.
James M. Neal	do	do	Mar. 2, 1866.
Henry Nabring	do	do	Mar. 2, 1866.
George W. Noble	do	do	Mar. 2, 1866.
J. B. Nave	do	do	Sept. 11, 1865.
James Nunn	do	Governor Parsons, W. R. R. Wyatt, J. B. Wilkinson, Thomas Underwood, A. J. Hall, A. T. Smith, and L. Howard.	Sept. 8, 1865.
Theodore Nunn	do	do	Sept. 8, 1865.
E. T. Napier	do	Governor Parsons	Aug. 21, 1865.
William O. Nixon	do	do	Oct. 11, 1865.
William J. Norris	do	do	Oct. 24, 1865.
Nathaniel Nuckolls	do	do	Oct. 23, 1865.
Robert W. Nicolson	do	do	Dec. 15, 1865.
Josiah C. Nott	do	do	Oct. 14, 1865.
T. F. Nolan	do	do	Oct. 14, 1865.
James Nance	do	do	Oct. 18, 1865.
H. E. Owens	Member of secession convention, and worth over $20,000.	do	Sept. 11, 1865.
D. C. Oates	Ex-United States and rebel postmaster, and worth over $20,000.	Governor Parsons, R. S. Walkins, C. Womble, judge of probate, J. B. Moore, and William Skrivner.	Oct. 26, 1865.
James F. Orr	Rebel postmaster, and worth over $20,000	Governor Parsons	Dec. 15, 1865.
R. H. Offut	Rebel contractor, and worth over $20,000	do	Sept. 12, 1865.
William Otis	do	do	Oct. 2, 1865.
Thomas Ormond	Worth over $20,000	Governor Parsons, S. M. Hollaway, William M. Lewis, E. K. Fulton, L. D. Godfrey, H. P. Snow, M. V. Lacy, G. B. Mobley, A. D. Hall, and S. W. Barnes.	Oct. 7, 1865.
Robert Otis	do	Governor Parsons	Dec. 18, 1865.
A. H. Otey	do	do	Sept. 29, 1865.
Lewis Owen	do	do	Sept. 12, 1865.
J. J. Ormond	do	do	Sept. 12, 1865.
Lewellin Oliver	do	Governor Parsons, B. Garner, W. E. Chambliss, William V. Stanton, D. R. Dunlap, G. L. Wilder, James Ballard, J. A. Mooring, T. Adams, and Frank P. Snedecor.	Sept. 12, 1865.

Alabama—Continued.

Name.	Exemption under amnesty proclamation of May 29, 1865.	By whom recommended.	Date of pardon.
R. M. Patton	Agent for the sale of rebel bonds, and worth over $20,000.	Governor Parsons and Benjamin Fitzpatrick	Aug. 8, 1865.
W. R. Palmer	Ex-United States and rebel postmaster	Governor Parsons	Sept. 26, 1865.
Jackson Phillips	do	do	Mar. 2, 1866.
W. D. Parks	do	Governor Parsons and Joseph C. Bradley	Sept. 29, 1865.
W. W. Pruitt	Rebel postmaster	Governor Parsons	Oct. 4, 1865.
Pleasant Ponder	do	do	Mar. 2, 1866.
Isaac M. Pool	do	do	Feb. 20, 1866.
Thomas W. Price	do	do	Sept. 12, 1865.
Lewis A. Pow	Rebel tax assessor	Governor Parsons, W. R. Wyatt, J. B. Wilkinson, A. J. Hall, and Charles M. Howard.	Oct. 18, 1865.
J. Q. Perry	do	Governor Parsons	Nov. 17, 1865.
W. W. Peck	do	Attorney General	June 25, 1866.
Benjamin F. Price	Rebel tax collector	Governor Parsons	Mar. 2, 1866.
Benjamin F. Petty	do	Governor Parsons, and Benjamin S. Dartt, major of 7th Pennsylvania cavalry, post commander.	Sept. 12, 1865.
William R. Patton	Rebel tax collector, and worth over $20,000	Governor Parsons and Joseph C. Bradley	Sept. 29, 1865.
Martha L. Patton	Worth over $20,000	Attorney General	Sept. 29, 1865.
Wesley Plattenberg	do	Governor Parsons	Oct. 25, 1865.
Mrs. F. E. Perine	do	do	Sept. 23, 1865.
J. C. Phares	do	do	Nov. 1, 1865.
C. D. Parke	do	do	Nov. 1, 1865.
George C. Phillips	do	do	Oct. 21, 1865.
John B. Phillips	do	do	Oct. 21, 1865.
William S. Phillips	do	Governor Parsons, F. L. Johnson, J. R. John, William M. Smith, and Benj. M. Woolsey.	Oct. 21, 1865.
William Perkins	do	Governor Parsons	Dec. 2, 1865.
S. B. Paine	do	do	Mar. 2, 1866.
G. C. Player	do	do	Mar. 2, 1866.
E. M. Perine	do	do	Mar. 2, 1866.
E. A. Pearce	do	Governor Parsons, A. B. Fannin, W. C. McIver, J. M. Newman	Mar. 2, 1866.
J. P. Pride	do	Governor Parsons	Jan. 29, 1866.
Malcolm Purcell	do	do	Jan. 29, 1866.
Richard C. Parker	do	do	Mar. 19 1866.
John F. Pride	do	do	Dec. 29, 1865.
H. J. Pride	do	do	Dec. 29, 1865.
W. H. Pratt	do	do	Dec. 18, 1865.
E. F. Pearson	do	do	Dec. 22, 1865.
W. M. Pleasant	do	do	Dec. 22, 1865.
J. E. Poellnitz	do	do	Dec. 22, 1865.
Joseph S. Powell	do	do	Dec. 22, 1865.
Thomas H. Perkins	do	do	Oct. 26, 1865.
A. J. Pool	do	do	Oct. 25, 1865.
William Powers	do	Governor Parsons and Joseph C. Bradley	Oct. 21, 1865.
Cyrus Phillips	do	Governor Parsons	Oct. 21, 1865.
Stephen M. Potts	do	Governor Patton	Oct. 19, 1866.

A. H. Powell	do	Governor Parsons	Oct. 4, 1865.
John Powell	do	do	Oct. 4, 1865.
James R. Powell	do	Governor Parsons and Ben. Fitzpatrick	Aug. 2, 1865.
Charles T. Pollard	do	Governor Parsons and J. J. Sickles	Aug. 12, 1865.
John Peters	do	Governor Parsons	Sept. 29, 1865.
Thomas Peters	do	Governor Sharkey, of Mississippi	Mar. 2, 1866.
Jas. M. Pearson	do	Governor Parsons	Mar. 2, 1866.
John M. Parkman	do	Brevet Major General McArthur	July 25, 1865.
Nelson W. Perry	do	Governor Parsons	Oct. 6, 1865.
R. W. Price	do	do	Sept. 12, 1865.
Mrs. Ann T. Perrin	do	do	Oct. 30, 1865.
John W. Prewett	do	do	Oct. 14, 1865.
Mrs. Mary G. Pickens	do	do	Oct. 30, 1865.
Wm. R. Powell	do	do	Oct. 10, 1865.
Socrates Parker	do	do	Oct. 6, 1865.
C. A. Poellnitz	do	do	Oct. 13, 1865.
Joseph Pow	do	do	Dec. 2, 1865.
E. B. Perrin	do	do	Aug. 14, 1865.
James T. Persons	do	do	Sept. 12, 1865.
Daniel F. Prout	do	do	Oct. 12, 1865.
Chillian Palmer	do	Governor Parsons, John A. Winton, John E. Brown, M. V. Lacy, E. K. Fulton, D. Mitchell, D. C. White, E. H. Watts, J. A. Gibbs, E. N. King, H. P. Snow, L. D. Godfrey, James B. Ivy, W. T. Dimick, and A. A. Winston.	Oct. 7, 1865.
James Porter	do	Governor Parsons	Sept. 12, 1861.
Richard H. Powell	do	do	Sept. 12, 1865.
Joseph Patton	do	do	Sept. 29, 1865.
J. E. Prestridge	do	Attorney General Speed	Oct. 23, 1865.
Samuel Peete	do	Governor Parsons	Sept. 29, 1865.
John H. Prince	do	do	Sept. 12, 1865.
L. B. Parker	do	do	Sept. 12, 1865.
James L. Price	do	do	Sept. 12, 1865.
R. R. Pickering	do	Governor Parsons and E. G. Sebree	Oct. 2, 1865.
Charles H. Patton	do	Governor Parsons and Joseph C. Bradley	Sept. 29, 1865.
Daniel Pratt	do	Governor Parsons	Sept. 29, 1865.
John Patton	do	do	Sept. 29, 1865.
Thomas J. Portis	do	do	Sept. 11, 1865.
P. H. Pitts	do	do	Sept. 12, 1865.
W. R. Pickett	do	do	Sept. 12, 1865.
A. Philipe	do	do	Sept. 13, 1865.
James M. Pruett	do	Governor Parsons, A. Stow, Eli S. Shorte, and Wm. H. Thornton	Sept. 12, 1865.
Caleb Price	do	Governor Parsons	Sept. 29, 1865.
Mrs. A. Perrin	do	do	Aug. 14, 1865.
A. Pope	do	do	Sept. 12, 1865.
Richard Pruit	do	do	Sept. 15, 1865.
Wm. H. Pollard	do	do	Aug. 21, 1865.
Francis M. Peterson	do	do	Feb. 2, 1866.
Cornelius Robinson	Member of rebel provisional congress, and worth over $20,000.	do	Sept. 8, 1865.
T. Reavis	Rebel agent to receive subscriptions to the fifteen-million loan, and worth over $20,000.	Governor Parsons and D. C. Thomas, colonel commanding	Sept. 9, 1865.
Patrick Ragland	Rebel commissioner under the sequestration act	Governor Parsons, D. C. Humphreys, and Benj. Jolley	Dec. 2, 1865.
A. H. Roebuck	Rebel agent to collect provisions for the army	Governor Parsons	Oct. 18, 1865.

Alabama—Continued.

Name.	Exemption under amnesty proclamation of May 29, 1865.	By whom recommended.	Date of pardon.
A. J. Requier	Ex-United States and rebel district attorney	Governor Parsons	Oct. 12, 1865.
V. M. Robertson	Rebel postmaster	Governor Patton	Apr. 25, 1866.
Elias Read	do	Governor Parsons	Mar. 2, 1866.
George Riser	Rebel postmaster, and worth over $20,000	do	Dec. 2, 1865.
John Rowe	Rebel tax collector	do	Mar. 2, 1866.
S. K. Rayburn	do	do	Mar. 2, 1866.
John Robbins	Rebel tax collector, and worth over $20,000	do	Sept. 12, 1865.
Wm. T. Rice	Rebel receiver of tax	Governor Parsons, Charles S. G. Doster, M. D. La Mar, John L. Alexander, H. Brown, Mills Rogers, and A. G. Smith.	Oct. 28, 1865.
John M. Robertson	Property libelled for confiscation, and worth over $20,000.	Governor Parsons	Mar. 15, 1866.
James B. Robinson	Property in possession of United States, and worth over $20,000.	do	Sept. 15, 1865.
J. C. Ray	Worth over $20,000	do	June 9, 1866.
D. M. Russell	do	S. C. Pomeroy, United States senator	Sept. 11, 1865.
Mrs. Sarah J. Rives	do	Governor Parsons	Feb. 2, 1866.
Samuel Ruffin	do	do	Oct. 6, 1865.
Mrs. Eliza A. Reese	do	do	Feb. 2, 1866.
John Robinson	do	do	Sept. 15, 1865.
Carlos Reese	do	do	Sept. 29, 1865.
Mrs. E. S. Richardson	do	do	Dec. 22, 1865.
Mary P. Rice	do	do	Nov. 9, 1865.
Walker Reynolds	do	do	Sept. 11, 1865.
O. T. Rogers	do	do	Sept. 8, 1865.
Josiah Robbins	do	Governor Parsons and A. B. Cooper	Mar. 19, 1866.
A. J. Reese	do	Governor Parsons	Sept. 11, 1865.
Thomas H. Reynolds	do	do	Sept. 11, 1865.
S. B. Rutledge	do	do	Sept. 11, 1865.
John E. Reese	do	Governor Parsons and M. J. Saffold	July 9, 1866.
Neal Rowell	do	Governor Patton	Oct. 20, 1866.
Peyton Rowan	do	Governor Parsons	Mar. 2, 1866.
Hopkins Rice	do	Governor Parsons, James Carpenter, W. S. Means, J. A. Walker, E. H. Sholl, John A. Winston, J. G. Sears, A. M. Woods, A. A. Archibald, and A. A. Winston.	Nov. 7, 1865.
John D. Ragland	do	Governor Parsons	Nov. 2, 1865.
B. B. Rudolph	do	do	Jan. 29, 1865.
F. Raowl	do	do	Sept. 8, 1865.
Wm. Robinson	do	do	Sept. 12, 1865.
B. F. Randolph	do	do	Sept. 12, 1865.
Elisha Reynolds	do	do	Feb. 20, 1866.
John B. Rudolph	do	do	Sept. 12, 1865.
George Rapelje	do	do	Dec. 29, 1865.
Wm. C. Ray	do	Governor Parsons, M. A. Chisholm, J. W. Roberts, and W. Bibb	Sept. 12, 1865.

Mary F. Russell	do	Attorney General of the United States	Mar. 2, 1866.
Thomas Robinson	do	Governor Parsons	Dec. 2, 1865.
Wm. M. Rumph	do	do	Sept. 18, 1865.
Thomas J. Riley	do	do	Sept. 29, 1865.
James Robinson	do	do	Aug. 14, 1865.
John B. Read	do	Governor Patton	Aug. 23, 1866.
Abraham Ricks	do	Governor Parsons	Dec. 29, 1865.
J. W. Rutland	do	Governor Parsons, S. C. Posey, R. M. Patton, and C. Womble	Jan. 29, 1866.
M. S. Relfe	do	Governor Parsons, L. Owen, M. A. Chisholm, and W. J. Bibb	Mar. 2, 1866.
George Rix	do	Governor Parsons	Mar. 2, 1866.
James Rumph	do	do	Nov. 9, 1865.
James R. Rogers	do	do	Oct. 7, 1865.
Robert Rives	do	do	Oct. 13, 1865.
Mills Rogers	do	do	Oct. 28, 1865.
O. G. Rencher	do	Governor Parsons, T. D. Bell, M. V. Lacy, G. B. Mobley, R. W. Hatch, John S. Roberts, Geo. H. Dunlap, H. P. Snow, W. O. Winston, J. A. Walker, W. S. Means, and A. A. Winston.	Oct. 7, 1865.
Samuel F. Rice	do	Governor Parsons	Oct. 24, 1865.
John Reid, jr	do	do	Oct. 21, 1865.
Ajax Royster	do	do	Oct. 6, 1865.
William Rowse	do	Robert S. Banker, L. Merchant & Co., and J. M. Hollingsworth	Oct. 6, 1865.
R. C. Randolph	do	Governor Parsons	Oct. 18, 1865.
Marcus Rogers	do	do	Oct. 18, 1865.
L. Ratcliff	do	do	Oct. 18, 1865.
G. L. Ragland	do	do	Oct. 25, 1865.
William Rix	do	Paul Dillingham, governor of Vermont, G. Horton, F. Drombery, and Williard Freeman, of Alabama.	Dec. 2, 1865.
Joseph C. Russell	do	Governor Parsons	Dec. 2, 1865.
Chas. G. Richards	do	do	Sept. 8, 1865.
Wm. F. Ricks	do	Governor Parsons and Jos. C. Bradley	Sept. 8, 1865.
W. F. Rogers	do	Governor Parsons	Mar. 2, 1866.
James Riley	do	do	Sept. 8, 1865.
Jacob Ramser	do	do	Sept. 8, 1865.
Wm. J. A. Russell	do	do	Sept. 18, 1865.
Thomas Riggs	do	do	Dec. 15, 1865.
Richard M. Robertson	do	do	Dec. 29, 1865.
George Robbins	do	do	Sept. 29, 1865.
John W. Rand	do	Governor Parsons and Jos. C. Bradley	Sept. 29, 1865.
John P. Rice	do	Governor Parsons	Nov. 7, 1865.
T. B. Randolph	do	do	Oct. 2, 1865.
Levi W. Reeves	do	do	Sept. 12, 1865.
Chas. J. Reynolds	do	do	Sept. 12, 1865.
Wm. H. Ross	do	do	Sept. 12, 1865.
Zach. Roquemore	do	do	Sept. 12, 1865.
John M. Raiford	do	do	Sept. 12, 1865.
A. H. Ryland	do	do	Sept. 12, 1865.
Richard H. Redwood	do	do	Sept. 12, 1865.
Richard Randolph	do	do	Sept. 12, 1865.
Bradley H. Ridgway	do	Governor Parsons, John W. Taylor, and Wm. P. Webb	Sept. 12, 1865.
Henry W. Reese	do	Governor Parsons	Sept. 12, 1865.
Daniel Rast	do	do	Sept. 12, 1865.
I. W. Roberts	do	do	Sept. 12, 1865.

Alabama—Continued.

Name.	Exemption under amnesty proclamation of May 29, 1865.	By whom recommended.	Date of pardon.
John D. Rother	Worth over $20,000	By order of the President	May 19, 1866.
W. T. Reid	do	do	Mar. 29, 1866.
Walker Richardson	do	Governor Parsons	Dec. 22, 1865.
Henry P. Reed	do	do	Oct. 13, 1865.
A. C. Ramsay	do	do	Oct. 4, 1865.
Jas. C. Rupert	do	do	Oct. 4, 1865.
Isaac Ross	do	do	Oct. 4, 1865.
Robert H. Smith	Member of rebel provisional congress	do	Nov. 4, 1865.
W. M. Smith	Member of rebel State legislature, depositary, and worth over $20,000.	do	Sept. 12, 1865.
John W. Scruggs	Member of legislature and worth over $20,000	Governor Parsons and Jos. C. Bradley	Oct. 21, 1865.
Lewis M. Stone	Member of secession convention and commissioner of rebel court.	Governor Parsons	Sept. 12, 1865.
S. S. Scott	Rebel commissioner of Indian affairs	do	Sept. 12, 1865.
M. J. Saffold	Rebel commissioner for examination of "political prisoners," and State printer.	do	Aug. 7, 1865.
J. Little Smith	Rebel receiver	Governor Parsons and James Q. Smith	Dec. 29, 1865.
P. T. Sayre	do	Governor Parsons	Aug. 19, 1865.
Daniel M. Seals	do	do	Oct. 18, 1865.
Frank W. Siddons	Rebel agent of the produce loan and worth over $20,000.	do	Aug. 11, 1865.
Daniel Stewart	Bonded agriculturist	do	Oct. 13, 1865.
S. B. Severs	Ex-United States and rebel mail contractor	Governor Parsons and Jos. C. Bradley	July 14, 1866.
P. A. Stamps	Rebel mail contractor	Governor Parsons	Oct. 21, 1865.
Wm. L. Sanders	Rebel contractor and worth over $20,000	do	Oct. 18, 1865.
E. T. Sturdivant	Rebel agent to make nitre	do	Oct. 2, 1865.
W. H. Stone	Rebel enrolling officer	do	Sept. 12, 1865.
Merit Street	Ex-United States and rebel postmaster	do	Mar. 2, 1866.
John W. Sandlin	Rebel postmaster	do	Nov. 17, 1865.
F. L. Spigener	do	do	Mar. 2, 1866.
Wm. H. Spigener	do	do	Mar. 2, 1866.
Jas. T. Skelton	do	do	Aug. 13, 1865.
D. T. Seals	do	do	Oct. 25, 1865.
Wm. T. Shaw	do	do	Mar. 2, 1866.
A. M. Simmons	Ex-United States and rebel postmaster	do	Sept. 12, 1865.
Geo. B. Saunders	Rebel tax assessor	do	Sept. 12, 1865.
T. J. Seals	do	Governor Parsons and Benj. S. Dartt, major and post commander	Dec. 18, 1865.
L. Spigener	do	Governor Parsons, Chas. S. G. Dostin, Jas. A. Reynolds, and M. D. LaMar	Oct. 28, 1865.
Wm. W. Selman	do	Governor Parsons	Sept. 12, 1865.
F. H. Smith	do	do	Sept. 8, 1865.
W. H. Spiers	do	do	Mar. 2, 1866.
Wm. A. Schoolar	Rebel tax collector	do	Mar. 2, 1866.
L. P. Saxon	do	Governor Parsons and Hon. M. Blair	Aug. 2, 1865.
Wm. B. Shields	Rebel tax collector and worth over $20,000	Governor Parsons	Sept. 18, 1865.

T. Sanford	Rebel collector of the port of Mobile	do	Nov. 17, 1865.
L. B. Sheffey	Proceedings commenced for confiscation	do	Aug. 17, 1866.
M. C. Stokes	Proceedings commenced for confiscation and worth over $20,000.	do	Nov. 17, 1865.
M. H. Sinclair	Violated his oath	do	Mar. 2, 1866.
Robt. S. Spragins	Left United States military lines	do	Sept. 29, 1865.
Chas. C. Seed	Left a loyal State and worth over $20,000	Governor Parsons, S. D. Weakley, and L. T. Thurston, United States army	Nov. 4, 1865.
Wm. S. Smith	Worth over $20,000	Governor Parsons	Sept. 18, 1865.
Samuel Swoddy	do	Governor Parsons and Wm. P. Webb	Jan. 29, 1866.
Robt. W. Smith	do	Governor Parsons	Sept. 8, 1865.
John M. Stark	do	Governor Parsons and Major Dartt, post commander	Sept. 12, 1865.
E. R Showalter	do	Governor Parsons	Sept. 12, 1865.
W. S. Stone	do	Governor Parsons, James Berney, J. Saffold, and M. A. Chisholm	Sept. 12, 1865.
George Sayre	do	Governor Parsons	Sept. 12, 1865.
Carol ne V. Sayre	do	do	Sept. 12, 1865.
A. K. Shepard	do	do	Sept. 11, 1865.
J. J. Seawell	do	do	Sept. 11, 1865.
E. W. Swoope	do	Governor Parsons, Brev. Maj. Gen. R. S. Granger, D. C. Humphreys, and D. P. Lewis	Sept. 15, 1865.
Mrs. Lucy L. Steele	do	Governor Parsons	Dec. 15, 1865.
W. T. Simpson	do	do	Dec. 2, 1865.
James Scott	do	do	Sept. 11, 1865.
Mrs. E. R. Steele	do	do	Dec. 15, 1865.
W. G. Swanson	do	do	Nov. 6, 1865.
D. S. Steele	do	do	Oct. 18, 1865.
Josiah Springer	do	do	Jan. 4, 1866.
Barton W. Stone	do	do	Sept. 12, 1865.
Geo. W. Stone	do	do	Aug. 21, 1865.
Isaac D. Spear	do	do	Feb. 24, 1866.
Thos. J. Sorsby	do	do	Dec. 22, 1865.
Robt. S. Saunders	do	do	Oct. 25, 1865.
Mrs. S. M. Sanford	do	do	Dec. 22, 1865.
Thomas W. Sims	do	do	Nov. 9, 1865.
Thomas B. Sprott	do	do	Dec. 22, 1865.
Hampton S. Smith	do	do	Oct. 14, 1865.
Joseph Silver	do	do	Dec. 2, 1865.
Mrs. Mary E. Seawell	do	do	Sept. 11, 1865.
Sylvester Steele	do	do	Oct. 18, 1865.
James C. Scott	do	do	Sept. 11, 1865.
Anthony Stow	do	Moses H. Grinnell, Lewis W. Brown, Thos. W. Phelps, Betts, Nicholas & Co., Duryee & Jaques, Fenner, Bennett & Bowman, of New York.	June 16, 1865.
Mrs. C. Smith	do	Jos. C. Bradley	Oct. 4, 1865.
Thos. L. Scott	do	Governor Parsons	Oct. 4, 1865.
David B. Scott	do	do	Sept. 11, 1865.
James H. Smith	do	do	Sept. 12, 1865.
H. L. Smith	do	do	Aug. 15, 1865.
Mrs. R. J. Smith	do	do	Oct. 18, 1865.
W. K. Simpson	do	do	Mar. 15, 1866.
Samuel P. Steele	do	do	Oct. 18, 1865.
H. D. Smith	do	do	Sept. 29, 1865.
H. A. Stollenmerck	do	do	Sept. 8, 1865.
Wm. M. Seldon	do	do	Nov. 1, 1865.
N. Smith	do	do	Oct. 24, 1865.

Alabama—Continued.

Name.	Exemption under amnesty proclamation of May 29, 1865.	By whom recommended.	Date of pardon.
D. A. Steele	Worth over $20,000	Governor Parsons	Oct. 18, 1865.
S. Schwesler	do	do	Sept. 12, 1865.
R. D. Shackelford	do	do	Sept. 18, 1865.
A. Sutter	do	do	Sept. 12, 1865.
Henry C. Sample	do	do	Aug. 19, 1865.
Jason G. Sears	do	do	Mar. 17, 1866.
J. P. Strother	do	do	Sept. 8, 1865.
John P. Streety	do	do	Dec. 2, 1865.
Daniel C. Sellers	do	do	Sept. 18, 1865.
C. H. Sanford	do	do	Mar. 2, 1866.
George C. Scott	do	do	Oct. 17, 1866.
John B. Scott	do	do	Aug. 19, 1865.
Chas. C. Swoope	do	do	Oct. 2, 1865.
Isaac Stone	do	do	Oct. 12, 1865.
John Sears	do	do	Oct. 7, 1865.
Daniel B. Sample	do	do	Feb. 2, 1866.
Reuben Seay	do	do	Mar. 17, 1866.
Dudley Sale	do	By order of the President	April 30, 1866.
Albert Stein	do	Governor Parsons	Oct. 28, 1865.
George Stewart	do	do	Oct. 12, 1865.
T. B. Stallworth	do	do	Oct. 6, 1865.
John G. Shine	do	do	Sept. 29, 1865.
Thomas R. Smith	do	Governor Parsons and Jos. C. Bradley	Sept. 29, 1865.
Thomas St. John	do	Governor Parsons	Sept. 8, 1865.
James E. Saunders	do	Governor Parsons, David P. Lewis, D. C. Humphreys, and Nicholas Davis	Sept. 15, 1865.
Jos. H. Speed	do	Attorney General Speed	Oct. 2, 1865.
Eli S. Shorter	do	Governor Parsons, B. S. Dartt, major and post commander	Sept. 5, 1865.
Robt. L. Steele	do	Governor Parsons	Mar. 2, 1866.
C. W. Strong	do	Governor Patton	May 16, 1866.
E. L. Shuford	do	Governor Parsons	Sept. 12, 1865.
Henry A. Schroeder	do	Isaac Bell, W. H. Vandyck, James Kelley, C. A. Edwards, Geo. F. Talman, Moses Taylor, M. H. Grinnell, John J. Cisco, Jas. Gallatin, and L. A. Waller, all of New York	Oct. 2, 1865.
Wm. D. Smith	do	Governor Parsons, Chas. S. G. Dosten, A. Y. Smith, A. J. Briggs, M. D. LaMar, J. L. Alexander, and G. W. Benson.	Sept. 8, 1865.
Jed. M. Spencer	do	Governor Parsons, J. W. Pennington, John Hunter, J. H. Kendall, Joseph Terry, B. Garner, A. A. Winston, W. O. Winston, T. J. Templeton, James Stephens, and G. B. Mobley.	Oct. 7, 1865.
F. E. Stollenwreck	do	Governor Parsons	Oct. 18, 1865.
F. N. Strudwick	do	do	Oct. 12, 1865.
M. C. Stokes	do	do	Nov. 17, 1865.
George Scovel	do	do	Mar. 2, 1866.
Robert D. Sturdivant	do	do	Sept. 18, 1866.
H. V. Smith	do	do	Sept. 12, 1865.
Edward Stoudemire	do	do	Sept. 12, 1865.

W. C. Sherrod	do	Governor Parsons and Joseph C. Bradley	Jan. 6, 1866.
William A. Smith	do	Governor Parsons	Sept. 12, 1865.
L. L. Stone	do	do	Oct. 21, 1865.
O. D. Sledge	do	do	Oct. 21, 1865.
Lewis E. Smith	do	do	Oct. 24, 1865.
F. A. Saunders	do	do	Mar. 2, 1866.
Isaiah B. Smaw	do	do	Sept. 8, 1865.
Charles Snow	do	do	Mar. 2, 1866.
Samuel Strudwick	do	do	Sept. 12, 1865.
H. Steinhart	do	do	Mar. 2, 1866.
Albert Strassburger	do	do	Sept. 12, 1865.
C. L. Stickney	do	do	Mar. 2, 1866.
A. S. Steele	do	do	Sept. 12, 1865.
S. Stoudenmire	do	do	Sept. 8, 1865.
William H. Smith	do	do	Sept. 12, 1865.
George L. Stewart	do	do	Nov. 13, 1865.
L. A. Sledge	do	do	Sept. 12, 1865.
Fred. O. Sherrod	do	do	Jan. 29, 1866.
Robert H. Slough	do	Attorney General of the United States	Jan. 29, 1866.
F. H. Smith	do	Lacy, Meeken & Co.; Hotchkiss, Fenner & Bennett; Belt, Nicholas & Co.; Lucus Hopkins; and John Allen, of New York.	Sept. 8, 1865.
Joseph Selden	do	Attorney General of the United States	Dec. 2, 1865.
B. F. Seary	do	Governor Parsons	Dec. 2, 1865.
John F. Terry	Rebel purchasing agent	Hon. Lewis E. Parsons, provisional governor of Alabama	Sept. 12, 1865.
H. B. Thompson	Rebel purchasing agent, and worth over $20,000	do	Oct. 13, 1865.
Harris Tinker	Rebel justice of the peace, and worth over $20,000	do	Sept. 12, 1865.
F. G. Thweatt	Ex-United States and rebel postmaster	Hon. R. M. Patton, governor of Alabama	Mar. 2, 1866.
James A. Tallman	Rebel postmaster	Governor Parsons	Sept. 12, 1865.
R. D. Twombly	do	do	Mar. 2, 1866.
L. F. Townsend	do	do	Oct. 24, 1865.
Henry Townsend	do	do	Oct. 24, 1865.
R. E. Tweedie	do	do	Oct. 16, 1865.
Noah R. Turner	Rebel postmaster, and worth over $20,000	do	Sept. 12, 1865.
M. K. Taylor	Tax assessor	Governor Parsons and Joseph C. Bradley	Oct. 21, 1865.
Felix Tankersley	do	Governor Parsons	Sept. 12, 1865.
Sam. Thompson	do	do	Oct. 18, 1865.
Henry Turner	do	do	Oct. 18, 1865.
I. J. Tucker	do	do	Mar. 2, 1865.
James B. Taylor	do	do	Sept. 8, 1865.
F. M. Thomason	Proceedings instituted for confiscation	do	Mar. 2, 1866.
Jesse Thompson	Proceedings instituted for confiscation, and worth over $20,000.	Governor Parsons and Hon. James Speed, Attorney General of the United States	Jan. 13, 1866.
B. F. Tarner	Worth over $20,000	Governor Parsons	Oct. 18, 1865.
B. Tardy	do	do	Oct. 12, 1865.
Amos Travis	do	do	Sept. 12, 1865.
Felix Tate	do	do	Sept. 12, 1865.
William Taylor	do	do	Sept. 12, 1865.
William Tinker	do	do	Sept. 12, 1865.
L. C. Tutt	do	do	Sept. 29, 1865.
James A. Turner	do	do	Sept. 11, 1865.
R. M. Tate	do	do	Sept. 12, 1865.
Benjamin Trimble	do	do	Sept. 12, 1865.

Alabama—Continued.

Name.	Exemption under amnesty proclamation of May 29, 1865.	By whom recommended.	Date of pardon.
Joseph Tanenbaum	Worth over $20,000	Governor Parsons	Oct. 30, 1865.
J. S. Triplett	do	do	Oct. 6, 1865.
C. E. Thames	do	do	Sept. 12, 1865.
George Thomas	do	do	Sept. 12, 1865.
James C. Turner	do	do	Oct. 4, 1865.
John A. Tyson	do	George S. Cox, M. A. Chisholm, and Hon. Judge Saffold	Sept. 29, 1865.
P. S. Townsend	do	Governor Parsons, Joseph C. Bradley, and P. M. Dox	Sept. 29, 1865.
J. G. Tyson	do	Governor Parsons	Dec. 2, 1865.
John T. Taylor	do	Hon Lewis E. Parsons, provisional governor of Alabama	Sept. 29, 1865.
T. T. Tyree	do	Governor Parsons and Hon. James Speed, Attorney General of the United States	Oct. 24, 1865.
Archibald Tyson	do	Governor Parsons	Aug. 7, 1865.
J. W. Tayloe	do	do	Sept. 12, 1865.
Lewis Tyus	do	do	Oct. 12, 1865.
Elizabeth F. Terrell	do	do	Oct. 12, 1865.
E. T. Tayloe	do	do	Nov. 2, 1865.
Thomas B. Taylor	do	do	Sept. 12, 1865.
E. G. Tolbert	do	do	Oct. 18, 1865.
Dr. William H. Thornton	do	do	Sept. 18, 1865.
J. Y. Thompson	do	do	Mar. 2, 1866.
George W. Tarlton	do	do	Mar. 2, 1866.
E. W. Tarver	do	do	Mar. 2, 1866.
W. C. Thompson	do	do	Oct. 25, 1865.
J. M. Taylor	do	Ordered by the President	May 21, 1866.
E. Tartt	do	do	Aug. 8, 1866.
Robert Taylor	do	R. M. Patton, governor of Alabama	Aug. 13, 1866.
T. M. Tartt	do	Governor Parsons, A. W. Dillard, E. H. Watts, John Dillard, F. M. Kirksey, Z. Trueman, R. Beck, M. V. Lacy, A. D. Hall, E. C. Sanders, J. M. Taylor, J. M. Barnes, W. A. Patton, C. J. McMahon, L. D. Godfrey, P. Weir, W. B. Peters, and J. A. Winston.	Oct. 7, 1865.
R. S. Tinker	do	Governor Parsons	Sept. 12, 1865.
C. B. Taliifero	do	do	Mar. 2, 1866.
W. F. Teat	do	do	Oct. 6, 1865.
Samuel F. Ticker	do	do	Sept. 8, 1865.
Drury Thompson	do	Governor Parsons, George N. Stewart, and Robert H. Smith	Sept. 8, 1865.
James Torbert	do	Governor Parsons	Oct. 18, 1865.
James Tait	do	do	Dec. 29, 1865.
B. L. Turner	do	do	Dec. 29, 1865.
William Thompson	do	do	Dec. 2, 1865.
R. D. Thompson	do	do	Sept. 8, 1865.
William B. Taber	do	do	Apr. 10, 1866.
W. C. Tunstall	do	do	Sept. 11, 1865.
S. J. Thomas	do	do	Nov. 2, 1865.
James B. Turner	do	do	Oct. 2, 1865.
James L. Terrell	do	do	Oct. 12, 1865.

Mrs. Ann Torbett	do	do	Feb. 20, 1866.
Jarvis Turner	do	do	Dec. 21, 1865.
James P. Tarry	do	do	Sept. 11, 1865.
James Throckmorton	do	Hon. Lewis E. Parsons, provisional governor of Alabama	June 7, 1866.
S. A. Tarrant	do	do	July 6, 1866.
S. M. Thompson	do	do	Dec. 29, 1865.
G. W. Thompson	do	do	Sept. 14, 1865.
George A. Tuthill	do	Hon. Lewis E. Parsons and J. M. Withers	Oct. 19, 1866.
Jack Thorington	do	Governor Parsons	Aug. 19, 1865.
Edmund Toney	do	do	Jan. 4, 1866.
Moses Thompson	do	do	Dec. 2, 1865.
George W. Tait	do	do	Oct. 25, 1865.
Mrs. Mary A. Taylor	do	do	Sept. 19, 1865.
Matthew Turner	do	do	Nov. 2, 1865.
James I. Thornton	do	do	Nov. 2, 1865.
L. C. Tutt	do	do	Sept. 29, 1865.
Wm. H. Timmons	do	Governor Parsons and Joseph C. Bradley	Oct. 21, 1865.
Miss Mary J. Tart	do	Governor Parsons	Dec. 18, 1865.
Dr. George Terrill	do	Hon. James Speed, Attorney General of the United States	Oct. 26, 1865.
N. H. Thomas	do	Governor Parsons	Mar. 2, 1866.
N. M. Thornton	do	do	Mar. 2, 1866.
Henry W. Todd	do	do	Oct. 31, 1865.
Joseph Tucker	do	do	Oct. 9, 1865.
Henry Tutwiler	do	Governor Parsons and Hon. James Speed, Attorney General of the United States	Oct. 31, 1865.
Henry P. Ulmer	do	Hon. Lewis E. Parsons, provisional governor of Alabama	Sept. 18, 1865.
James Underwood	do	do	Sept. 11, 1866.
Leroy Upshaw	do	do	July 6, 1866.
Benjamin J. Vincent	Rebel postmaster	do	Oct. 21, 1865.
William Varner	Worth over $20,000	C. L. Sayre, agent for the State of Alabama	Apr. 23, 1866.
W. P. Van Derveer	do	Governor Parsons	Sept. 12, 1865.
James H. Vaughan	do	do	Sept. 18, 1865.
S. W. Vaughan	do	Hon. James Speed, Attorney General of the United States	Oct. 21, 1865.
F. C. Vinson	do	Governor Parsons, D. P. Lewis, and Joseph C. Bradley	Sept. 29, 1865.
Fielding Vaughan	do	Governor Parsons	Oct. 21, 1865.
Thomas G. Vicker	do	do	Oct. 21, 1865.
Littlebery Vasser	do	do	Oct. 25, 1865.
E. B. Vaughan	do	do	Sept. 12, 1865.
R. W. Walker	Member of rebel congress	Russell Houston	Aug. 9, 1865.
S. P. Walker	do	Ordered by President	Sept. 28, 1865.
Percy Walker	do	T. Reavis, D. C. Anderson, W. H. Fowler, W. H. Jennison, P. Phillips, L. W. Lewler, C. A. Lochram, of Georgia, Duff Green, A. T. Caperton, of West Virginia, T. S. Gholson of Virginia, A. C. B. Mitchell, H. L. Jurnagan, S. J. Gholson, J. L. Alcorn, and W. of T. Withers, of Mississippi.	Sept. 28, 1865.
John M. Withers	Rebel major general and graduate of West Point	Hon. Lewis E. Parsons, provisional governor of Alabama	Dec. 28, 1865.
H. P. Watkins	Adjutant and inspector general of Alabama, and worth over $20,000.	H. C. Semple, J. W. Roberts, and James Birney	Oct. 13, 1865.
J. H. Witherspoon	Member of the rebel legislature, and worth over $20,000.	Russell Houston	June 12, 1865.
John J. Walker	West Point three years. Did not graduate	Governor Parsons	Nov. 26, 1866.

Alabama—Continued.

Name.	Exemption under amnesty proclamation of May 29, 1865.	By whom recommended.	Date of pardon.
T. H. Watts	Member of the rebel convention, and voted for the ordinance of secession, colonel in the rebel army, attorney general of the would-be southern confederacy, rebel governor of Alabama, and worth over $20,000.	Governor Parsons, Ben. Fitzpatrick, and Hon. Attorney General of the United States	Oct. 18, 1865.
R. H. Wynne	Sergeant at-arms of the rebel congress	Governor Parsons	Mar. 2, 1866.
N. L. Whitfield	Commissioner to receive loan to rebel government	do	Nov. 1, 1865.
T. Y. Ware	Member of the rebel advisory board, and worth over $20,000.	do	Sept. 12, 1865.
T. B. Witmore	Rebel receiver	do	Oct. 21, 1865.
Abner Williams	Rebel purchasing agent	do	Jan. 4, 1866
James Wilson	do	do	Mar. 2, 1865.
J. L. Wainwright	do	do	Oct. 2, 1865.
M. L. Walker	Rebel agent to receive tithes	do	Oct. 14, 1865.
Hardy Wilkins	Rebel deputy marshal	do	Mar. 2, 1866.
J. B. Wilkinson	Petty civil officer	do	Sept. 8, 1865.
D. S. Walker	Rebel justice of the peace and worth over $20,000	do	Sept. 12, 1865.
Thomas Williams	Aided the rebellion	do	Oct. 1, 1865.
J. U. Whiteside	Ex-United States and rebel postmaster	do	Mar. 2, 1866.
James P. Wood	do	do	Mar. 2, 1866.
Larkin Willis	do	J. A. Kerchevul, H. H. Kyle, and A. J. Fletcher, secretary of state	Aug. 16, 1865.
Allen Walls	do	Governor Parsons	Jan. 4, 1866.
W. J. Whisennat	Ex-U. S. and rebel postmaster; worth over $20,000	do	Mar. 2, 1866.
Daniel Wallis	Rebel postmaster	do	May 17, 1866.
Wm. W. Wilkins	do	do	Mar. 2, 1866.
Andrew J. Ward	do	do	Jan. 11, 1866.
J. N. Winston	do	do	Feb. 20, 1866.
Nathaniel Welch	do	do	Oct. 21, 1865.
A. W. White	do	do	Oct. 14, 1865.
Wm. H. Wood	Rebel tax assessor	do	Mar. 2, 1866.
Wm. Williams	do	do	Mar. 2, 1866.
E. B. Woodfin	Rebel tax assessor and worth over $20,000	Governor Parsons and G. W. Lee	Sept. 12, 1865.
D. A. Walker	Rebel tax assessor	Governor Parsons	Oct. 18, 1865.
Thomas Walker	Worth over $20,000	do	Sept. 18, 1865.
G. L. Wallace	do	do	Sept. 29, 1865.
J. T. Whitsitt	do	do	Sept. 11, 1865.
Wm. N. Wyatt	do	do	Sept. 11, 1865.
Wm. B. Woods	do	do	Mar. 2, 1866.
B. W. Whitfield	do	do	Sept. 12, 1865.
W. R. Westcott	do	Governor Parsons, Israel Roberts, James Berney, J. J. Sickles, M. A. Chisholm, and Wm. Falconer.	Sept. 12, 1865.
Samuel Wallace	do	Governor Parsons	Dec. 2, 1865.
L. W. Walker	do	do	Dec. 2, 1865.
Gaines Whitfield	do	do	May 30, 1866.

Lewis T. Woodruff	do	Hon. W. Dennison, Postmaster General, H. L. Burnett, L. W. Lawler, and Milton Brown.	Sept. 29, 1865.
J. T. Walton	do	Governor Parsons	Oct. 12, 1865.
J. L. Winter	do	Hon. Lewis E. Parsons, provisional governor of Alabama, Israel W. Roberts, R. D. Ware, and M. A. Chisholm.	Sept. 12, 1865.
Charles Wise	do	Governor Parsons	June 18, 1866.
D. H. Williams	do	do	Sept. 12, 1865.
W. O. Winston	do	do	Sept. 12, 1865.
Samuel S. Webb	do	do	Oct. 6, 1865.
H. H. Ware	do	do	June 28, 1866.
W. W. Waller	do	do	Oct. 4, 1865.
E. T. Watts	do	do	Oct. 2, 1865.
Price Williams	do	do	Oct. 12, 1865.
R. L. Watkins	do	do	Sept. 12, 1865.
Moses Waring	do	do	Dec. 2, 1865.
Charles Walsh	do	do	Oct. 13, 1865.
Addison White	do	do	Sept. 12, 1865.
S. D. Weakley	do	Hon. James Speed, Attorney General of the United States	June 12, 1865.
George N. Ware	do	Governor Parsons	Sept. 12, 1865.
J. A. Winston	do	do	Sept. 12, 1865.
W. H. Winston	do	do	Sept. 12, 1865.
J. E. Windham	do	do	Sept. 12, 1865.
William Ware	do	do	Sept. 12, 1865.
A. F. Woolley	do	do	Sept. 12, 1865.
F. A. Woodson	do	do	Sept. 2, 1865.
T. A. Walker	do	do	Aug. 12, 1865.
John M. Weston	do	do	Sept. 12, 1865.
Alexander Williams	do	do	Dec. 15, 1865.
R. Westfeldt	do	do	Dec. 21, 1865.
George M. White	do	do	Sept. 12, 1865.
R. S. Williams	do	do	Sept. 12, 1865.
Peter Weir	do	do	Sept. 12, 1865.
J. M. Winston	do	do	Sept. 12, 1865.
John J. Winston	do	do	Sept. 12, 1865.
J. J. V. Wanroy	do	do	Sept. 12, 1865.
James W. Wallace	do	do	Sept. 12, 1865.
Osmun A. Wynne	do	do	Oct. 30, 1865.
R. J. Ware	do	Governor Parsons, E. A. Carr, J. T. Leeper, M. B. Locke, J. B. Hunter, J. P. Cornan, A. Collins, W. C. Winston, Jonathan Ware, B. B. McKenzie, Daniel Crawford, T. B. Cooper, W. H. Crenshaw, T. B. Cooper, J. S. Clark, J. A. Elmore, E. T. Fare, Ben. Fitzpatrick, C. C. Langdon, C. P. Gage, James Bond, Moses McGuire, J. T. Rather, J. H. Hastie, J. Lawrence, C. P. Gage, S. J. Cumming, W. J. Boon, John Lawrence, and J. C. Foster.	Oct. 14, 1865.
Joseph N. Williams	do	Governor Parsons	Oct. 14, 1865.
James M. Wright	do	do	Sept. 12, 1865.
R. D. Ware	do	do	Sept. 12, 1865.
R. B. Waller	do	do	Sept. 12, 1865.
N. Waller	do	do	Mar. 1, 1866.
Charles Walsh	do	do	Oct. 13 1865.
Henry H. Ware	do	do	June 28, 1865.
John R. Webster	do	do	Oct. 30, 1865.
M. P. Watts	do	do	Oct. 12, 1865.
Mrs. C. B. Winston	do	do	Jan. 29, 1866.

Alabama—Continued.

Name.	Exemption under amnesty proclamation of May 29, 1865.	By whom recommended.	Date of pardon.
Miss E. W. Winston	Worth over $20,000	Governor Parsons	Jan. 29, 1866.
E. R. Woods	do	do	Oct. 18, 1865.
J. T. Wiswall	do	do	Oct. 18, 1865.
Bryce Wilson	do	Governor Parsons, R. S. Watkins, C. Womble, S. C. Posey, and Joseph C. Bradley	Jan. 29, 1866.
R. Y. Ware	do	Governor Parsons	Sept. 12, 1865.
R. Weaver	do	do	Oct. 7, 1865.
A. A. Winston	do	do	Dec. 29, 1865.
R. G. Windham	do	do	Sept. 12, 1865.
A. G. Wray	do	do	Sept. 12, 1865.
J. A. White	do	do	Sept. 12, 1865.
F. A. Woodson	do	Ordered by the President	Sept. 2, 1865.
A. J. Withers	do	Governor Parsons and J. C. Bradley	Sept. 29, 1865.
W. A. Welch	do	Governor Parsons	Dec. 2, 1865.
J. L. Watkins	do	do	Sept. 12, 1865.
Weil Henry	do	do	April 4, 1866.
Charles Walsh	do	do	Oct. 13, 1865.
N. Woodruff	do	do	Mar. 2, 1866.
William Wilson	do	do	Nov. 3, 1865.
C. A. Wise	do	do	June 18, 1866.
T. M. Walthall	do	do	Sept. 11, 1865.
L. M. Whetstone	do	do	Sept. 18, 1865.
James A. Ware	do	do	Sept. 23, 1865.
L. F. Whitehead	do	do	Sept. 18, 1865.
A. P. Watt	do	do	Aug. 10, 1866.
J. Y. Wallace	do	do	Sept. 11, 1865.
L. J. Wilson	do	do	Feb. 21, 1866.
Dr. A. A. Wilson	do	do	Sept. 13, 1865.
J. W. Walton	do	do	Sept. 8, 1865.
T. W. White	do	Governor Parsons and J. C. Bradley	Aug. 19, 1865.
J. A. Wemyss	do	do	Sept. 8, 1865.
John A. Walker	do	do	Mar. 17, 1866.
J. H. Ware	do	do	Sept. 8, 1865.
H. Wingate	do	Hon. Lewis E. Parsons, provisional governor of Alabama, and B. S. Dartt, major of seventh Pennsylvania cavalry.	Sept. 8, 1865.
Charles Walker	do	Governor Parsons	Nov. 9, 1865.
Mike L. Woods	do	do	Oct. 2, 1865.
John N. Walthall	do	Governor Parsons, Levi W. Lawler, and Hon. James Speed, Attorney General U. S.	Oct. 2, 1865.
Albert Williams	do	Governor Parsons	Sept. 8, 1865.
P. J. Weaver	do	do	Oct. 2 1865.
Stanhope L. Wallace	do	do	Sept. 11, 1865.
L. M. Wilson	do	C. Walsh and H. A. Schroeder	Aug. 16, 1865.
L. N. Walthall	do	Hon. James Speed, Attorney General of the United States, and L. W. Lawler	Sept. 29, 1865.
John Whiting	do	Governor Parsons, L. Owen, I. W. Roberts, E. H. Metcalf, R. D. Ware, M. A. Chisholm, F. Bugbee, T. B. Maddox, and James Berney.	Sept. 2, 1865.

Benjamin J. Wilson	do	Governor Parsons	Mar. 2, 1866.
Joel White	do	do	Nov. 3, 1865.
Mrs. W. G. Wine	do	do	Nov. 1, 1865.
Horace Ware	do	do	Oct. 2, 1865.
John White	do	do	Oct. 2, 1865.
Henry Ware	do	do	Oct. 23, 1865.
A. G. Watters	do	do	Mar. 2, 1866.
E. L. Woodward	do	do	Mar. 2, 1866.
J. H. Y. Webb	do	do	Sept. 8, 1865.
N. B. Whitfield	do	do	Nov. 1, 1865.
Samuel Wolff	do	do	Sept. 29, 1865.
R. A. Wiggins	do	do	Jan. 4, 1866.
A. F. Williams	do	do	Sept. 20, 1865.
W. C. Yonge	Ex-United States and rebel postmaster, and worth over $20,000.	do	May 17, 1866.
J. E. Young	Worth over $20,000	do	Jan. 29, 1866.
Edward B. Young	do	do	Oct. 18, 1865.
Hardaway Young	do	do	Sept. 18, 1865.
J. M. Yeldell	do	Governor Parsons and J. H. Watts	Oct. 4, 1865.
Harriet C. Young	do	Governor Parsons	Mar. 19, 1866.

VIRGINIA.

J. R. Anderson	Rebel brigadier general, and worth over $20,000	Governor Peirpoint, Hon. J. K. Moorhead, of Pennsylvania, Wm H. Macfarland, Asa Snyder, C. L. Mosby, James Johnson, John W. Duncan, Richard Peters, C. A. Lochran, and Dilworth, Porter & Co., Pittsburg, Pa.	Sept. 21, 1865.
G. W. Alexander	Rebel privateer	Governor Peirpoint and Hons. J. M. Howard and Z. Chandler, United States senators.	Nov. 7, 1865.
B. F. Almond	Ex-United States and rebel postmaster	Governor Peirpoint	Sept. 23, 1865.
John D. Alderson	Rebel postmaster	do	Sept. 4, 1865.
W. C. Agee	do	do	Aug. 1, 1865.
C. B. Anderson	do	do	Aug. 1, 1865.
T. C. M. Alderson	do	Governor Peirpoint, S. W. Asten, H. D. Ferguson, John G. Davis, E. D. Kernan, D. J. Egras, A. Hendrix, J. V. Fulkerson, W. H. Gray, Charles Carrell, P. S. Fulkerson, G. G. Bruce, and L. D. Fulkerson.	July 21, 1865.
W. B. Allegre	do	Governor Peirpoint	July 29, 1865.
J. H. Arbogast	do	do	Aug. 4, 1865.
D. A. Ammen	do	Governor Peirpoint and D. H. Hoge	Sept. 16, 1865.
J. W. F. Allemong	Rebel postmaster, and worth over $20,000	Governor Peirpoint and Hon. C. H. Lewis	
A. P. Abell	Rebel depositary, and worth over $20,000	Governor Peirpoint	Aug. 11, 1865.
James Adams	Proceedings instituted for confiscation of property	Governor Peirpoint and Lewis McKenzie	Sept. 14, 1865.
John T. Antrim	Rebel tax assessor, and worth over $20,000	Governor Peirpoint	July 29, 1865.
Jacob Acker	Aided the rebellion	do	July 5, 1866.
Joseph Augustine	Worth over $20,000	Governor Peirpoint, R. M. Thorne, and Mrs. Eliza L. Van Lew	July 29, 1865.
W. H. Armistead	do	Governor Peirpoint and Hon. Thomas M. Bowden, attorney general of Virginia	July 29, 1865.
J. B. Anderson	do	Governor Peirpoint and Horace L. Kent	Sept. 9, 1865.
Wm. C. Allen	do	Governor Peirpoint, Charles Palmer, and Francis J. Smith	Sept. 7, 1865.
J. B. Alexander	do	Governor Peirpoint and Daniel H. Hoge	Aug. 10, 1865.
W. M. Ambler	do	Governor Peirpoint, F. J. Smith, Franklin Stearns, R. B. Davis, and Thos. K. Pendleton.	Aug. 10, 1865.

Virginia—Continued.

Name.	Exemption under amnesty proclamation of May 29, 1865.	By whom recommended.	Date of pardon.
John Aldridge	Worth over $20,000	Governor F. H. Peirpoint, Lewis McKenzie, Wm. Brown, jr., N. E. Janney, Thomas Brown, A. M. Janney, William Hoge, D. J. Hoge, S. N. Brown, and Joshua Hatcher.	Aug. 15, 1865.
R. S Allen	do	Governor Peirpoint and Wm. Macfarland	July 29, 1865.
J. B. Anderson	do	Governor Peirpoint	Sept. 9, 1865.
Mark Alexander	do	do	Aug. 4, 1865.
Rhesa Allen	do	do	Aug. 4, 1865.
John D. Alexander	do	Governor Peirpoint and C. L. Mosby	Aug. 4, 1865.
Thos. H. Allen	do	Governor Peirpoint	Sept. 23, 1865.
William Allen	do	Governor Peirpoint and Hon. Joseph Segar, United States senator, Virginia	July 7, 1865.
Mrs. Louisa G. Allen	do	Governor Peirpoint	Sept. 20, 1865.
Israel Allen	do	Governor Peirpoint and F. W. Butterfield, colonel 192d O. V. I., commanding	Aug. 14, 1865.
William Allen	do	Governor Peirpoint	July 21, 1865.
John J. Allen	do	Governor Peirpoint and C. L. Mosby	Aug. 14, 1865.
Wm. G. Allan	do	Governor Peirpoint	Aug. 1, 1865.
Francis Allison, sr	do	do	Aug. 10, 1865.
Wm. H. Allison	do	do	Aug. 19, 1865.
James W. Allison	do	do	July 22, 1866.
Samuel Andrews	do	do	Aug. 10, 1865.
George W. Anderson	do	do	Aug. 10, 1865.
Thos. N. Ashley	do	Governor Peirpoint and Chas. H. Lewis, secretary commonwealth of Virginia	Sept. 4, 1865.
R. Archer	do	Governor Peirpoint	Sept. 22, 1865.
R. S. Archer	do	do	Sept. 22, 1865.
Archibald Atkinson	do	do	Sept. 4, 1865.
Jo. M. Adams	do	do	July 17, 1865.
Mark Alexander	do	do	July 5, 1866.
John G. Andrews	do	do	Sept. 16, 1865.
Thomas Avent	do	do	Aug. 24, 1865.
R. W. Ashlin	do	do	July 29, 1865.
Tamlin Avent	do	do	Aug. 24, 1865.
J. T. Anderson	do		June 26, 1865.
E. J. Amiss	do	do	Aug. 2, 1865.
Eli Ames	do	do	Sept. 9, 1865.
John Alexander	do	do	Sept. 16, 1865.
F. S. Anderson	do	Governor Peirpoint and C. L. Mosby	July 21, 1865.
John J. Ambler	do	Governor Peirpoint	Sept. 4, 1865.
P. St. G. Ambler	do	Governor Peirpoint and C. L. Mosby	July 31, 1865.
David Amentrout	do	Governor Peirpoint and Samuel R. Sterling, collector internal revenue, dist. Virginia	July 25, 1865.
John P. Aylor	do		July 25, 1865.
J. L. Apperson	do		June 24, 1865.
R. T. Alvey	do	Governor Peirpoint	July 29, 1865.
John Arehart	do	do	Aug. 10, 1865.
George Adams	do	do	July 13, 1865.
Wm. C. Adams	do	do	July 14, 1865.

Obedience Adams	do	do	Nov. 6, 1865.
R. C. Ambler	do	do	Aug. 5, 1865.
John Alsop	do	do	Aug. 3, 1865.
S. W. Anderson	do	do	Aug. 19, 1865.
Joseph Alsop	do	do	July 18, 1865.
Catharine Alston	do	do	Aug. 1, 1865.
John B. Baldwin	Member of rebel congress	Hon. Reverdy Johnson, Md., C. H. Lewis, secretary commonwealth of Virginia, A. A. H. Stewart, and J. C. G. Kennedy.	Sept. 28, 1865.
Thomas Branch	Member of secession convention, and worth over $20,000.	Governor F. H. Peirpoint	Aug. 1, 1855.
John Brannon	Member of rebel senate, (State,) and worth over $20,000.	do	July 29, 1865.
A. S. Buford	Member of rebel house of delegates, and worth over $20,000.	do	July 21, 1865.
Edward C. Burks	do	do	Dec. 5, 1865.
Reese T. Bowen	do	Governor F. H. Peirpoint and Daniel H. Hoge	July 14, 1865.
William Branch	do	Governor Peirpoint and John R. Woods	Sept. 13, 1865.
W. T. Booker	Depositary of the treasury, and worth over $20,000		*June 26, 1865.
James Burk	Ex-United States and rebel postmaster, and worth over $20,000.	Governor Peirpoint	Aug. 25, 1865.
Cæsario Bias	do	do	Aug. 25, 1865.
Albert Baldwin	Ex-United States and rebel postmaster	do	Aug. 1, 1865.
N. L. Blackmore	do	do	July 25, 1865.
J. W. Bardine	do	do	Oct. 12, 1865.
Joseph Burkholder	do	do	July 5, 1865.
George P. Burtner	Rebel postmaster	do	Aug. 16, 1865.
A. G. Barnes	do	do	Aug. 7, 1865.
Alpheus Balling	do	do	Aug. 29, 1865.
T. M. Butterworth	do	do	Aug. 29, 1865.
Robert L. Bonham	do	do	Sept. 29, 1865.
John W. Barnes	do	do	Aug. 24, 1865.
J. S. Buchanan	do	do	Nov. 9, 1865.
A. S. Blair	do	do	
Robert Beverly	do	Governor Peirpoint and J. M. Botts	July 21, 1865.
Abraham F. Bradley	do	Governor Peirpoint	Aug. 16, 1865.
Louis Bremond	do	do	July 29, 1865.
C. P. Bigger	do	do	Aug. 19, 1865.
A. L. Burwell	Rebel postmaster, and worth over $20,000		July 5, 1866.
Thomas Brown	do	do	Sept. 13, 1865.
David M. Brand	Deputy postmaster	do	Oct. 5, 1865.
Wm. J. Berryman	Rebel tax assessor	do	Aug. 4, 1865.
David Baker, jr.	do	do	Sept. 20, 1865.
William Bradley	do	do	Aug. 14, 1865.
J. L. Barnell	do	do	Aug. 16, 1865.
F. H. Booker	Tax collector	do	Aug. 4, 1865.
James Boisseau	do	Hon. James Speed, Attorney General United States, and Governor Peirpoint	Aug. 12, 1865.
John W. Barclay	do	Governor F. H. Peirpoint	July 17, 1865.
Lee A. Beckham	Left a loyal State	Governor F. H. Peirpoint, Hons. J. Minor Botts, Va., and J. K. Moorhead, Pa.	Aug. 5, 1865.
Thos. A. Ball	do	Governor Peirpoint	Sept. 9, 1865.
S. G. Baxter	Left District of Columbia	do	
Richard L. Brown	Left District of Columbia, and ex-United States and rebel department clerk.	do	Apr. 25, 1866.

Virginia—Continued.

Name.	Exemption under amnesty proclamation of May 29, 1865.	By whom recommended.	Date of pardon.
Arthur Broadwater	Proceedings commenced for confiscation	Governor Peirpoint	Sept. 15, 1865.
O. S. Braden	do	Governor Peirpoint and Lewis McKenzie	Sept. 19, 1865.
George Booker	do	Governor Peirpoint, Hon. John Minor Botts, and Brevet Major Gen. Nelson A. Mills.	Sept. 29, 1865.
Albert S. Bart	do	Governor Peirpoint and L. McKenzie	Aug. 16, 1865.
R. V. Boykin	do	Governor Peirpoint and L. H. Chandler, esq., United States district attorney	July 17, 1865.
Isaiah Beans	do	Governor Peirpoint	Aug. 16, 1865.
R. G. Bowie	do	Governor Peirpoint, Lewis McKenzie, and Charles Albert	Oct. 5, 1865.
James Bolton	do	Hon. John Minor Botts	July 15, 1865.
R. H. Baker, sr	do	Hon. James Speed, Attorney General United States, Governor Peirpoint, and L. H. Chandler, United States district attorney.	Sept. 23, 1865.
G. W. Ball	Property confiscated	L. H. Chandler, esq., United States district attorney	July 17, 1865.
R. H. Baker, jr	Proceedings commenced as abandoned property	L. H. Chandler, esq., U. S. district attorney, Governor Peirpoint, and S. G. P. Cowper	
R. L. Brown	Rebel mail contractor, and worth over $20,000	Governor Peirpoint	Aug. 25, 1865.
G. S. Bruce	Rebel mail contractor	do	Aug. 29, 1865.
John G. Beckham	Rebel agent for quartermaster and navy departments, and worth over $20,000.	do	Aug. 11, 1865.
Henry A. Ball	Rebel agent for purchasing quartermasters' supplies, and worth over $20,000.	do	Aug. 31, 1865.
P. H. Booth	District purchasing agent, and worth over $20,000	do	Aug. 1, 1865.
Taylor Berry	Rebel bonded agent	do	Aug. 10, 1865.
Andrew J. Blair	do	do	Sept. 29, 1865.
A. J. Blair	Ex-United States and rebel mail agent	Governor Peirpoint and Captain John Teed	Aug. 24, 1865.
John C. Bowyer	Resigned government clerkship at Washington, D. C.; went south and was appointed rebel commissioner.	W. Hunter, esq., chief clerk State Department, and J. W. Fisher, colonel 195th Pennsylvania volunteers.	Aug. 3, 1865.
J. M. Bennett	Rebel auditor	Governor F. H. Peirpoint and John C. Chiles	July 11, 1865.
Franklin L. Brockett	Accountant in rebel treasury department	Governor Peirpoint	July 31, 1865.
G. A. Baker	Depositary of the rebel treasury	do	Aug. 1, 1865.
Edward C. Bruce	Clerk in rebel quartermasters' department	do	Oct. 5, 1865.
T. P. A. Bibb	Clerk in rebel post office department	Hon. James Speed, Attorney General United States	June 12, 1865.
Wm. J. Bromwell	Clerk under rebel authorities	Governor Peirpoint, W. Hunter, chief clerk State Department, Marmaduke Johnson, A. B. Grigon, James Anson, S. S. Hall, and John S. Caskie.	Oct. 3, 1866.
A. T. Bledsoe	Petty civil officer	Hon. O. H. Browning	June 26, 1866.
John J. Coleman	Worth over $20,000	S. Woods, T. M. Dickinson, John C. Collins, and D. A. Wibb	Aug. 11, 1865.
George W. Bassell	do	Governor Peirpoint, Charles Palmer, and Horace L. Kent	Aug. 11, 1865.
Charles Boswell	do	Governor Peirpoint	Aug. 11, 1865.
Robert A. Banks	do	do	Aug. 11, 1865.
Henry S. Bowens	do	Governor Peirpoint, Daniel H. Hoge, and E. E. Willey	July 15, 1865.
Mrs. V. B. Burwell	do	Governor Peirpoint	Aug. 5, 1865.
Paschal Buford	do	Governor Peirpoint and J. F. Johnson	Aug. 16. 1875.
John R. Bryan	do	Governor Peirpoint	Aug. 19, 1865.
O. F. Baxter	do	L. E. Chandler, esq., United States district attorney, E. C. Robinson, H. M. Bowdery, and John S. Millson.	Aug. 19, 1865.
Thomas L. Bendeerant	do	Governor Peirpoint	Aug. 19, 1865.

A. P. Beirne	do	do	Aug. 16, 1865.
John Brown	do	do	Aug. 16, 1865.
Josiah Burruss	do	do	Aug. 16, 1865.
D. J. Burr	do	Hon. J. M. Botts and George W. Riggs	June 29, 1865.
J. R. Bryan	do	Governor Peirpoint and Wm. Mumford	July 6, 1865.
Alex. Baylor	do	do	July 5, 1866.
Daniel C. Brubaker	do	do	Aug. 3, 1865.
Wood Bouldin	do	do	July 13, 1865.
William Baldwin	do	do	July 13, 1865.
John D. Betts	do	do	Oct. 26, 1865.
Beverly Barksdale	do	do	Sept. 27, 1865.
James Bumgardner	do	do	July 5, 1866.
J. W. Bowen	do	do	Nov. 9, 1865.
John B. Bransford	do	do	Aug. 7, 1865.
Christ. T. Brown	do	do	Nov. 6, 1865.
Alfred M. Barbour	do	do	Aug. 11, 1865.
John A. Belvin	do	Governor Peirpoint and G. A. Myers	July 18, 1865.
John Roy Baylor	do	Governor Peirpoint, Charles Palmer, F. J. Smith, and Franklin Stearns	July 22, 1865.
James R. Branch	do	Governor Peirpoint, N. Nunnly, and James Custrie	July 18, 1865.
James Bickers	do	Governor Peirpoint, Lewis P. Nelson, and William L. Early	Aug. 5, 1865.
Francis E. Brooke	do	Governor Peirpoint	July 25, 1865.
C. R. Barksdale	do	do	July 18, 1865.
B. Brown	do	do	July 5, 1865.
S. F. Barnes	do	Governor Peirpoint, William Jeter, and E. T. James	July 15, 1865.
F. C. Brawer	do	Governor Peirpoint, J. L. Apperson, H. L. Kent, and W. Goddin	July 15, 1865.
John W. Backhouse	do	Governor Peirpoint	Aug. 31, 1865.
F. Brawer	do	Governor Peirpoint, J. L. Apperson, W. Goddin, and William I. Smith	July 17, 1865.
C. M. Blackford	do		June 26, 1865.
James M. Brown	do	Governor Peirpoint and Charles Palmer	July 22, 1865.
Joseph A. Buss	do	Governor Peirpoint, George W. Jones, and Samuel P. Wingo	July 22, 1865.
William B. Byars	do	Governor Peirpoint	July 14, 1865.
B. Briel	do	do	July 17, 1865.
William Beale	do	do	Oct. 5, 1865.
William R. Baskerville	do	do	July 5, 1866.
Isaac R. Barksdale	do	Governor Peirpoint and John R. Woods	Sept. 25, 1865.
Carey Breckenridge	do	Governor Peirpoint	July 18, 1865.
Robert S. Bagley	do	Governor Peirpoint, R. R. Cralli, Fred. N. Robertson, Edward G. Bagley, A. G. Barnes, and Henry S. Richards.	July 5, 1865.
Richard Bagly	do	Governor Peirpoint	Aug. 14, 1865
C. J. Baldwin	do	Governor Peirpoint, Francis J. Smith, and James Palmer	Aug. 25, 1865.
A. C. Bowman	do	Governor Peirpoint	Sept. 11, 1865.
Robert U. Brooking	do	do	Aug. 5, 1865.
William B. Beverly	do	do	Aug. 10, 1865.
B. R. Baird	do	do	Aug. 10, 1865.
W. O. Bannon	do	Hon. James Speed, Attorney General United States, and John Minor Botts	July 20, 1865.
C. C. Beckham	do	do do	July 20, 1865.
W. H. Browning	do	do do	July 20, 1865.
Edmund Berkeley	do	Governor Peirpoint	Aug. 16, 1865.
Charles F. Berkeley	do	do	Aug. 16, 1865.
Norburn Berkeley	do	do	Aug. 16, 1865.
Thomas C. Bowen	do	do	Aug. 16, 1865.
William A. Bowen	do	do	Aug. 16, 1865.

Virginia—Continued.

Name.	Exemption under amnesty proclamation of May 29, 1865.	By whom recommended.	Date of pardon.
Francis Bell	Worth over $20,000	Governor Peirpoint	Aug. 10, 1865.
A. R. Blakey	do	do	Aug. 10, 1865.
John A. Britton	do	do	Aug. 10, 1865.
Slith Bouldin	do	do	Aug. 10, 1865.
Alfred T. Blanks	do	do	Aug. 10, 1865.
David S. Bell	do	do	Aug. 10, 1865.
George H. Burwell	do	do	Aug. 24, 1865.
William H. Beasley	do	do	Aug. 24, 1865.
Dr. George W. Briggs	do	do	Aug. 24, 1865.
William D. Boaz	do	Governor Peirpoint, E. R. Watson, W. W. Gilmer, James F. Fry, William T. Early, J. A. Marhio, S. W. Martin, J. S. Barksdale, and D. E. Watson.	Aug. 24, 1865.
R. J. Barksdale	do	Governor Peirpoint	Aug. 24, 1865.
J. W. Brown	do	do	July 22, 1865.
John Brownlee	do	do	July 5, 1866.
George M. Bowen	do	do	Mar. 7, 1865.
Mary Baylor	do	do	Oct. 5, 1865.
A. G. Boyd	do	do	
Richard E. Byrd	do	do	July 5, 1866.
Bartholomew Bowers	do	do	Aug. 24, 1865.
Nathan Burwell	do	do	Aug. 24, 1865.
H. M. Bower	do	do	Aug. 24, 1865.
William W. Boyd	do	do	Aug. 12, 1865.
A. G. Boyd	do	do	Aug. 4, 1865.
John Bowman, sr	do	do	Aug. 4, 1865.
William E. Bradshaw	do	do	Aug. 4, 1865.
Jacob Baylor	do	Governor Peirpoint, A. A. H. Stewart, and John B. Baldwin	July 17, 1865.
A. N. Bernard	do	Governor Peirpoint	Sept. 29, 1865.
G. H. Brown	do	do	July 31, 1865.
John R. Baylor	do	Governor Peirpoint and Charles Palmer	July 20, 1865.
James H. Barnley	do	Governor Peirpoint	July 23, 1865.
M. P. Burks	do	do	Sept. 4, 1865.
Blair Burwell	do		June 26, 1865.
C. S. Bliss	do	Governor Peirpoint	Sept. 20, 1865.
William Breeden	do	Governor Peirpoint, Charles Palmer, Francis J. Smith, and Franklin Stearns	July 20, 1865.
H. W. Bowyer	do	Governor Peirpoint	Sept. 26, 1865.
J. W. Bell	do	do	July 25, 1865.
Robert G. Bickle	do	Governor Peirpoint and David Feelty	July 25, 1865.
J. M. Booker	do	Governor Peirpoint and G. W. Redd	Aug. 14, 1865.
George M. Bohannon	do	Governor Peirpoint	Aug. 25, 1865.
Benjamin W. Belches	do	do	Aug. 25, 1865.
Jacob Bowman	do	do	July 25, 1865.
H. M. Bell	do	do	July 25, 1865.
William A. Burke	do	do	Aug. 1, 1865.
William Baskerville, jr	do	Governor Peirpoint, Charles Palmer, and William H. Mumford	July 3, 1865.

George Baylor	do	Governor Peirpoint	Aug. 1, 1865.
Richard Baylor	do	do	Oct. 5, 1865.
James M. Bickers, jr.	do	Governor Peirpoint, Joseph K. Pendleton, J. L. Gordon, J. C. Cammack, John Hunter, and G. W. Trice.	July 5, 1866.
H. E. C. Baskerville	do	Governor Peirpoint	July 3, 1865.
J. G. Brooks	do	do	July 3, 1865.
John L. Bacon	do	do	Sept. 29, 1865.
H. Boyd	do	do	July 14, 1865.
Jesse S. Burks	do	do	Oct. 9, 1865.
Neill Barnett	do	do	Sept. 4, 1865.
Thomas F. Buck	do	do	Sept. 4, 1865.
William Bennett	do	do	Sept. 4, 1865.
Marcus B. Buck	do	Governor Peirpoint and Charles Lewis	Sept. 4, 1865.
J. M. Barber	do	do	Sept. 4, 1865.
William A. Bell	do	Governor Peirpoint	Aug. 7, 1865.
M. A. Blankman	do	do	Aug. 24, 1865.
D. C. Booth	do	do	Sept. 13, 1865.
Bridget Bolin	do	do	Aug. 16, 1865.
David Baylor	do	do	Aug. 16, 1865.
Dr. James Beale	do	do	Aug. 2, 1865.
William N. Berkeley	do	do	Sept. 14, 1865.
Robert Bland	do	do	Aug. 2, 1865.
D. W. Burton	do	do	June 26, 1865.
Samuel H. Bell	do	do	Aug. 4, 1865.
Jacob Bear	do	do	Aug. 29, 1865.
John P. Branch	do	do	Aug. 1, 1865.
Henry Berry	do	do	Aug. 13, 1865.
Anne B. Baylor	do	do	Sept. 9, 1865.
Ann B. Burke	do	do	Sept. 9, 1865.
George C. Brown	do	do	Sept. 9, 1865.
James S. Buster	do	do	Aug. 1, 1865.
Thomas Bolling	do	do	Aug. 2, 1865.
A. J. Brodnax	do	do	Aug. 2, 1865.
A. J. Bondurant	do	do	Aug. 2, 1865.
H. W. Barksdale	do	do	Aug. 29, 1865.
William Brounley	do	do	
A. J. Boulware	do	do	July 14, 1865.
James H. Bradley	do	do	July 17, 1865.
E. W. Bayly	do	Governor Peirpoint, Charles W. Carrigan, and Hon. John W. Forney	July 25, 1865.
Archibald Brock	do	Governor Peirpoint	Oct. 31, 1865.
P. B. Borst	do	Governor Peirpoint, John S. Calvert, and H. W. Thomas	July 6, 1865.
Charles W. Button	do	Hon. James Speed, Attorney General U. S., and Governor Peirpoint	Sept. 7, 1866.
Robert B. Bolling	do	Hon. John Minor Botts	July 21, 1865.
J. M. Booker	do		June 26, 1865.
F. J. Barnes	do	Governor Peirpoint	Oct. 9, 1865.
Willis Browning	do	do	July 25, 1865.
Samuel Baldwin	do	do	July 13, 1865.
George W. Bolling	do	do	July 29, 1865.
Elijah Baker	do	Governor Peirpoint, L. N. Ellett, M. Burton, Francis J. Smith, Franklin Stearns, John N. Van Lew, and —— Dudley.	July 29, 1865.
Samuel D. Burke	do	Governor Peirpoint	July 29, 1865.
I. L. Boutwell	do	do	Sept. 16, 1865.

Virginia—Continued.

Name.	Exemption under amnesty proclamation of May 29, 1865.	By whom recommended.	Date of pardon.
John Bowers	Worth over $20,000	Governor Peirpoint	July 29, 1865.
Thomas E. Ballard	do	Governor Peirpoint and L. H. Chandler, U. S. district attorney	July 29, 1865.
William B. Bruce	do		July 14, 1865.
Daniel C. E. Brady	do	Governor Peirpoint	July 17, 1865.
John A. Brown	do	do	Aug. 24, 1865.
Alexander Bruce	do		July 14, 1865.
R. Barksdale	do	Governor Peirpoint	Aug. 24, 1865.
George Booker	do	do	July 21, 1865.
William P. Braxton	do	do	Aug. 11, 1865.
John Bowman, jr	do	do	July 13, 1865.
G. A. Burks	do	do	Oct. 9, 1865.
John Buford	do	do	Aug. 29, 1865.
Wilkins Bruce	do	do	July 21, 1865.
T. T. Broocks	do	do	Sept. 20, 1865.
Mrs. Juliet M. Boyd	do	do	
John A. Browning	do	do	July 25, 1865.
J. M. Byers	do	Governor Peirpoint and John R. Carmack, of Memphis, Tenn	Aug. 19, 1865.
W. H. Bell	do	Governor Peirpoint	Nov. 3, 1865.
John R. Bennett	do	Governor Peirpoint, R. C. Morris, C. L. Mosby, and C. W. Britton	Oct. 19, 1865.
Samuel T. Bayley	do	Governor Peirpoint	Oct. 19, 1865.
H. C. Boyd	do	Governor Peirpoint and Charles Palmer	June 28, 1865.
William A. Baynham	do	Governor Peirpoint	
S. A. Buckner	do	Governor Peirpoint and Lewis McKenzie	Aug. 16, 1865.
John P. De Butts	do	do	Aug. 19, 1865.
Charles T. Beale	do	Governor Peirpoint	Aug. 11, 1865.
R. T. Bibb	do	Governor Peirpoint and Francis J. Smith	Aug. 11, 1865.
William Beverly	do	Governor Peirpoint	Aug. 11, 1865.
Jacob Bonsack	do	do	Sept. 13, 1865.
Massena Beazley	do	do	July 29, 1865.
Robert Boyd	do	do	July 5, 1866.
Jacob Brubaker	do	do	Aug. 3, 1865.
Elisha Barksdale, jr	do	John M. Speed and J. F. Johnson	July 5, 1865.
Christian Brunk	do	Governor Peirpoint	July 13, 1865.
H. F. Bocock	do	do	July 14, 1865.
R. H. Burke	do	do	Nov. 7, 1865.
John G. Boyd	do		June 26, 1865.
William Barret	do	Governor Peirpoint	July 29, 1865.
Nathaniel Burwell	do	do	July 29, 1865.
Isaac N. Buck	do	Governor Peirpoint and C. W. Lewis, secretary of commonwealth	Sept. 4, 1865.
N. S. Braden	do	Governor Peirpoint	Sept. 4, 1865.
B. K. Buchanan	do	Governor Peirpoint and E. Longley	Oct. 2, 1865.
George H. Burch	do	Governor Peirpoint and Lawreston & Co.	July 26, 1865.
I. J. Bowcock	do		Oct. 25, 1865.
George A. Barksdale	do	Governor Peirpoint, Charles A. Rose, and William H. Lyons	Aug. 10, 1865.

Robert P. Baylor	do	Governor Peirpoint	Aug. 10, 1865.
Benjamin B. Brock	do	do	Aug. 10, 1865.
William H. Brooke	do	do	Aug. 10, 1865.
Mrs. Elizabeth Brenner	do	do	Aug. 10, 1865.
Spotswood Bradford	do	do	Aug. 7, 1865.
John S. Bourbour	do	H. H. Marshal	June 26, 1865.
Helen S. Baylor	do	Governor Peirpoint	Oct. 5, 1865.
Elisha Barksdale, jr	do	do	July 5, 1865.
Harriet R. Baylor	do	do	Oct. 5, 1865.
Charles Bruce	do	do	July 13, 1865.
William J. D. Bell	do		July 27, 1865.
Catherine B. Baylor	do	Governor Peirpoint	Oct. 5, 1865.
Nunnie W. Baylor	do	do	Oct. 5, 1865.
Henry L. Baylor	do	do	Oct. 5, 1865.
A. Bodeker	do	do	July 11, 1865.
Alfred Boyd	do	Governor Peirpoint and Charles Palmer	July 3, 1865.
John P. Ballard	do	Governor Peirpoint	July 18, 1865.
George Blow, sr	do	do	Oct. 5, 1865.
Thos. B. B. Baber	do	do	Oct. 5, 1865.
John Boucher	do	do	Aug. 24, 1865.
N. F. Bowe	do	do	July 6, 1865.
Edward S. Brown	do	do	Sept. 16, 1865.
William Boulware	do	do	July 13, 1865.
John R. Bryan	do	Hon. Edward Bates of Missouri	July 6, 1865.
T. L. Bondurant	do	Governor Peirpoint	Aug. 14, 1865.
Robert Beatie	do	Governor Peirpoint and John R. Carmack	
S. P. Bayly	do	Governor Peirpoint, J. V. Brooke, and Lewis McKenzie	Aug. 16, 1865.
Robert Beverly	do	Governor Peirpoint	July 21, 1865.
Gray Boulware	do	do	Sept. 4, 1865.
James H. Carson	Rebel brigadier general, member of State senate, and worth over $20,000.	Governor F. H. Peirpoint	Aug. 16, 1865.
W. W. Crump	Assistant secretary of rebel treasury	Charles Palmer	June 26, 1865.
A. C. Cummings	Member of the rebel legislature, and worth over $20,000.	Governor Peirpoint	Aug. 7, 1865.
R. Crockett	do	do	
A. L. Carter	do	do	Aug. 10, 1865.
Samuel Carpenter	do	do	Aug. 25, 1865.
W. F. Carter	Lieutenant in rebel navy; went to Europe and rendered assistance to rebel navy.	do	Sept. 29, 1865.
L. B. Conway	Rebel depositary	do	Aug. 19, 1865.
David P. Curry	Bonded agent	do	Aug. 1, 1865.
W. B. Compton	Condemned to be hung as a rebel spy; escaped from Fort McHenry.	do	July 13, 1865.
Odin G. Clay	Rebel commissioner of public works, and worth over $20,000.	Governor Peirpoint and C. L. Mosby	July 29, 1865.
John O. Chiles	Doorkeeper of rebel congress	Hon. James Speed, Attorney General of the United States	June 30, 1865.
E. Y. Cannon	Commissioner to take affidavits in admiralty causes and worth over $20,000.	Governor Peirpoint	July 15, 1865.
Thomas H. Campbell	Receiver under the sequestration act and worth over $20,000.	do	July 3, 1865.
Charles F. Chelf	Ex-United States and rebel postmaster	do	Sept. 23, 1865.
Kennerly Craig	do	do	Aug. 16, 1865.

Virginia—Continued.

Name.	Exemption under amnesty proclamation of May 29, 1865.	By whom recommended.	Date of pardon.
J. K. Cooke	Ex-United States and rebel postmaster, and purchasing agent for rebel government.	Governor Peirpoint	Nov. 10, 1865.
R. J. Chappell	Rebel postmaster	Governor Peirpoint and Charles Palmer	July 3, 1865.
John G. Cootes	do	Governor Peirpoint and John L. Thomas, ex-State attorney for Baltimore	Sept. 13, 1865.
P. A. Chalkley	do	Governor Peirpoint	July 29, 1865.
James M. Conway	do	do	Aug. 19, 1865.
William B. Chalkley	do	Governor Peirpoint, Rev. Samuel Taylor, G. N. Winpre, A. H. Drewry, A. E. Cogbell, late commonwealth attorney, J. W. Howard, J. A. Stracharis, P. H. Wilkinson, S. O. Duval, Dan. Adkins, commissioner of election at C. H., H. K. Graves, and T. G. C.	July 29, 1865.
T. A. Chappell	do	Governor Peirpoint	July 5, 1866.
William J. Crabtree	do	do	Oct. 9, 1865.
W. D. Coleman	do	do	July 13, 1865.
J. D. Crawley	Rebel postmaster and worth over $20,000	Governor Peirpoint, J. W. Dunnington, A. D. Dickinson, Dr. Woods & Bro., and J. M. McNutt.	Aug. 14, 1865.
John J. Coleman, sr.	do	Governor F. H. Peirpoint	Oct. 5, 1865.
George W. Coleman	Rebel deputy postmaster	do	Aug. 19, 1865.
John H. Caldwell	do	do	Sept. 13, 1865.
Annie E. Carrington	Rebel postmistress	do	Sept. 4, 1865.
A. D. Campbell	Rebel tax assessor	do	Aug. 4, 1865.
George R. Cowan	do	do	Aug. 29, 1865.
R. P. Carson	do	do	Sept. 29, 1865.
W. H. Clarke	R bel tax collector	do	Aug. 9, 1865.
W. T. Carrington	Rebel tax collector and worth over $20,000	do	July 5, 1865.
J. R. Cunningham	Rebel commissioner of revenue and tax assessor	Governor Peirpoint, B. J. Wooster, and A. Vaughan	July 15, 1865.
Joseph W. Caldwell	Clerk of rebel district court	Governor Peirpoint	Sept. 11, 1865.
Alfred Chapman	Rebel clerk	Governor Peirpoint, Hon. John M. Botts, and C. H. Lewis, secretary of the commonwealth of Virginia.	....
M. B. Carrington	Rebel tobacco agent	Governor Peirpoint	July 29, 1865.
J. E. Crowder	Rebel justice of the peace	do	July 29, 1865.
Thomas W. Cecil	Left a loyal State	do	July 14, 1865.
Dr. William A. Carrington	do	Governor Peirpoint and Charles Palmer	July 18, 1865.
W. N. Cansey	Left the federal lines	Hons. James Speed, Attorney General of the United States, Thomas R. Bowden, attorney general of Virginia, and W. W. Wing, treasurer of Virginia.	July 29, 1865.
W. G. Cazenove	Left loyal district	Governor Peirpoint, R. Johnston, Lewis McKenzie, and A. Jamierson, collector of customs.	Aug. 14, 1865.
Silas Copeland	Proceedings commenced for confiscation	Governor Peirpoint	Aug. 16, 1865.
John Clendening	do	do	Aug. 16, 1865.
James H. Clendening	do	do	Aug. 16, 1865.
William Clendening	do	do	Aug. 16, 1865.
A. M. Clarke	do	do	Sept. 19, 1865.
William H. Cockerille	do	do	Aug. 29, 1865.
James R. Crenshaw	Interested in steamers running the blockade and worth over $20,000.	do	July 13, 1865.
William G. Crenshaw	do	do	July 13, 1865.

David Currie	Aided the rebellion	do	Sept. 16, 1865.
B. F. Carter	do	do	July 31, 1865.
G. W. Clark	Worth over $20,000	do	Aug. 3, 1865.
W. A. Chapman	do	do	Aug. 19, 1865.
S. S. Cottrell	do	Governor Peirpoint, F. J. Smith, Franklin Stearns, H. L. Kent, and H. G. Fant	July 17, 1865.
E. A. Cralle	do	Governor Peirpoint, J. Brown, A. Balling, R. R. Cralle, F. J. N. Robertson, E. G. Bagley, A. G. Barnes, and H. B. Richards.	July 5, 1865.
J. G. Cabell	do	Governor Peirpoint, T. R. Bowden, attorney general of Virginia, and Charles Palmer	July 11, 1865.
O. H. Chalkley	do	Governor Peirpoint, R. F. Walker, F. J. Smith, and Charles Palmer	July 11, 1865.
H. A. Claiborne	do	Hon. James Speed, Attorney General of the United States, Governor Peirpoint, and H. L. Kent.	June 29, 1865.
A. H. Christian	do	Governor Peirpoint	July 7, 1865.
R. H. Carter	do	do	July 11, 1865.
C. P. Chilton	do	Governor Peirpoint and H. L. Kent	Aug. 11, 1865.
James H. Cox	do	Governor Peirpoint, Paul Chaelbourne, major and provost marshal, Chesterfield county, Va., Captain J. Wilson, Franklin Stearns, M. Burton, and Charles Palmer.	July 3, 1865.
George M. Carter	do	Governor Peirpoint, W. H. Ryan, lieutenant Maryland rifles, Ward Bros., John Leary & Co., H. Wendebaught & Co., Howard, Cole & Co., Shipley, Roane & Co., W. A. Dean, Armstrong & Co., J. S. Berry.	Sept. 29, 1865.
John Cowen	do	Governor Peirpoint and C. H. Lewis	July 5, 1865.
S. A. Coffman	do	Governor Peirpoint and John F. Lewis, collector of internal revenue, and C. H. Lewis, secretary of the commonwealth of Virginia.	July 5, 1865.
Eugene Carrington	do	C. L. Mosby and H. H. Marshal	June 21, 1865.
C. B. Claiborne	do	Governor Peirpoint and C. L. Mosby	Aug. 14, 1865.
Thos. H. Claggett	do	Governor Peirpoint, H. T. Harrison, William H. Gray, A. W. Gray, and Lewis McKenzie.	Aug. 5, 1865.
William G. Carr	do	Governor Peirpoint	Aug. 1, 1865.
William Crawford	do	Governor Peirpoint and John F. and S. H. Lewis	Aug. 1, 1865.
Thomas Campbell	do	Governor Peirpoint and J. F. Johnson	Aug. 5, 1865.
John B. Cocke	do	Governor Peirpoint and W. H. Macfarland	July 6, 1865.
John H. Coleman	do	Governor Peirpoint, J. C. Hill, John O. Lewis, E. R. Watson, and S. V. Southall	Oct. 9, 1865.
John Caddall	do	Governor Peirpoint and Daniel H. Hoge	Aug. 10, 1865.
G. H. Chisman	do	Governor Peirpoint	July 5, 1865.
R. S. Cabell	do	do	Oct. 25, 1865.
N. F. Cabell	do	do	Oct. 25, 1865.
N. C. Clarkson	do	do	Sept. 23, 1865.
B. T. Chinn	do	do	Aug. 29, 1865.
P. B. Cabell	do	do	Oct. 29, 1865.
R. F. Cole	do	do	Aug. 4, 1865.
F. M. Cabell	do	do	Aug. 25, 1865.
L. W. Cabell	do	do	Aug. 25, 1865.
G. G. Collins	do	do	Aug. 31, 1865.
W. C. Claiborne	do	do	Nov. 17, 1865.
Rev. John H. Cawthon	do	do	July 5, 1866.
H. C. Clay	do	do	July 14, 1865.
I. H. Carrington	do	do	Sept. 20, 1865.
A. N. Chaffin	do	do	Oct. 9, 1865.
J. K. Childrey	do	do	July 11, 1865.
William Cocke	do	do	July 5, 1866.
H. Cannon	do	do	July 21, 1865.
J. L. Carrington	do	do	July 18, 1865.
R. G. Cabell	do	do	July 18, 1865.
H. C. Cabell	do	do	Aug. 1, 1865.

Virginia—Continued.

Name.	Exemption under amnesty proclamation of May 29, 1865.	By whom recommended.	Date of pardon.
George Carrington	Worth over $20,000	Governor Peirpoint	Aug. 19, 1865.
H. Carrington	do	do	July 13, 1865.
Paul S. Carrington	do	Governor Peirpoint and Charles Palmer	July 18, 1865.
B. G. Carter	do	Governor Peirpoint and Lewis McKenzie	Aug. 5, 1865.
R. H. Carter	do	Governor Peirpoint	Aug. 2, 1865.
Dale Carter	do	do	Oct. 26, 1865.
John R. Carter	do	do	Sept. 13, 1865.
Francis M. Carter	do	do	July 31, 1865.
John S. Cocke	do	do	Aug. 5, 1865.
John H. Cocke	do	do	July 6, 1865.
C. C. Cocke	do	Governor Peirpoint and William H. McFarland	July 6, 1865.
Benjamin Crawford	do	Governor Peirpoint	July 25, 1865.
J. S. Callaway	do	do	Aug. 16, 1865.
Joseph Cloyd	do	do	Aug. 7, 1865.
C. H. Carter	do	do	July 22, 1865.
William J. Cheatham	do	do	Aug. 24, 1865.
Samuel Coiner, sr	do	Governor Peirpoint and Hon. C. H. Lewis	Aug. 4, 1865.
George K. Crutchfield	do	Governor Peirpoint and Hon. John M. Botts	July 1, 1865.
Thomas Cook	do	Governor Peirpoint	July 5, 1866.
H. V. Coleman	do	do	Aug. 11, 1865.
E. R. Chambers	do	Governor Peirpoint and Charles Palmer	July 3, 1865.
J. W. Chambers	do	Governor Peirpoint	July 5, 1866.
A. B. Chambers	do	do	July 13, 1865.
Philip Coiner	do	do	Aug. 4, 1865.
E. A. Coleman	do	do	June 26, 1865.
Walter Coles	do	do	July 25, 1865.
Edward Coles	do	do	July 25, 1865.
J. L. Clayton	do		July 26, 1865.
G. T. Cralle	do	Governor Peirpoint	July 22, 1865.
John W. Chappell	do	do	Aug. 2, 1865.
W. C. Cunell	do	do	Aug. 1, 1865.
William Cowherd	do	do	Aug. 1, 1885.
A. P. Cranshaw	do	do	Aug. 4, 1865.
John Clark	do	do	Aug. 1, 1865.
Mrs. R. E. Clayton	do	do	July 3, 1865.
Charles Campbell	do	do	July —, 1865.
Samuel Chancellor	do	do	Nov. 3, 1865.
L. D. Crenshaw	do	do	June 19, 1865.
John S. Cowherd	do	do	Aug. 1, 1865.
W. F. Cheek	do	do	Sept. 16, 1865.
David Chalmers	do	do	July 14, 1865.
O. A. Crenshaw	do	do	Aug. 1, 1865.
B. F. P. Conway	do	do	Aug. 11, 1865.
Gibbon S. Conway	do	do	Aug. 11, 1865.

F. J. Chapman	do	do	Aug. 7, 1865.
N. B. Clarke	do	do	Aug. 11, 1865.
Jacob Coyner, sr	do	do	Aug. 16, 1865.
Ro. B. Cunningham	do	do	Aug. 19, 1865.
William E. Clark	do	do	Aug. 19, 1865.
James M. Cloyd	do	do	Aug. 19, 1865.
R. W. Crenshaw	do	do	Aug. 16, 1865.
John E. Crowder	do	Governor Peirpoint and Charles Palmer	Nov. 3, 1865.
William J. Crems	do	Governor Peirpoint	July 13, 1865.
A. Cunningham	do	do	July 13, 1865.
S. W. Corbin	do	do	July 21, 1865.
C. G. Coleman	do	do	Aug. 3, 1865.
R. T. Chappell	do	do	July 5, 1866.
J. J. Crems	do	do	July 13, 1865.
J. C. Cochran	do	do	July 25, 1865.
G. W. Cochran	do	do	July 25, 1865.
Samuel Cline	do	do	July 29, 1865.
Gray Carrall	do	do	Aug. 11, 1865.
William T. Clark	do	do	July 29, 1865.
Ruffin H. Coleman	do	do	Aug. 31, 1865.
John A. Carter	do	Hon. James Speed, Attorney General of the United States	Aug. 29, 1865.
Bowling Clark	do		July 14, 1865.
Hiram Cheatwood	do	Governor Peirpoint	Aug. 16, 1865.
James H. Coiner	do	do	Aug. 16, 1865.
Raleigh Colston	do	do	Aug. 19, 1865.
C. Claybrook	do	do	Sept. 4, 1865.
William W. Carrington	do	Governor F. H. Peirpoint and William L. Oliver	Sept. 4, 1865.
Alfred Castleman	do	Governor Peirpoint	Sept. 4, 1865.
W. H. Crouch	do	Governor F. H. Peirpoint and D. H. Hoge	Sept. 4, 1865.
William H. Clark	do	Governor Peirpoint	Aug. 10, 1865.
H. O. Clagett	do	do	Aug. 10, 1865.
T. D. Crawford	do	do	July 14, 1865.
William D. Cabell	do	do	Oct. 26, 1865.
John T. Clark	do	do	Aug. 16, 1865.
Middleton Chambers	do	do	Oct. 9, 1865.
Pat. Cullan	do	do	Oct. 2, 1865.
John C. Coleman	do	do	Aug. 16, 1865.
Jacob Cohn	do	do	Sept. 4, 1865.
David Cook	do	do	Aug. 16, 1865.
H. E. Coleman	do	do	Aug. 4, 1865.
John Coleman	do	do	Aug. 4, 1865.
James D. Coleman	do	do	Aug. 24, 1865.
Tucker Carrington	do	do	Aug. 5, 1865.
W. L. Carrington	do	do	Oct. 2 1865.
Charles S. Carrington	do	Hon. James Speed, Attorney General United States	July 20, 1865.
Peyton S. Coles	do		June 15, 1865.
John S. Coles	do	Governor Peirpoint	July 29, 1865.
Tucker S. Coles	do	do	July 29, 1865.
J. A. Cowardin	do	Governor Peirpoint and C. C. Fulton	July 13, 1865.
George Carter	do	Governor Peirpoint	Aug. 1, 1865.
Samuel J. Campbell	do	do	July 17, 1865.
John Christian	do	do	Aug. 4, 1865.

Virginia—Continued.

Name.	Exemption under amnesty proclamation of May 29, 1865.	By whom recommended.	Date of pardon.
William K. Clemmer	Worth over $20,000	Governor Peirpoint	Sept. 16, 1865.
Jonas Chamberlin	do	do	Oct. 5, 1865.
C. J. Cabaniss	do	do	July 5, 1866.
Thomas Croxton	do	do	April 12, 1866.
Benjamin F. Cochran	do	do	July 28, 1865.
John Churchman	do	do	July 25, 1865.
John M. Cole	do	do	Aug. 5, 1865.
C. J. Cabaniss	do	Governor Peirpoint and L. H. Chandler, esq., United States district attorney	Oct. 6, 1865.
James Chieves	do		June 26, 1865.
James E. Carson	do	Governor Peirpoint	May 31, 1866.
W. L. Cowardin	do	do	Aug. 24, 1865.
George Carr	do	do	July 29, 1865.
Charles Corling	do	do	July 29, 1865.
John Cochran	do	do	July 29, 1865.
Francis J. Clemer	do	do	July 29, 1865.
J. H. Cooper	do	do	Sept. 9, 1865.
James D. Crawley	do	do	July 22, 1865.
H. Carter	do	do	July 17, 1865.
R. H. Cunningham	do	Governor F. H. Peirpoint and Horace L. Kent	July 17, 1865.
George A. Cralle	do	Governor Peirpoint	July 22, 1865.
Joseph W. Chinn	do	do	Sept. 9, 1865.
Martin Coyner	do	do	Sept. 16, 1855.
Thomas Carter	do	do	Aug. 29, 1865.
Bushrod Carr	do	do	Sept. 16, 1865.
Johnathan T. Cowherd	do	do	Sept. 11, 1865.
William J. Cheatnam	do	Governor Peirpoint and Brevet Colonel S. R. Clark	Aug. 24, 1865.
J. H. Crenshaw	do	Governor Peirpoint	June 28, 1865.
S. S. Crockett	do	Governor Peirpoint and D. H. Hoge	Aug. 25, 1865.
Charles Carrell	do	Governor Peirpoint	July 5, 1866.
Campbell Cornelius	do	do	Sept. 4, 1865.
Henry Cox	do	Governor Peirpoint and J. M. Botts	July 3, 1865.
Belfield Cave	do	Governor Peirpoint	Sept. 4, 1865.
Mayo Cabell	do	do	Oct. 25, 1865.
Franklin Coiner	do	do	Aug. 4, 1865.
John J. Coleman	do	S. Woods, T. W. Dickinson, J. C. Colamer, and D. A. Webb	Aug. 11, 1865.
William Crawley	do	Governor Peirpoint	Sept. 26, 1865.
J. W. Custis	do	do	July 13, 1865.
Dr. George W. Clement	do	do	Aug. 19, 1865.
A. D. Dickinson	Member rebel legislature and worth over $20,000	do	July 15, 1865.
R. K. Dunlap	Left a loyal State	do	Aug. 7, 1865.
Benjamin Dennis	do	do	July 29, 1865.
C. W. C. Dunnington	Left District of Columbia	B. B. French	June 12, 1865.
W. R. Drinkard	do	Attorney General Speed	Feb. 2, 1866.
John E. Deans	Left federal lines and went south	Governor Peirpoint	Aug. 31, 1866.

B. W. Dobyns	Ex-United States and rebel postmaster	do	July 5, 1866.
Jonathan Draper	do	do	July 5, 1866.
John J. Deal	do	do	Oct. 26, 1865.
J. M. Davis	do	do	Oct. 14, 1865.
James H. Dickinson	do	do	Sept. 4, 1865.
R. B. Davis	Ex-United States and rebel postmaster, and worth over $20,000.	Governor Peirpoint, T. K. Pendleton, Joseph M. Baker, J. B. Eastham, G. W. Price, J. C. Cammack, J. L. Gordon, and G. A. Bluhaugh.	Aug. 7, 1865.
Martin E. Davis	Ex-United States and rebel postmaster	Governor Peirpoint	Aug. 4, 1865.
G. G. Dougherty	Rebel postmaster	do	Oct. 5, 1865.
James H. Darts	do	do	Oct. 5, 1865.
T. W. Davis	do	do	Aug. 29, 1865.
Cornelius Dull	do	do	July 29, 1866.
Leonard Daniels, jr	do	do	July 29, 1865.
J. J. Deal	do	do	Aug. 1, 1865.
G. W. Dyson	do	do	Sept. 9, 1865.
D. D. M. Digges	Rebel tax assessor	Governor Peirpoint, T. J. Elliott, captain 11th Pennsylvania cavalry, and assistant provost marshal; and Lewis C. Hunt, lieutenant colonel and provost marshal.	Aug. 10, 1865.
Joseph W. Davis	do	Governor Peirpoint and E. Longley	July 21, 1865.
W. T. Dudley	Assessor of war tax	Governor Peirpoint	Nov. 3, 1865.
George W. Deskins	Rebel tax collector	Governor Peirpoint and Daniel H. Hoge	July 14, 1865.
Giles Devier	do	Governor Peirpoint	Aug. 31, 1865.
T. B. Doe	Rebel tax collector and worth over $20,000	do	July 13, 1865.
James Dorrell	Proceedings commenced for confiscation	do	Aug. 16, 1865.
Robert Drane	do	do	Oct. 5, 1865.
Thomas W. Dorrell	do	Governor Peirpoint and L. McKenzie	Aug. 16, 1865.
W. W. Davis	do	L. H. Chandler, United States district attorney	July 17, 1865.
James W. Downey	Property confiscated	Governor Peirpoint	Sept. 26, 1865.
Daniel Dodson	Rebel agent for sale of bonds	do	Oct. 7, 1865.
Alexander Dudley	Rebel purchasing agent and worth over $20,000	do	July 6, 1865.
Archimedes Davis	Rebel receiver	do	July 21, 1865.
John C. Dunn	Absentee	do	Aug. 1, 1865.
M. M. Davis	Absentee and worth over $20,000	Hon. James Speed, Attorney General United States; R. G. Greene, postmaster, Petersburg, Va.	June 20, 1865.
G. B. Davenport	Rebel clerk	Governor Peirpoint, H. L. Kent, and F. J. Smith	July 29, 1865.
G. E. Dabney	do	Governor Peirpoint, J. A. Meredith, and Wm. H. Lyons	Aug. 10, 1865.
Samuel Donald	Rebel clerk and worth over $20,000	Governor Peirpoint and Hon. T. R. Bowden, attorney general of Virginia	July 29, 1865.
W. S. Donnan	Scotch rebel		June 26, 1865.
W. H. Dennis	Worth over $20,000	Governor Peirpoint	July 13, 1865.
Wm. A. Deitrick	do	Governor Peirpoint, Franklin Sterns, and J. J. Smith	July 29, 1865.
J. J. Daly	do	Governor Peirpoint and Charles Palmer	July 3, 1865.
Thomas Doswell	do	Governor Peirpoint and R. W. Hughes	July 26, 1865.
J. A. Dalby	do	Governor Peirpoint, F. N. Watkins, attorney at law, Richard McIlwaine, pastor Presbyterian church, Wm. E. Judkins, pastor M. E. church, south, R. P. Walton, M. D., and Wm. G. Venable, teller Farmers' Bank of Virginia, Farmville.	July 20, 1865.
George Davis, sr.	do	Governor Peirpoint	July 29, 1865.
Mark Davis, jr., and Goodman Davis.	do	D. D. Moore, mayor, G. H. Barny, county clerk, Alfred Ely, G. W. Updike, postmaster, S. P. Allen, collector of internal revenue, E. D. Smith, and John C. Chumatero, Monroe county judge.	
Samuel E. Dove	do	Governor Peirpoint, F. J. Smith, Jacob S. Atlee, and Franklin Stearns	Aug 4, 1865.
James W. Dunnington	do	Governor Peirpoint, A. D. Dickinson, attorney at law and late senator of Virginia, Dr. Wood & Brother, druggists, and James M. McNull, planter.	Aug. 14, 1865.
Robert M. Dunlop	do	Governor Peirpoint and J. D. Osborne	Aug. 24, 1865.

Virginia—Continued.

Name.	Exemption under amnesty proclamation of May 29, 1865.	By whom recommended.	Date of pardon.
Alex. Donnan	Worth over $20,000	Governor Peirpoint and John Mann, notary public	Aug. 1, 1865.
Samuel D. Denoon	do	Governor Peirpoint, A. J. Crane, R. A. Lancaster, H. K. Ellzson, Franklin Stearns, and F. J. Smith.	July 25, 1865.
John Dodson	do	Governor Peirpoint, Thomas Wallace, and Alexander Donnan	July 29, 1865.
S. P. Daniel	do	Governor Peirpoint	July 22, 1865.
Benjamin Davis	do	Governor Peirpoint, Charles Palmer, Samuel D. Denoon, and Smith Ford	July 18, 1865.
Jacob Van Doren	do	Governor Peirpoint, D. H. Strother, and Adjutant General of Virginia	Oct. 6, 1865.
Wm. F. Dowell	do	Governor Peirpoint, C. A. Ward, mayor of Alexandria, R. Johnston, and Lewis McKenzie	Aug. 7, 1865.
A. H. Drewry	do	Governor Peirpoint, James H. Cox, and Charles Palmer	July 3, 1865.
R. H. Dulany	do	Hon. L. H. Chandler, United States district attorney for Virginia, and C. M. Stewart	Sept. 19, 1865.
James Dunlop	do	J. D. Osborne	June 26, 1865.
H. T. Drewry	do	Charles H. Lewis, secretary commonwealth of Virginia	Nov. 1, 1865.
Wm. J. Dickinson	do	Governor Peirpoint	July 25, 1865.
Charles T. Davis	do	Governor Peirpoint and William Greer	Nov. 9, 1865.
G. W. Dillard	do	Governor Peirpoint and Alexander Rives	July 20, 1865.
Clay Drewry	do	Governor Peirpoint, Francis J. Smith, Benj. H. Nash, W. Goddin, and Wm. F. Tayler	Aug. 1, 1865.
B. F. Dew	do	Governor Peirpoint and A. Broaddus, jr., minister of the gospel	July 31, 1865.
Robert Douthal	do	Hons. John Minor Botts and Jos. Segar	June 26, 1865.
H. L. Destler	do	Governor Peirpoint and Franklin Stearns	July 17, 1865.
J. Dunlop	do	Governor Peirpoint, Alexander Donnan, David May, John Kevan, Thomas Wallace, and W. F. Taylor.	July 17, 1865.
Joseph Dupuy	do	Governor Peirpoint, George W. Redd, and James M. Booker	Aug. 14, 1865.
D. S. Delaplane	do	Governor Peirpoint, C. A. W——, mayor of Alexandria, Lewis McKenzie, and R. Johnston.	Aug. 25, 1865.
J. H. De Jarnette	do	Governor Peirpoint	July 29, 1865.
David Dinges	do	do	Aug. 14, 1865.
Wm. R. Dunlap	do	do	Aug. 4, 1865.
John Dodson	do	do	July 13, 1865.
John J. Dickinson	do	do	Sept. 23, 1865.
George Dull	do	do	Sept. 16, 1865.
Wm. P. Dickinson	do	do	July 22, 1865.
H. G. Dulany	do	do	Oct. 2, 1866.
Benj. A. Davis	do	do	Aug. 19, 1865.
Martin Dalton	do	do	Aug. 19, 1865.
Wm. W. Dabney	do	do	Aug. 19, 1865.
Thos. S. Davidson	do	do	Aug. 19, 1865.
Felix S. Dodson	do	do	Aug. 19, 1865.
Benjamin Deyerb	do	do	Aug. 7, 1865.
F. B. Doane, jr	do	do	June 16, 1865.
F. Brown Doane	do	do	June 16 1865.
Madison Dunlap	do	do	July 29, 1865.
Thos. W. Doswell	do	do	June 24, 1865.
John Dooley	do	do	June 24, 1865.
Samuel D. Drewry	do	do	Oct. 24, 1865.

Mark Davis, sr	do	do	July 29, 1865.
Henry Davis	do	do	Sept. 13, 1865.
Mary A. Downman	do	do	July 29, 1865.
W. W. Donaghe	do	do	July 25, 1865.
R. H. Dudley	do	do	July 25, 1865.
Dr. B. B. Donaghe	do	do	July 25, 1865.
Samuel Daniel	do	do	July 13, 1865.
John Doman	do	do	Aug. 4, 1865.
Thos. R. Dew	do	do	Aug. 31, 1865.
Isaac B. Davis	do	do	July 5, 1866.
John B. Davis	do	do	July 11, 1865.
Braxton Davis	do	do	Aug. 1, 1865.
J. S. Davis	do	do	Sept. 11, 1865.
John T. Davis	do	do	Aug. 19, 1865.
Rev. R. T. Davis	do	do	Oct. 9, 1865.
Solomon Davis	do	do	July 29, 1865.
R. J. Davis	do	do	July 14 1865.
John D. Davis	do	do	Oct. 9, 1865.
George D. Davis	do	do	July 14, 1865.
C. H. Davidson	do	do	July 17, 1865.
B. F. Dulaney	do	do	Sept. 15, 1865.
John P. Dulaney	do	do	Sept. 11, 1865.
C. C. Dulaney	do	do	Sept. 29, 1865.
E. K. Durrett	do	do	Sept. 4, 1865.
D. D. Doval	do	do	Aug. 10, 1865.
Randolph Dickinson	do	do	Oct. 26, 1865.
Joseph Deyerle	do	do	Aug. 7, 1865.
R. A. Duncan	do	do	Aug. 7, 1865.
William Dillard	do	do	Aug. 11, 1865.
Dr. F. H. Deane	do	do	Aug. 5, 1865.
J. K. Dabney	do	do	Nov. 15, 1865.
James Drewry	do	do	Aug. 5, 1865.
Mark Downey	do	do	July 18, 1865.
John E. Drake	do	do	Aug. 31, 1865.
C. M. Dahlen	do	do	Aug. 7, 1865.
J. H. Downing	do	do	Aug. 5, 1865.
J. D. Davidson	do	do	June 26, 1865.
R. R. Dickson	do	do	Sept. 4, 1865.
Samuel M. Dold	do	do	Aug. 4, 1865.
P. V. Daniel, jr	do	do	July 3, 1865.
B. A. Donald	do	do	Aug. 2, 1865.
Francis Dyson	do	do	July 22, 1865.
Isaac Davenport, jr	do	do	Aug. 1, 1865.
Joseph B. Dunn	do	do	July 11, 1865.
E. H. Dillard	do	do	July 14, 1865.
George W. Daniel	do	do	July 22, 1865.
Josiah L. Dean	do	do	Aug. 24, 1865.
John A. Davidson	do	do	Aug. 1, 1865.
Adolph Dill	do	do	July 7, 1865.
R. H. Dibrell	do	do	June 24, 1865.

Virginia—Continued.

Name.	Exemption under amnesty proclamation of May 29, 1865.	By whom recommended.	Date of pardon.
J. J. English	Representative in the State legislature	J. M. Humphreys, president Union Association; George H. Baldwin, vice-president; Franklin Stearns, H. J. Smith, C. C. Burton, Wm. E. Burton, J. C. Japlin, E. W. Tompkins, and F. J. Smith.	June 15, 1865.
Arthur Emmerson	Left a loyal State and worth over $20,000	Governor Peirpoint and J. S. Tucker	May 10, 1866.
John Early	Ex-United States and rebel postmaster	Governor Peirpoint	Aug. 10, 1865.
W. H. Eubank	do	do	Aug. 19, 1865.
J. P. Everitt	do	do	Sept. 11, 1865.
A. R. Edmonds	Ex-United States and rebel postmaster, and indicted for treason.	do	Sept. 15, 1865.
W. K. Echard	Rebel postmaster	do	July 17, 1865.
Wm. Easley	Rebel postmaster, and worth over $20,000	do	Sept. 16, 1865.
S. H. Emory	Tax assessor	B. F. Winger, military commander of Surry county	July 13, 1865.
E. H. Edmunds	do	Governor Peirpoint and Wm. S. Bailey, major second Pennsylvania artillery	Aug. 1, 1865.
E. J. Early	Tax collector	Governor Peirpoint	Aug. 1, 1865.
T. W. Edwards	Proceedings instituted for confiscation	do	Aug. 25, 1865.
Charles Ellis	Property libelled for confiscation	do	Sept. 26, 1865.
R. S. Ellis	do	do	Sept. 26, 1865.
L. N. Ellett	Rebel clerk of court and worth over $20,000	Governor Peirpoint, Hon. J. M. Botts, E. L. Van Lew, Mrs. Eliza L. Van Lew, John L. Van Lew, and Charles Palmer.	June 30, 1865.
Wm. English	Aided the rebellion	Governor Peirpoint	July 26, 1865.
N. M. Elliott	do	Hon. J. M. Botts, Governor Peirpoint, and R. Ridgway	June 23, 1865.
Samuel H. Early			Oct. 2, 1865.
Thos. F. Epes	Worth over $20,000	Governor Peirpoint and Fred. Pryor	July 22, 1865.
M. H. Effinger	do	Governor Peirpoint and John F. Lewis	July 5, 1865.
Geo. Earhart	do	Governor Peirpoint and Daniel H. Hoge	Aug. 24, 1865.
Andrew E. Ellett	do	Governor Peirpoint, Miss E. L. Van Lew, and John N. Van Lew	June 30, 1865.
Francis H. Epes	do	Governor Peirpoint, P. J. Wright, and R. A. Lancaster	July 22, 1865.
B. R. Eldridge	do	Governor Peirpoint and C. W. Smith, brevet major general volunteers	Aug. 3, 1865.
James Early	do	Governor Peirpoint and D. H. Hoge	Aug. 19, 1865.
John Enders	do	Governor Peirpoint, Horace L. Kent, and Brevet Brigadier General J. E. Mumford	Aug. 14, 1865.
Edwin Edmunds	do	Governor Peirpoint, F. N. Watkins, Hy. Stokes, Locker & McKinney, B. S. Scott, and H. E. Watkins.	July 20, 1865.
Henry Edson	do	Governor Peirpoint and David Feelly	July 25, 1865.
J. B. Evans	do	Governor Peirpoint	July 25, 1865.
David R. Edley	do	do	July 5, 1865.
John Enders	do	do	June 24, 1865.
Wm. L. Early	do	do	July 25, 1865.
Robert Early	do	do	June 26, 1865.
W. T. Early	do	do	July 29, 1865.
Richard Early	do	do	Aug. 25, 1865.
James S. Early	do	do	June 27, 1865.
Alex. M. Earle	do	do	Sept. 4, 1865.
W. J. Eppes	do	do	Nov. 17, 1865.
Richard Eppes	do	do	June 28, 1865.

John W. Eppes	do	do	April 4, 1866.
Richard S. Eppes	do	do	July 22, 1865.
V. M. Eppes	do	do	Sept. 23, 1865.
Samuel F. Epes	do	do	July 22, 1865.
Francis W. Epes	do	do	July 22, 1865.
W. O. English	do	do	Aug. 5, 1865.
H. E. Edmunds	do	do	Aug. 16, 1865.
Peter Engleman	do	do	Aug. 16, 1865.
John R. Edmunds	do	do	June 16, 1865.
R. S. Ellis	do	do	Aug. 1, 1865.
R. Edmond	do	do	June 26, 1865.
Andrew L. Ellett	do	do	July 12, 1865.
Chas. C. Ellett	do	Governor Peirpoint and Hon. J. M. Botts	June 30, 1865.
Curtis Eames	do	Governor Peirpoint	July 21, 1865.
Thos. Edmunds	do	do	Aug. 16, 1865.
D. C. Edmunds	do	do	July 21, 1865.
S. E. Edmunds	do		June 26, 1865.
N. S. Edmunds	do	Governor Peirpoint	Nov. 17, 1865.
Thos. Edmunds	do	do	June 16, 1865.
P. Echols	do	do	July 5, 1865.
Dr. Chas. D. Everett	do	Governor Peirpoint and A. C. Vont, brevet brigadier general	Oct. 5, 1865.
A. P. Estridge	do	Governor Peirpoint	Aug. 4, 1865.
B. Estes	do	do	----------
Samuel Eleys	do	do	Sept. 20, 1865.
J. E. Eskridge	do	do	Aug. 25, 1865.
Lawson Eastham	do	do	Aug. 7, 1865.
B. F. Eastham	do	do	Aug. 7, 1865.
Henry K. Ellyson	do	do	July 13, 1865.
T. B. Evans	do	do	Aug. 7, 1865.
J. R. Ewine	do	do	Aug. 24, 1865.
David Eugene	do	do	Aug. 19, 1865.
Jos. N. Edmonds	do	do	July 13, 1865.
John M. Forbes	Member of State legislature, and worth over $20,000.	do	Aug. 5, 1865.
O. Fairfax	Left a loyal district; property confiscated and sold.	do	July 25, 1865.
R. C. Fugate	Ex-United States and rebel postmaster	Governor Peirpoint, W. B. Aston, J. L. Boyd, R. B. Aston, E. R. Dorton, C. V. Dorton, Wm. Dorton, David Jessie, D. Bundy, T. Bundy, H. C. Bundy, Stephen Bundy, Wm. Riggs, L. A. Johnson, G. W. Mead, Joseph Johnson, J. C. Vicars, James Hartsock, Samuel Burk, J. V. Johnson, Jos. Johnson, James Jessee, E. Vanderpool, J. H. Vanderpool, A. J. Poter, Stephen Burk, L. D. Vaughan, H. Dickenson, and John W. Hackney.	Sept. 4, 1865.
R. M. Firth	do	James Mitchell, of Indiana	Nov. 22, 1866.
Wm. A. Frazier	do	Governor Peirpoint	Aug. 4, 1865.
William Frazer	Rebel postmaster and worth over $20,000	do	July 6, 1865.
Wm. T. C. Finch	do	do	Aug. 29, 1865.
James F. Fleenor	do	do	Jan. 19, 1865.
J. C. Fowler	do	do	Aug. 11, 1865.
P. B. Foster	do	do	Aug. 4, 1865.
Elbert Fowler	do	do	Aug. 11, 1865.
E. S. Fulton	Rebel tax assessor and postmaster	do	Sept. 26, 1865
Andrew Ferguson	Rebel tax collector	do	Aug. 29, 1865.
Robert S. Field	do	do	Aug. 14, 1865.
W. W. Forbes	do	Governor Peirpoint and C. W. Smith, brevet major general of volunteers	Aug. 5, 1865.

Virginia—Continued.

Name.	Exemption under amnesty proclamation of May 29, 1865.	By whom recommended.	Date of pardon.
John H. Flood	Rebel tax collector and worth over $20,000	Governor Peirpoint, James G. Brooks, and Charles Palmer	Aug. 3, 1865.
T. T. Fauntleroy, jr.	Rebel receiver	Attorney General Speed	Sept. 29, 1865.
George K. Fox, jr	Proceedings instituted for confiscation	Governor Peirpoint, L. H. Chandler, esq., United States district attorney	Sept. 9, 1865.
Daniel Forrer	Rebel contractor and worth over $20,000	Governor Peirpoint, J. F. Lewis, collector of internal revenue for the second district of Virginia, and C. H. Lewis, secretary of the Commonwealth of Virginia.	July 5, 1865.
R. H. Figgat	Rebel deputy marshal	Governor Peirpoint	July 17, 1865.
John Freeland	Aided rebellion	Attorney General Speed	June 29, 1865.
J. F. Ficklen	Rebel clerk	Governor Peirpoint	Sept. 29, 1865.
Andrew J. Farrish	Worth over $20,000	do	July 10, 1865.
O. R. Funsten	do	do	Aug. 10, 1865.
James W. Foster	do	do	Aug. 10, 1865.
Z. S. Farland	do	do	Aug. 11, 1865.
J. T. Fletcher	do	do	July 20, 1865.
Beverly R. Fleming	do	do	Aug. 16, 1865.
George Fleming	do	Governor Peirpoint, R. T. Brooke, and Charles Wortham	July 9, 1865.
James B. Ficklen	do	Governor Peirpoint	July 11, 1865.
Wm. W. Fulcher	do	Governor Peirpoint, W. Goddin, D. P. Winston, J. H. Sands, and Ro. Howard	Aug. 14, 1865.
Charles Friend	do	Governor Peirpoint, Thos. Wallace, Alex. Donnan, Wm. S. Simmons, and T. H. Daniel	July 25, 1865.
Ambrose Ford	do	Governor Peirpoint, F. J. Smith, and Franklin Stearns	July 31, 1865.
Wm. F. Fourqurean	do	Governor Peirpoint and William L. Owen	Aug. 29, 1865.
R. T. Foster	do	Governor Peirpoint and Charles Palmer	June 28, 1865.
Whitty Fullin	do	Governor Peirpoint, F. McMellen, and E. Longley	Oct. 26, 1865.
A. J. Ford	do	Governor Peirpoint, Charles Palmer, F. J. Smith, J. E. Lipscomb, Franklin Stearns, and William Taylor.	Aug. 19, 1865.
B. C. Flannagan	do	Governor Peirpoint, E. R. Watson, Edward Coles, and Lewis C. Hunt, lieutenant colonel, and provost marshal of Albemarle, Virginia.	Aug. 11, 1865.
A. G. Fuller	do	Governor Peirpoint, J. F. Ficklin, and R. V. Lanier	Nov. 13, 1865.
Edmund Fitzgerald	do	Governor Peirpoint	July 25, 1865.
Dr. Wm. A. Fuqua	do	do	Nov. 24, 1865.
H. M. Folke	do	do	Sept. 13, 1865.
S. W. Ficklin	do	do	July 29, 1865.
J. M. Ferguson	do	do	Aug. 7, 1865.
E. H. Fitzhugh	do	do	Aug. 11, 1866.
J. M. Fowlkes	do	do	Aug. 11, 1865.
P. H. Foster	do	do	Aug. 16, 1865.
George A. Farrow	do	do	Aug. 5, 1865.
John G. Fulton	do	do	Aug. 16, 1865.
Francis M. Finley	do	do	Aug. 10, 1865.
Thomas W. Fauntleroy	do	do	July 17, 1865.
Thomas R Foster	do	do	Aug. 10, 1865.
A. Findlay	do	do	Aug. 10, 1865.
Andrew Fudge	do	do	Aug. 25, 1865.
James W. Fletcher	do	do	July 25, 1865.
Wm. Fitzgerald	do	do	July 13, 1865.

C. C. Francisco	do	do	July 25, 1865.
John B. Faulkner	do	do	Aug. 7, 1865.
James Fife	do	do	Aug. 7, 1865.
T. L. Farish	do	do	July 20, 1865.
William P. Farish	do	do	July 20, 1865.
B. S. Ferrell	do	do	Aug. 2, 1865.
Joel W. Flood	do		July 6, 1865.
James Franklin	do		July 6, 1865.
T. C. S. Ferguson	do	Governor Peirpoint	June 26, 1865.
Joseph Faqua	do	do	Aug. 22, 1855.
T. M. Fleming	do	do	Aug. 1, 1865.
Calvin Ford	do	do	Dec. 23, 1865.
William Faber	do	do	July 5, 1866.
L. H. Frayser	do	do	June 26, 1865.
Sidney Fletcher	do	do	Aug. 14, 1865.
W. R. Fleming	do	do	Aug. 2, 1865.
John F. Field	do	Governor Peirpoint and Attorney General Speed	July 3, 1865.
Hugh W. Fry	do		June 26, 1865.
John W. Fairfax	do	Hon. Andrew Wylie, of Washington, D. C	July 3, 1865.
Thomas Ferguson	do		June 26, 1865.
L. E. Finch	do	Governor Peirpoint	Aug. 1, 1865.
Henry D. Flood	do	do	July 3, 1865.
Thomas R. Friend	do	do	June 18, 1866.
Frederick Foot	do	do	Aug. 31, 1865.
W. J. Fowlkes	do	do	Aug. 31, 1865.
C. W. Fitzgerald	do	do	July 22, 1865.
John Fitzgerald	do	do	July 22, 1865.
J. S. Field	do	do	July 3, 1865.
P. J. Fowlkes	do	do	July 22, 1865.
Samuel B. Fisher	do	do	Aug. 3, 1865.
C. F. Fadley	do	do	Sept. 4, 1865.
H. S. Fletcher	do	do	July 25, 1865.
J. W. Ford	do	do	July 5, 1865.
E. Ferneybough	do	do	July 29, 1865.
Thomas Fletcher	do	do	Aug. 7, 1865.
S. B. Furgusen	do	do	July 5, 1866.
John T. Foster	do	do	Oct. 26, 1865.
Alexander Findlay	do	do	Aug. 11, 1865.
Henry Forrer	do	do	July 13, 1865.
C. W. Flippin	do	do	Sept. 4, 1865.
Edmund Fontaine	do	Governor Peirpoint, Lewis McKenzie, and Charles Palmer	July 3, 1865.
D. Funston	Member of rebel congress	Governor Peirpoint	Sept. 20, 1865.
William L. Goggin	Member of secession conv'n and worth over $20,000.	do	Sept. 26, 1865.
D. H. Gordon	Member of State legislature and worth over $20,000		June 26, 1865.
James K. Gibson	Rebel depositary	Governor Peirpoint	July 21, 1865.
William Gibboney	Rebel receiver, and worth over $20,000	do	Aug. 25, 1865.
Robert Gibboney	Com'r of impressed property and worth over $20,000.	do	Aug. 25, 1865.
John Gardner	Ex-United States and rebel postmaster	do	Aug. 25, 1865.
A. F. Gregory	do	do	Nov. 9, 1865.
Benjamin F. Gravely	do	Governor Peirpoint, J. H. Gardner, Horace L. Kent, W. S. Dorman, and W. R. Isaacs	July 15, 1865.
H. P. Gill	Rebel postmaster	Governor Peirpoint	Aug. 29, 1865.
James S. Guy	do	do	Nov. 7, 1865.

Virginia—Continued.

Name.	Exemption under amnesty proclamation of May 29, 1865.	By whom recommended.	Date of pardon.
W. T. Gary	Worth over $20,000	Governor Peirpoint	Aug. 7, 1865.
E. Grove	do	Hon. J. F. Harris	July 25, 1865.
S. W. Gibson	do	Governor Peirpoint	Sept. 4, 1865.
Samuel Goode	do	Governor Peirpoint and John B. Baldwin	Aug. 16, 1865.
S. T. Gibson	do	Governor Peirpoint and Daniel H. Hoage	Oct. 9, 1865.
James C. Gregory	do	Governor Peirpoint	Aug. 4, 1865.
David Gose	do	do	Jan. 18, 1865.
J. Grabeel	Rebel deputy postmaster	do	Nov. 9, 1865.
Eugenia S. Gatewood	Rebel postmistress	do	Sept. 16, 1865.
N. B. Gray	Rebel tax assessor	do	Aug. 29, 1865.
C. H. Greever	do	Governor Peirpoint and Daniel H. Hoge	July 14, 1865.
J. W. Graves	do	Governor Peirpoint	Sept. 4, 1865.
William F. Gray	Rebel tax assessor and worth over $20,000	do	July 13, 1865.
Thomas H. Garrett	Rebel tax collector	do	Aug. 29, 1865.
William Green	Rebel tax collector and worth over $20,000	do	July 29, 1865.
George W. Green	Rebel tax receiver	Governor Peirpoint, Wm. J. Bailey, major and provost marshal, and G. H. McKibbin, brevet brigadier general.	July 29, 1865.
Ephraim Grabill	Rebel collector of revenue	Governor Peirpoint, Wm. Ott, and J. A. Snyder	Aug. 19, 1865.
Miles George	Clerk in rebel treasury department	Governor Peirpoint and Charles Palmer	July 15, 1865.
J. C. Green	Left a loyal State	Governor Peirpoint	July 5, 1866.
G. W. Grice	Proceedings instituted for confiscation	L. H. Chandler, United States district attorney	July 3, 1865.
D. J. Goodwin	do	do	July 3, 1865.
George G. Garrison	do	Governor Peirpoint and John S. Millum	Sept. 4, 1865.
John George	Proceedings instituted for confiscation and worth over $20,000.	Governor Peirpoint and Lewis McKenzie	Sept. 23, 1865.
A. S. Grigsby	do	Governor Peirpoint	Sept. 23, 1865.
John T. Giddings	Property libelled for confiscation	do	Sept. 16, 1865.
W. A. Graves	Property confiscated	L. H. Chandler, esq., United States district attorney	Sept. 9, 1865.
C. W. Grandy	Property withheld	Governor Peirpoint and L. H. Chandler, esq., United States district attorney, Va.	Sept. 9, 1865.
James Giles	Aided the rebellion	Governor Peirpoint	Oct. 5, 1865.
Robert J. Glendy	Worth over $20,000	do	Sept. 16, 1865.
Cornelius Gilbert	do	do	Aug. 29, 1865.
James Garnett	do	do	Aug. 3, 1865.
R. H. Gilliam	do	do	Nov. 3, 1865.
Franklin Greyson	do	do	July 5, 1866.
John Grame	do	do	July 29, 1865.
Benjamin F. Garrett	do	do	Aug. 16, 1865.
J. P. Gilliam	do	do	Aug. 2, 1865.
James F. Gouldin	do	do	Sept. 9, 1865.
Adam Garnand	do	do	Sept. 9, 1865.
Wesley Grigg	do	Governor Peirpoint and Thomas R. Bowden, attorney general of Virginia	July 29, 1865.
James H. Gardner	do	Governor Peirpoint and Charles Palmer	Aug. 24, 1865.
James B. Gardner	do	Governor Peirpoint, Wm. A. Macfarland, and J. C. Hobson	July 13, 1865.
Mrs. Mary L. Garland	do	Governor Peirpoint	Aug. 24, 1865.

W. G. Gammon	do	do	Aug. 24, 1865.
Chapman Glover	do	do	July 26, 1865.
William A. Gillespie	do	do	Aug. 31, 1865.
Robert T. Gooch	do	do	Aug. 31, 1865.
Fleming Griffin	do	do	July 15, 1865.
William Gravatt	do	do	July 25, 1865.
Thomas W. Gee	do	do	July 5, 1866.
Bazil Gordon	do	do	July 21, 1865.
Samuel S. Gatewood	do	do	Sept. 29, 1865.
Samuel Gordon	do	do	Nov. 1, 1865.
Thomas Gilbert	do	do	Sept. 29, 1865.
John H. Griffin	do	do	Oct. 5, 1865.
R. F. Gaines	do	do	July 22, 1865.
Hugh L. Gallagher	do	do	July 18, 1865.
S. D. Gooch	do	do	July 5, 1866.
W. K. Gordon	do	do	July 26, 1865.
C. H. Gordon	do	do	Oct. 5, 1865.
William Gray	do	do	July 17, 1865.
Fendall Griffin	do	do	Aug. 24, 1865.
C. Greer	do	do	July 25, 1865.
George Guest	do	do	May 28, 1866.
Samuel E. Goodson	do	V. Keebler and C. T. Pepper	Mar. 8, 1866.
A. G. Garnett	do	Governor Peirpoint	Nov. 17, 1865.
William Gee	do	do	Nov. 7, 1865.
Emanuel Gerst	do	Governor F. H. Peirpoint and Hon. Thomas R. Bowden, attorney general of Virginia.	July 5, 1865.
William F. Gaines	do	Governor Peirpoint	Aug. 14, 1865.
T. W. Gouldin	do	do	Sept. 9, 1865.
David Graham	do	do	Aug. 1, 1865.
James Galt	do	do	Aug. 1, 1865.
Roger Gregory	do	Governor Peirpoint, Charles Palmer, Horace L. Kent, and Hon. Thomas R. Bowden, attorney general of Virginia.	July 7, 1865.
John Garst	do	Governor Peirpoint	Aug. 25, 1865.
William A. Gregory	do	do	Aug. 1, 1865.
Henry Garst, sr	do	do	Aug. 2, 1865.
P. H. Gilmer	do	do	July 18, 1865.
George H. Gilmer	do	do	July 18, 1865.
T. J. Gilliam	do	do	July 17, 1865.
W. H. Gaines	do	Governor Peirpoint and H. L. Kent	Aug. 4, 1865.
R. V. Gaines	do	Governor Peirpoint	Aug. 5, 1865.
D. Grigg	do	do	
William J. Gilkeson	do	do	July 25, 1865.
David Graham	do	do	Aug. 3, 1865.
John C. Graham	do	do	Aug. 7, 1865.
Joseph Graham	do	do	Sept. 29, 1865.
Thomas P. Gantt	do	do	Aug. 10, 1865.
James A. Glenn	do	do	Sept. 27, 1865.
James W. Goss	do	do	Aug. 19, 1865.
Mary E. C. Gilliam	do	do	Dec. 23, 1865.
R. M. Garrett	do	do	Aug. 16, 1865.
Wellington Goddin	do	Governor Peirpoint and Charles Palmer	July 13, 1865.
Lewis Graves	do	Governor Peirpoint	Sept. 26, 1865.
John Gibson, sr	do	do	July 17, 1865.

Virginia—Continued.

Name.	Exemption under amnesty proclamation of May 29, 1865.	By whom recommended.	Date of pardon.
W. Goddin	Worth over $20,000	Governor F. H. Peirpoint	Oct. 26, 1865.
Andrew Grinnan	do	do	July 29, 1865.
C. G. Goodman	do	do	Sept. 13, 1865.
Charles W. Gill	do	do	Aug. 11, 1865.
James Garnett	do	do	Aug. 3, 1865.
Hugh G. Guthrie	do	do	July 25, 1865.
Ebenezer Gloss	do	do	Aug. 19, 1865.
Price P. Gnatt	do	do	July 26, 1865.
W. D. Gresham	do	Governor Peirpoint and Hon. James Speed, Attorney General United States	Aug. 7, 1865.
J. W. Garth	do	Governor Peirpoint	July 29, 1865.
R. A. Gibbons	do	do	July 29, 1865.
L. W. Glazebrook	do	do	June 24, 1865.
Robert Gentry	do	do	Sept. 9, 1865.
W. E. Green	do	do	July 13, 1865.
William Gaines	do	do	July 13, 1865.
W. B. Green	do	do	July 13, 1865.
Samuel B. Gardner	do	do	Aug. 7, 1865.
David Greenway	do	do	Aug. 16, 1865.
P. M. Geurrant	do	do	Aug. 16, 1865.
Henry Gantt	do	Governor Peirpoint, Francis J. Smith, and William T. Taylor	Aug. 16, 1865.
Braxton Garlick	do	Governor Peirpoint	Aug. 16, 1865.
James C. Greenway	do	do	Aug. 16, 1865.
Alexander M. Glasgow	do	do	Aug. 16, 1865.
Richard P. Graves	do	do	July 17, 1865.
R. C. Garnett	do	do	Aug. 1, 1865.
William Greaner	do	do	Aug. 5, 1865.
Samuel Geld	do	do	Sept. 18, 1865.
William G. Gurrant	do	do	July 17, 1865
Wellington Gordon	do	do	Aug. 25, 1865.
Joel Garnett	do	do	Aug. 5, 1865.
W. H. Gray	do	do	July 5, 1866.
Edward Gresham	do	do	Aug. 10, 1865.
Thomas T. Giles	do	Governor Peirpoint and John M. Speed, esq., Lynchburg, Va	Oct. 2, 1865.
George W. Gretler	do		June 16, 1865.
John B. Glazebrook	do	Governor Peirpoint	July 13, 1865.
W. B. Gates	do	Governor Peirpoint, Franklin Stearns, Benjamin H. Nash, and Francis J. Smith	July 13, 1865.
H. Gresham	do	Governor Peirpoint	July 13, 1865.
Jonathan B. Gardner	do	do	Sept. 4, 1865.
E. Garth	do	do	Sept. 4, 1865.
W. H. Grant	do	do	July 20, 1865.
John H. Greaner	do	do	Aug. 7, 1865.
Peter Goobrick	do	do	Aug. 10, 1865.
William Gordon	do	do	Aug. 7, 1865.
			Oct. 14, 1865

William Graves	do	do	Aug. 5, 1865.
John D. Glass	do	do	Aug. 5, 1865.
William H. Goodwin	do	do	Aug. 24, 1865.
William C. George	do	Governor Peirpoint, Charles Palmer, M. Burton, and Francis J. Smith	Sept. 4, 1865.
James H. Grant	do	Hon. James Speed, Attorney General United States, Governor Peirpoint, Brevet Major General Curtis, William H. McFarland, J. A. Meredith, W. Gaddin, W. H. Lyons, and T. M. Dudley.	June 30, 1865.
John N. Hendren	Treasurer of the rebel States	Governor Peirpoint	July 15, 1865.
E. G. Hall	Rebel privateer	do	Oct. 26, 1865.
J. P. Holcombe	Rebel agent abroad	do	Dec. 28, 1865.
F. B. Huot	Rebel Depository	do	June 26, 1865.
A. J. Hamilton	Rebel bonded agent	do	Aug. 19, 1865.
W. Horner	Rebel agent commissary dedartment, and worth over $20,000.	do	Sept. 9, 1865.
W. N. Habersham	Rebel sub agent of produce, and worth over $20,000.	do	July 14, 1865.
E. W. Hubard	Rebel commissioner of appraisement, and worth over $20,000.	do	June 27, 1865.
M. G. Harman	Rebel mail contractor, and worth over $20,000	Brigadier General J. D. Stevenson	July 10, 1865.
G. A. Hancock	County magistrate	Governor Peirpoint	Oct. 9, 1865.
R. B. Higginbotham	Ex-United States and rebel postmaster	do	July 14, 1865.
A. D. Harding	do	do	Aug. 14, 1865.
R. S. Hines	do	do	Aug. 14, 1865.
J. Y. Hardy	do	do	Aug. 14, 1865.
Isaac Hass	do	do	Aug. 14, 1865.
J. M. Hawson	do	do	Sept. 4, 1865.
E. B. Hill	do	do	Aug. 3, 1865.
John Hammon, sr	do	do	Aug. 7, 1865.
Henry Horn	do	do	July 5, 1865.
Lewis Housman, jr	do	do	Nov. 6, 1865.
J. Humphreys	Rebel postmaster	do	Aug. 1, 1865.
E. K. Herren	do	do	Aug. 19, 1865.
H. F. Hanks	do	do	Oct. 5, 1865.
Jackson Higgins	do	do	Sept. 16, 1865.
G. W. Hunks	do	do	Aug. 24, 1865.
W. B. Hackley	Rebel tax assessor	do	Aug. 7, 1865.
B. W. Haxall	Rebel assessor of agricultural products	Hon. James Speed, Attorney General	June 29, 1865.
George P. Holman	Tax collector, and worth over $20,000	Governor Peirpoint	July 6, 1865.
John Hunter	Rebel clerk	do	Sept. 4, 1865.
Thomas Hume	Violated his oath	Governor Peirpoint and L. H. Chandler, Esq., United States district attorney, Va	Sept. 9, 1866.
J. A. Hooe	Left a loyal State	Governor Peirpoint	July 5, 1866.
C. E. Haas	Left a loyal State, and rebel government clerk	do	July 17, 1865.
H. St. G. Hopkins	Left loyal district	Governor Peirpoint and General Torbert	Aug. 29, 1865.
George R. Head	Proceedings commenced for confiscation	do	Sept. 11, 1865.
Benjamin F. Hudgins	do	Governor Peirpoint and L. H. Chandler	Oct. 5, 1865.
R. S. Hudgins	do	United States district attorney, Va	Oct. 5, 1865.
Bernard Hough	do	Governor Peirpoint and L. McKenzie, Esq	Aug. 5, 1865.
M. Harrison	Property seized for confiscation	Governor Peirpoint and L. H. Chandler, Esq., United States district attorney	Sept. 9, 1865.
T. Hume	Property libelled for confiscation		Sept. 9, 1865.
J. D. Hammearsley	Went abroad to avoid conscription, and worth over $20,000.	Governor Peirpoint	July 11, 1865.
T. E. Hambleton	Blockade runner, and worth over $20,000	do	Oct. 2, 1865.

Virginia—Continued

Name.	Exemption under amnesty proclamation of May 29, 1865.	By whom recommended.	Date of pardon.
D. B. Hall	Worth over $20,000	Governor Peirpoint	Sept. 29, 1865.
John Henry	do	do	July 23, 1866.
J. M. Harris	do	do	July 5, 1865.
T. J. Higginbotham	do	do	July 14, 1865.
Samuel Hobson	do	do	Sept. 26, 1865.
Walker Hogan	do	do	Sept. 4, 1865.
Joshua Hightower	do	do	Sept. 4, 1865.
A. G. Hancock	do		June 26, 1866.
S. H. Hairston	do	Governor Peirpoint, E. Barksdale, sr., and A. Y. Stokes	Aug. 2, 1865.
B. Herring	do	Governor Peirpoint	Sept. 16, 1865.
W. K. Heiskell	do	do	Aug. 12, 1865.
J. W. Henry	do	Hon. Attorney General Speed	Sept. 21, 1865.
H. St. George Harris	do	Governor Peirpoint	Aug. 24, 1866.
J. D. Howe	do	do	Aug. 24, 1865.
D. L. Hopkins	do	do	July 17, 1865.
William Howell	do	do	Sept. 16, 1865.
Kenton Harper	do	Governor Peirpoint, Hon. Henry Stanbery, Attorney General United States, and N. K. Trout, mayor of Staunton, Virginia.	Aug. 20, 1866.
Joseph Hodgson	do	Governor Peirpoint	July 17, 1865.
F. W. Hancock	do	do	July 29, 1865.
Lewis Hyman	do	do	Aug. 24, 1865.
J. H. Hausberger	do	do	July 17, 1865.
Mrs. J. V. Henry	do	do	Aug. 14, 1865.
T. N. Harrison	do	do	Aug. 5, 1865.
E. Hogshead	do	do	July 25, 1865.
Howson Hooe	do	F. Minor and P. C. Minor	Oct. 7, 1865.
John Hamilton	do	Governor Peirpoint	Aug. 1, 1865.
George E. Harrison	do	do	Aug. 14, 1865.
George Hankins	do	do	Aug. 14, 1865.
A. R. Holliday	do	do	Aug. 29, 1865.
R. T. Hubard	do	do	June 27, 1865.
J. H. Hathaway	do	do	Aug. 19, 1865.
Robert Hough	do	do	Aug. 24, 1865.
A. T. Harris	do	Governor Peirpoint, Charles Palmer, and F. J. Smith	July 7, 1865.
M. E. Hinton	do	Governor Peirpoint	Aug. 1, 1865.
Benjamin Harrison	do	do	Aug. 10, 1865.
A. W. Harman	do	do	July 5, 1865.
L. E. Harvie	do	Hon. James Speed, Attorney General United States	June 29, 1865.
W. A. Harrison	do	Governor Peirpoint	Aug. 14, 1865.
W. H. Hall	do	do	July 3, 1865.
Julian Harrison	do		July 3, 1865.
John M. Herndon	do	Governor Peirpoint	July 13, 1865.
J. G. Hurkamp	do	do	July 18, 1865.
E. W. Hudgins	do	do	Aug. 1, 1865.

N. W. Harris	do	do	Aug. 2, 1865.
D. J. Harstook	do	do	July 6, 1865.
Henry Harrison	do	do	July 13, 1865.
C. S. Hutchison	do	do	Nov. 3, 1865.
R. M. Hughes	do	Governor Peirpoint, Hons. John Minor Botts and Joseph Segar	Oct. 26, 1865.
Peter Hanger, sr	do	Governor Peirpoint	Aug 2, 1865.
Samuel J. Harrison	do	do	July 22, 1865.
S. B. Hughes	do	Governor Peirpoint and H. L. Kent	July 3, 1865.
Hugh Hamilton	do	Governor Peirpoint	Aug. 19, 1865.
Edward Hammet	do	do	Aug. 1, 1865.
Charles Harris	do	do	Sept. 20, 1865.
W. B. Harrison	do	do	Aug. 25, 1865.
E. E. Hundley	do	Governor Peirpoint, Hon. Attorney General James Speed, R. L. Owen	July 7, 1865.
William Hocker	do	Governor Peirpoint	Aug. 24, 1865.
W. H. Haxall	do	Hon. Attorney General James Speed	June 29, 1865.
Hugh Hagan	do	Governor Peirpoint	July 11, 1865.
Robert Healey	do	John Hopkins	Dec. 1, 1865.
E. Helm	do	Governor Peirpoint	Aug. 4, 1865.
Hooe Howson	do	do	Sept. 9, 1865.
J. W. Harwood	do	do	July 14, 1865.
John Howlett	do	do	Aug. 2, 1865.
Thomas Harrison	do	do	Aug. 19, 1865.
W. D. Hart	do	do	Sept. 9, 1865.
Marshall Hairston	do	do	Aug. 2, 1865.
Randolph Harrison	do		July 3, 1865.
R. B. Haxall	do	Hon. James Speed, Attorney General United States	June 29, 1865.
Robert Hamsberger	do	Governor Peirpoint	Aug. 1, 1865.
John A. Herring	do	Governor Peirpoint, J. F. Lewis, and Charles H. Lewis	July 5, 1865.
John Harrison	do	Governor Peirpoint	July 20, 1865.
G. C. Hannah	do	do	July 14, 1865.
S. H. Holland	do	do	July 13, 1865.
George Hawn	do	do	Aug. 4, 1865.
R. M. Haxall	dc	do	July 17, 1865.
N. B. Hill	do	Governor Peirpoint, J. H. Sands, and W. Goddin	July 17, 1865.
D. E. Harrison	de	Governor Peirpoint	Aug. 16, 1865.
Alfred Harris	do	do	Oct. 5, 1865.
William H. Harris	do	do	Oct. 5, 1865.
William B. Harris	do	Governor Peirpoint and J. H. Clark	Sept. 19, 1865.
A. B. Hooe	do	Governor Peirpoint	July 5, 1866.
R. R. Howison	do	do	Sept. 4, 1865.
Jacob Howdershell	do	do	Aug. 31, 1865.
D. W. Haxall	do	do	July 15, 1865.
J. J. Hunton	do	do	Aug. 31, 1865.
William L. Harrison	do	do	Nov. 17, 1865.
William E. Hoge	do	do	Aug. 25, 1865.
Houlder Hudgins	do	Governor Peirpoint and Hon. Joseph Segar	Jan. 18, 1866.
Joseph L. Howard	do	Governor Peirpoint	July 5, 1866.
John H. Harding	do	do	Sept. 11, 1865.
William Harding	do	do	Sept. 11, 1865.
W. H. Hosley	do	do	Oct. 25, 1865.
E. S. Hammond	do		July 14, 1865.
John H. Hawkins	do	Governor Peirpoint	Aug. 10, 1865.

Virginia—Continued.

Name.	Exemption under amnesty proclamation of May 29, 1865.	By whom recommended.	Date of pardon.
James C. Howlett	Worth over $20,000	Governor Peirpoint	Aug. 10, 1865.
William H. Hall	do		July 14, 1865.
Robert Hudgin	do	Governor Peirpoint	Aug. 5, 1865.
James Harts	do	do	Sept. 13, 1865.
Jeremiah Harrisberger	do	do	July 29, 1865.
W. M. Hannah	do	do	Oct. 24, 1865.
D. E. Hancock	do	do	Aug. 19, 1865.
G. J. Hite	do	do	Aug. 19, 1865.
Samuel Hairston	do	do	Aug. 19, 1865.
William Hatcher	do	do	July 29, 1865.
John S. Hardaway	do	Governor Peirpoint, Thomas T. Giles, and R. H. Meade	July 29, 1865.
James E. Horner	do	Governor Peirpoint	Aug. 11, 1865.
George Harston	do	do	July 29, 1865.
Dr. G. W. Hamsberger	do	do	Aug. 10, 1865.
A. E. Huff	do	do	Aug. 7, 1865.
John B. Harvie	do	Governor Peirpoint, W. Goddin, and Thomas T. Giles	July 29, 1865.
J. C. Hutcheson	do	Governor Peirpoint	July 5, 1865.
A. E. Heneberger	do	do	July 5, 1866.
Willis Huckstep	do	do	July 5, 1866.
M. Haden	do	do	July 5, 1866.
E. F. Hill	do	do	Aug. 3, 1865.
John O. Harris	do	do	July 25, 1865.
John W. Holland	do	do	July 13, 1865.
F. L. Hale	do	Governor Peirpoint and D. H. Hoge	Aug. 19, 1865.
E. Hershberger	do	Governor Peirpoint	Aug. 3, 1865.
Henry Howard	do	do	Aug. 19, 1865.
R. E. Haskins	do	do	Nov. 7, 1865.
John Harrold	do	do	July 11, 1865.
R. Y. Horsley	do	do	July 14, 1865.
R. H. Hairston	do	do	Nov. 3, 1865.
C. Y. Horsley	do	do	July 21, 1865.
Ann Hollins	do	do	July 26, 1865.
L. W. Hough	do	do	Sept. 4, 1865.
M. H. Hobbs	do	do	Aug. 16, 1865.
E. D. Hundley	do	do	Aug. 16, 1865.
R. Harrison	do	do	July 23, 1865.
Peter Harman	do	do	July 29, 1865.
Joseph Heirholyer	do	do	July 15, 1865.
J. M. Hinegardner	do	do	Aug. 10, 1865.
Samuel Hawbert	do	do	Aug. 16, 1865.
F. Henderson	do	do	Aug. 25, 1865.
David Hansbrough	do	do	Aug. 5, 1865.
James Harris	do	do	Aug. 5, 1865.

C. G. Holland	do	do	July 14, 1865.
John W. Hurt	do	do	Aug. 7, 1865.
Robert A. Hamilton	do	do	July 11, 1865.
Seth Halsey	do	do	Nov. 3, 1865.
S. B. Hunter	do	do	Nov. 3, 1865.
W. C. Hebener	do	Governor Peirpoint, B. H. Nash, Francis J. Smith, Franklin Stearns, and W. F. Taylor.	July 21, 1865.
Ludwig Hoyer	do	Governor Peirpoint	July 3, 1865.
A. W. Harris	do	do	Aug. 12, 1865.
Ambrose Hord	do	Governor Peirpoint and H. L. Kent	Aug. 4, 1865.
W. M. Harrison	do	Governor Peirpoint	Aug. 2, 1865.
J. D. Harvey	do		June 26, 1865.
Joseph H. Hoge	do	Governor Peirpoint and Daniel H. Hoge	Aug. 14, 1865.
Dr. Isaac Hull	do	Governor Peirpoint	July 25, 1865.
Madison Hook	do	do	Aug. 25, 1865.
R. G. Haden	do	do	Aug. 25, 1865.
Joel Hayes	do	do	Sept. 11, 1865.
William King Heiskell	do	do	Sept. 11, 1865.
John C. Hobson	do	do	July 18, 1865.
George A. Hundley	do	do	July 21, 1865.
George B. Hannah	do	do	July 18, 1865.
R. N. Hudson	do	Governor Peirpoint and W. Goddin	July 29, 1865.
E. D. Hundley	do		July 14, 1865.
O. P. Hare	do	Governor Peirpoint	Aug. 24, 1865.
John W. Hamilton	do	do	July 17, 1865.
Nathaniel B. Harvey	do	do	Aug. 24, 1865.
John Hunter	do	do	Aug. 11, 1865.
Richard M. Harrison	do	do	Aug. 16, 1865.
Thomas Harvey	do		July 13, 1865.
John Horsely	do	Governor Peirpoint	July 21, 1865.
Clinton B. Haddox	do	do	Sept. 23, 1865.
Alexander Hunter	do	do	Sept. 4 1865.
A. W. Ireson	Ex-United States and rebel postmaster	do	Aug. 16, 1865.
R. H. Isbell	Rebel postmaster	do	Sept. 13, 1865.
J. J. Irby	Deputy marshal, and worth over $20,000		June 26, 1865.
William B. Isaacs	Worth over $20,000		June 26, 1865.
Richard Irby	do	Governor Peirpoint and T. W. Campbell	July 22, 1865.
J. A. Inloes	do	Governor Peirpoint	July 17, 1865.
A. B. Irick	do	do	July 11, 1865.
Thos. M. Isbell	do	do	Aug. 4, 1865.
William T. Joynes	Judge of the rebel circuit court, and worth over $20,000.	do	July 1, 1865.
J. M. Johnston	Rebel depositary	George D. Ruggles, brevet brigadier general of volunteers	Aug. 29, 1865.
John M. Johnston	do	Governor Peirpoint	Aug. 29, 1865.
John W. Johnston	Rebel receiver	do	Aug. 11, 1865.
J. G. Jefferson	Rebel agent, and worth over $20,000	Governor Peirpoint and H. L. Kent	Nov. 31, 1865.
William B. Jones	Mail contractor, and worth over $20,000	Governor Peirpoint	Aug. 25, 1865.
Robert A. Jackson	Ex-United States and rebel postmaster	do	Aug. 5, 1865.
A. G. Jeffress	Ex-United States and rebel postmaster, and worth over $20,000.	do	July 15, 1865.
G. H. Jewett	Rebel postmaster	do	July 29, 1865.
S. R. Johnson	do	do	July 3, 1865.

Virginia—Continued.

Name.	Exemption under amnesty proclamation of May 29, 1865.	By whom recommended.	Date of pardon.
Robert Jackson	Rebel postmaster	Governor Peirpoint	Sept. 11, 1865.
S. F. Jordan	Rebel postmaster, and worth over $20,000	do	July 17, 1865.
Decatur Jones	Rebel tax assessor	do	Aug. 19, 1865.
E. S. Joynes	Clerk in rebel war department, and worth over $20,000.	do	July 15, 1865.
Jacob Henry Jones, M. D.	Left loyal State	Governor Peirpoint, Lewis McKenzie, William Arnold, W. D. Massey, James T. Close, and T. A. Stoutenburgh.	Aug. 12, 1865.
Charles T. Jones	Left District of Columbia, and clerk in rebel register office.	Hon. Senator Hendricks, Indiana	May 26, 1866.
J. W. Jones	Proceedings instituted for confiscation	Governor Peirpoint	Aug. 31, 1865.
James H. Johnston	Property confiscated	do	Sept. 20, 1865.
William H. Jones	Worth over $20,000	do	Aug. 29, 1865.
H. T. Jones	do	do	July 11, 1865.
Mrs. Helen Jones	do	do	Aug. 4, 1865.
R. H. Jones	do	do	Aug. 4, 1865.
George M. Jones	do	do	Dec. 14, 1865.
O. H. Jones	do		July 24, 1865.
B. C. Jones	do	Governor Peirpoint	July 22, 1865.
Gabriel Jones	do	do	Nov. 17, 1865.
R. Y. Jones	do	do	July 17, 1865.
Archer Jones	do	do	July 22, 1865.
Philip B. Jones	do	do	Aug. 19, 1865.
Richard Jones	do	do	July 25, 1865.
John B. Jones	do	do	Oct. 26, 1865.
J. B. Jones	do	do	July 3, 1865.
W. S. Jones	do	do	Sept. 9, 1865.
T. M. Jones	do	do	July 20, 1865.
P. B. Jones	do	do	Aug. 19, 1865.
James Alfred Jones	do	do	July 3, 1865.
James F. Jones	do	do	Aug. 5, 1865.
Joseph P. Jones	do	do	July 5, 1865.
William R. Johnson	do	do	July 11, 1865.
Benjamin Johnson	do	do	Nov. 17, 1865.
James F. Johnson	do	Governor Peirpoint and Hon. J. M. Botts	June 28, 1865.
John H. Johnson	do	do	July 5, 1865.
A. J. Johnson	do	Governor Peirpoint	July 6, 1865.
Silas L. Johnson	do	Governor Peirpoint and H. L. Kent	July 6, 1865.
Silvanus Johnson	do	Governor Peirpoint	Aug. 14, 1865.
J. T. Johnson	do	do	Nov. 3, 1865.
Zichariah Johnston	do	do	Aug. 19, 1865.
Andrew Johnston	do	Hon. O. H. Browning	June 26, 1865.
Morgan Johnston	do	Governor Peirpoint and C. H. Lewis, of South Carolina	Sept. 14, 1865.
Thomas Johnston	do	Governor Peirpoint	July 29, 1865.
T. H. Johnston	do		June 26, 1865.

C. I. Johnston	do	Governor Peirpoint	Aug. 31, 1865.
Enoch Jeffries	do	do	Aug. 11, 1865.
John B. Jeffries	do	do	Aug. 11, 1865.
Joseph Jeffries	do	do	Aug. 11, 1865.
James H. Jeffries	do	do	Aug. 4, 1865.
William C. Jeffress	do	do	July 22, 1865.
E. T. Jeffress	do	do	July 22, 1865.
Joseph Jackson, jr	do	do	July 15, 1865.
Joseph Jackson	do	do	July 17, 1865.
P. H. Jackson	do	Governor Peirpoint, R. S. Paulett, T. M. Noble, and other names, miserably illegible	July 20, 1865.
F. W. Jackson	do	Governor Peirpoint	July 22, 1865.
Michael Jackson	do	do	Sept. 11, 1865.
Easthorn Jordon	do	do	Aug. 7, 1865.
John W. Jordan	do	do	July 17, 1865.
Ira F. Jordan	do	do	Aug. 25, 1865.
Francis Jordone	do	do	Aug. 1, 1865.
James Jett	do	do	July 25, 1865.
John Jett	do	do	July 25, 1865.
E. T. James	do	do	July 13, 1865.
Martin James	do	do	Aug. 1, 1865.
M. P. Jarnagin	do	do	July 20, 1865.
L. S. Joynes, M. D.	do	Governor Peirpoint and Hon. James Speed, U. S. Attorney General	June 19, 1865.
Joseph Jaques	do	Governor Brownlow, Tenn.; George B. Parker, and A. G. Jackson	July 15, 1865.
William B. Jennings	do	Governor Peirpoint	Sept. 27, 1865.
A. C. Jones	do	do	Aug. 10, 1865.
R. G. H. Kean	Chief of rebel bureau of war		June 27, 1865.
A. F. Kinney	Rebel depositary and collector of customs	Governor F. H. Peirpoint	July 25, 1865.
John Keys	Ex-United States and rebel postmaster	do	Oct. 14, 1865.
Samuel Kinney, jr	do	do	Aug. 19, 1865.
William P. Kindrick	do	do	Sept. 26, 1865.
David Kunkle	do	do	Aug. 24, 1865.
E. S. Kusling	do	do	Aug. 3, 1865.
E. S. Kemper	do	do	July 25, 1865.
Samuel X. Kerr	Ex-United States and rebel postmaster, and worth over $20,000.	do	Aug. 16, 1865.
C. Kinney	Ex-United States and rebel postmaster	do	Oct. 24, 1865.
R. B. Kasey	Rebel postmaster	Governor Peirpoint and R. F. Walker	Oct. 5, 1865.
Gilbraith Kyle	do	Governor Peirpoint	Aug. 25, 1865.
George Kelley	do	do	Oct. 9, 1865.
B. F. Kemper	do	do	July 5, 1866.
H. M. Keyser	do	do	Sept. 11, 1865.
James Kersey	Rebel tax assessor	Governor Peirpoint and —— Green	Nov. 9, 1865.
R. M. Kent	Rebel tax assessor, and worth over $20,000	Governor Peirpoint	Aug. 11, 1865.
W. C. Kloman	Left loyal State	do	Aug. 24, 1865.
E. F. Kloman	do	do	Aug. 24, 1865.
J. M. Kilgour	do	do	Aug. 31, 1865.
James M. Kilgour	Property seized	do	Aug. 16, 1865.
Edward Kearns	do		July 17, 1865.
William Knigh	Forced to resign a petty office in the United States navy.		June 13, 1865.
Andrew Kevan	Aided rebellion	Governor Peirpoint and L. H. McKinzie	July 7, 1865.
John Kevan	do	Governor Peirpoint	July 7, 1865.

Virginia—Continued.

Name.	Exemption under amnesty proclamation of May 29, 1865.	By whom recommended.	Date of pardon.
John Kelly	Worth over $20,000	Governor Peirpoint	Sept. 11, 1865.
J. F. Kent	do	do	Sept. 11, 1865.
S. E. Knight	do	do	July 22, 1865.
William Kyle	do	do	Sept. 26, 1865
R. M. Kirby	do	do	Sept. 27, 1865.
Jeff. Kinney	do	do	July 25, 1865.
John P. Kelly	do	do	Aug. 19, 1865.
D. C. Kiser	do	do	Sept. 13, 1865.
D. C. Kent	do	do	Sept. 13, 1865.
Isham Keith	do	do	Aug. 19, 1865.
A. Kendrick	do	do	Aug. 16, 1865.
William Kerr	do	do	Aug. 16, 1865.
John Kenney	do	do	Aug. 7, 1865.
G. J. Kelly	do	Governor Peirpoint, Charles Palmer, Franklin Stearns, and H. G. Fant, president of First National bank.	July 5, 1865.
Thomas Kasey	do	Governor Peirpoint	Nov. 6, 1865.
John R. Koogler	do	do	July 13, 1865.
Mrs. E. Kent	do	do	Aug. 24, 1865.
W. C. Knight	do	do	Sept. 14, 1865.
W. W. Keen	do	Governor Peirpoint, W. F. Tayler, A. Y. Stokes, and E. Barksdale, jr	July 3, 1865.
B. F. Kinsey	do	Governor Peirpoint	Aug. 7, 1865.
James Keith	do	do	Aug. 19, 1865.
Jeremiah Kyler	do	do	Aug. 25, 1865.
H. S. Kane	do	Governor Peirpoint, D. H. Hoge, R. C. Bennett, postmaster; W. D. Nottingham, and George H. Nottingham.	Mar. 14, 1865.
Henry Kisling	do	Governor Peirpoint	July 13, 1865.
G. C. Kent	do	do	Aug. 25, 1865.
Peter Keyser	do	do	July 21, 1865.
R. N. Kelso	do	do	Aug. 2, 1865.
Henry Koiner	do	do	Aug. 1, 1865.
J. McG. Kent	do	do	Aug. 1, 1865.
J. K. J. Kinker	do	do	Aug. 4, 1865.
J. R. Kent	do	do	April 3, 1866.
John H. Knight	do	do	Aug. 9, 1865.
Daniel S. Kerfoot	do	do	Oct. 5, 1865.
Dr. Harry Kyle	do	do	Aug. 16, 1865.
Alfred King	do	do	July 13, 1865.
George Koiner	do	do	Aug. 16, 1865.
Thomas F. Knox	do	do	Aug. 1, 1865.
John W. Lewis	Member of the rebel legislature, and worth over $20,000.	do	Oct. 23, 1865.
R. A. Lancaster	Rebel depositary, and worth over $20,000	Governor Peirpoint, Francis J. Smith, Franklin Stearns, and Charles Palmer	July 3, 1865.
John Lyon	Rebel mail contractor		June 8, 1865.
J J. Littell	Ex-United States and rebel postmaster	Governor Peirpoint	July 13, 1865.

John W. Lee	do	do	July 25, 1865.
T. K. Lear	do	do	Aug. 7, 1865.
A. S. Lara	Ex-United States and rebel postmaster, and worth over $20,000.	do	Aug. 1, 1865.
William Lipscomb	Rebel postmaster	do	Aug. 14, 1865.
James M. Lewis	do	do	Sept. 16, 1865.
H. A. Lockett	Rebel postmaster, and worth over $20,000	Governor Peirpoint and Charles Palmer	
John J. Larew	Rebel tax assessor	Governor Peirpoint	July 25, 1865.
Frederick Lloyd	Rebel assessor, worth over $20,000, and proceedings instituted for confiscation.	do	Oct. 12, 1865.
W. H. H. Lynn	Rebel tax assessor	do	Oct. 9, 1865.
Maria Louisa Long	Proceedings instituted for confiscation	do	Sept. 9, 1865.
William B. Lynch	do	do	Aug. 10, 1865.
Mrs. M. L. Longstreet	do	Hon. James Speed, Attorney General of the United States	Sept. 21, 1865.
P. D. C. Lee	do	Governor Peirpoint	Sept. 9, 1865.
R. C. Littleton	do	do	Sept. 9, 1865.
A. C. Landstreet	Property seized and condemned	Hon. Reverdy Johnson, Governor Peirpoint, and C. G. Phelps	Oct. 16, 1865.
Samuel L. Lewis } Catharine E. Lewis }	Left District of Columbia	Governor Peirpoint	Mar. 7, 1866.
R. D. Leaman	Aided the rebellion	do	Oct. 6, 1865.
James M. Langhorn	Worth over $20,000	do	Sept. 16, 1865.
James E. Lipscomb	do	do	Aug. 19, 1865.
Lucius L. Lanier	do	do	July 25, 1865.
C. L. Ludwig	do	Governor Peirpoint, F. J. Smith, Franklin Stearns, and Charles Palmer	July 15, 1865.
J. W. Lampkin	do	Governor Peirpoint and C. L. Mosby	Aug. 11, 1865.
John O. Lewis	do	Governor Peirpoint, Charles A. Rose, and W. Goddin	Aug. 10, 1865.
Robert Lampkin	do	Governor Peirpoint	July 17, 1865.
A. J. Lucass	do	Governor Peirpoint and Daniel H. Hoge	July 15, 1865.
James E. Lipscomb	do	Governor Peirpoint	July 29, 1865.
Augustine Leftwich	do	Governor Peirpoint and L. C. Moseby	Aug. 11, 1865.
R. H. Lyell	do	Governor Peirpoint	Sept. 9, 1865.
Z. R. Lewis	do	do	July 21, 1865.
R. D. Lee	do	do	Sept. 25, 1865.
John H. Lee	do	do	Aug. 31, 1865.
J. H. C. Leach	do	do	Aug. 31, 1865.
John A. Lee	do	do	Jan. 18, 1866.
A. J. Livingston	do	do	Nov. 3, 1865.
J. B. Lightfoot	do	do	Sept. 20, 1865.
W. H. Langhorn	do	do	Sept. 16, 1865.
J. W. Logan	do	do	July 29, 1865.
D. H. London	do	Governor Peirpoint, A. D. Chockley, A. S. Lee, R. W. Hughes, W. Giddin, R. A. Lancaster, J. B. Smith, Joseph Jackson, and Jos. Jackman, jr.	July 17, 1865.
T. A. Lacy	do	Governor Peirpoint and T. R. Bowden, attorney general of Virginia	July 17, 1865.
B. P. Lee, sr.	do	Governor Peirpoint and Nelson Smith	Sept. 25, 1865.
P. Lybrook	do	Governor Peirpoint	Aug. 31, 1865.
David Laird	do	do	Sept. 4, 1865.
John Lionberger	do	do	Aug. 3, 1865.
Daniel A. Langhorne	do	do	July 14, 1865.
Isaac Long	do	do	Aug. 3, 1865.
M. S. Langhorne	do		July 14, 1865.
J. D. Langhorne	do	Hon. Henry Stanbery, Attorney General United States, and Governor Peirpoint	Nov. 19, 1866.
John S. Langhorne	do	Governor Peirpoint and Hon. Simon Cameron	July 14, 1865.

Virginia—Continued.

Name.	Exemption under amnesty proclamation of May 29, 1865.	By whom recommended.	Date of pardon.
James Lobban	Worth over $20,000	Governor Peirpoint and L. C. Hunt, lieutenant colonel	Aug. 7, 1865.
A. F. Leonard	do	Governor Peirpoint	Nov. 7, 1865.
C. H. Lynch	do	do	July 14, 1865.
Philip Long	do	do	Aug. 3, 1865.
N. M. Lee	do	do	Aug. 19, 1865.
J. D. Ligon	do	do	July 20, 1865.
John Lightfoot	do	do	Aug. 3, 1865.
H. B. Lewis	do	do	Aug. 3, 1865.
Ed. Lightfoot	do	do	Aug. 3, 1865.
Ellen Lovell	do	do	Aug. 3, 1865.
Michael Long	do	do	Aug. 3, 1865.
G. V. Litchfield	do	do	Aug. 12, 1865.
H. H. Lewis	do	do	Sept. 23, 1865.
Charles C. Lee	do	do	Aug. 25, 1865.
Ludlow Lawrence	do	do	Aug. 24, 1865.
William Leitch	do	do	July 11, 1865.
P. D. Lipscomb	do	Governor Peirpoint, R. Johnston, Lewis McKenzie, and C. A. Ware, mayor	Aug. 5, 1865.
William Logan	do	Governor Peirpoint	Aug. 2, 1865.
Richard Logan	do	do	Aug. 2, 1865.
Ash Levy	do	do	July 26, 1865.
W. E. Lauck	do	do	July 21, 1865.
Anthony Lawson	do	do	July 17, 1865.
H. H. Lewis	do		Mar. 24, 1866.
A. J. Leavenworth	do	Governor F. H. Peirpoint and Hon. James Speed, Attorney General of United States	Sept. 7, 1865.
H. L. D. Lewis	do		Oct. 30, 1866.
E. P. C. Lewis	do		Oct. 30, 1866.
Gustavus Lersner	do	Governor Peirpoint	Aug. 14, 1865.
Alfred Leyburn	do	do	July 17, 1865.
Eli S. Lutwiler	do	do	July 17, 1865.
Lloyd Logan	do	do	Oct. 4, 1865.
Geo. W. Lewis	do		Oct. 30, 1866.
John G. Lane	do	Governor Peirpoint	July 25, 1865.
John A. Liggat	do	do	Aug. 10, 1865.
Robert Leslie	do	Governor Peirpoint, Charles Palmer, F. Stearns, M. Burton, J. H. Cox, and F. J. Smith	July 6, 1865.
Thomas Latané	do	Governor Peirpoint	Aug. 19, 1865.
Rev. J. H. C. Leach	do	do	Aug. 14, 1865.
J. W. Love	do	do	Aug. 1, 1865.
J. Horace Lacy	do	do	Aug. 25, 1865.
John C. Laird	do	do	Aug. 19, 1865.
I. J. Leftwich	do	do	Aug. 7, 1865.
Gilbert S. Meem	Rebel brigadier general	do	Aug. 7, 1865.
G. W. Munford	Rebel secretary of state of Virginia	do	Sept. 1, 1865.
Robert A. Mayo	Member of rebel legislature, and worth over $20,000	do	Sept. 26, 1865.
Franklin Minor	do	do	Aug. 1, 1865.

J. M. McCue	do	do	July 25, 1865.
C. McIver	Worth over $20,000	do	July 14, 1865.
C. W. Murdaugh	Member of house delegates, and property libelled	Governor Peirpoint and L. H. Chandler	Oct. 6, 1865.
William Martin	do	Governor Peirpoint	Aug. 4, 1865.
S. McD. Moore	Member of secession convention	do	Aug. 1, 1865.
T. J. Morrison	Rebel depositary, and worth over $20,000	do	Aug. 7, 1865.
J. R. McDaniel	do		June 26, 1865.
Henry W. Moncure	Rebel agent abroad, and worth over $20,000	Governor Peirpoint	Oct. 6, 1865.
T. J. Michie	Rebel receiver	do	July 25, 1865.
W. A. Maury	do	do	July 11, 1865.
Samuel F. McGehee	Rebel purchasing agent, and worth over $20,000	do	July 17, 1865.
C. R. Mason	Rebel mail contractor	do	July 25, 1865.
R. M. Mallory	do	do	July 29, 1865.
H. B. Miller	Rebel district attorney	do	Sept. 20, 1865.
John S. McNulty	Ex-United States and rebel postmaster	do	Aug. 25, 1865.
James C. Moir	do	do	Sept. 9, 1865.
H. A. Morrison	do	do	Aug. 10, 1865.
Elias Marshal	do	do	Nov. 13, 1865.
J. M. McCall	do	do	Oct. 9, 1865.
John N. Mauck	do	do	Sept. 4, 1865.
F. H. Mayse	Ex-U. S. and rebel postmaster; worth over 20,000	do	Aug. 25, 1865.
E. C. McCruw	Rebel postmaster	Governor Peirpoint and Brevet Brigadier General Smith	Aug. 1, 1865.
Creed Mucalls	do	Governor Peirpoint	Sept. 16, 1865.
J. L. Mitchell	do	do	Aug. 24, 1865.
B. D. Morton	do	do	Aug. 1, 1865.
J. A. Mann	do	do	Sept. 9, 1865.
M. J. Meyerhoeffer	do	Governor Peirpoint and Samuel R. Sterling, collector inter'l rev's second district of Va	July 25, 1865.
Jefferson Matney	do	Governor Peirpoint	Oct. 12, 1865.
W. B. Mason	do	do	July 28, 1866.
G. A. R. Merideth	do	do	Aug. 24, 1865.
F. M. McCraw	do	do	Aug. 24, 1865.
R. A. Marshal	do	do	Aug. 14, 1865.
John M. Muphies	do	do	Aug. 14, 1865.
A. A. Morehead	do	do	Aug. 10, 1865.
D. W. Meredith	do	do	Aug. 2, 1865.
Charles D. McKinney	Deputy postmaster	Governor Peirpoint and Brevet Major General Smith	Aug. 1, 1865.
G. Mosely	Rebel tax assessor	do	July 11, 1865.
George Mosely	do	Governor Peirpoint	July 29, 1865.
James D. Morrison	do	do	Aug. 1, 1865.
T. B. McRobert	do	do	Aug. 2, 1865.
J. R. McNutt	Rebel assistant assessor	do	Aug. 2, 1865.
Wm. H. McCorkle	do	do	Aug. 2, 1865.
E. T. Montegue	Rebel tax collector	do	Sept. 11, 1865.
E. T. Montague	do	do	Oct. 24, 1865.
S. H. Morrison	do	do	Aug. 10, 1865.
Wm. G. Miller	do	do	Aug. 7, 1865.
A. H. Mitchell	do	do	Aug. 24, 1865.
J. M. Montague	Deputy collector, and worth over $20,000	do	Aug. 25, 1865.
Patrick McCormick	Proceedings instituted for confiscation	do	July 5, 1866.
A. R. Mott	do	do	Aug. 24, 1865.
C. K. Mallory	do	L. H. Chandler, esq., United States district attorney, Virginia	July 3, 1865.
J. H. McVingle	do	Governor Peirpoint	Sept. 29, 1865.

Virginia—Continued.

Name.	Exemption under amnesty proclamation of May 29, 1865.	By whom recommended.	Date of pardon.
James Murdough	Property libelled for confiscation	L. H. Chandler, esq., United States district attorney, Virginia	July 17, 1865.
George W. Munford	do	Hon. Preston King	Sept. 1, 1865.
J. H. Manning	Property seized, and worth over $20,000	Governor Peirpoint	Sept. 16, 1865.
J. D. Myrick	do	Governor Peirpoint and Major General Thomas	Oct. 4, 1865.
Edward McCormick	Violated his oath, and worth over $20,000	Daniel T. Wood, C. L. Wood, L. R. Smith, and Samuel Trunday	June 26, 1865.
L. D. Merrall	Left a loyal district	Governor Peirpoint and Brevet Major General Smith	Aug. 5, 1865.
R. B. Worman	do	Governor Peirpoint	Aug. 7, 1865.
C. B. Maury	do	do	Aug. 5, 1865.
A. N. Marr	Left District of Columbia	James H. Marr	June 16, 1865.
Charles F. Myers	Left District of Columbia, and accepted clerkship in rebel treasury department.	Governor Peirpoint	Oct. 26, 1865.
John C. McCabe	Rebel chaplain		June 26, 1865.
R. H. Maury	Aided the rebellion		June 24, 1865.
John A. Merchant	Worth over $20,000	Governor Peirpoint	July 29, 1865.
O. C. Morris	do	do	July 25, 1865.
M. Moore	do		June 27, 1865.
Charles Mason	do	Governor Peirpoint	Oct. 26, 1865.
David McGavock	do	do	Aug. 17, 1865.
James Moore	do	do	Aug. 17, 1865.
Neal McCurdy	do	do	July 29, 1865.
James D. Maddock	do	do	Sept. 4, 1865.
George W. Morton	do	do	Aug. 3, 1865.
William Mathews	do	do	Oct. 26, 1865.
Thomas C. Miller	do	do	Aug. 19, 1865.
James M. Mathews	do	do	Sept. 23, 1865.
William M. Michaux	do	do	July 6, 1865.
S. Maupin	do	do	Aug. 19, 1865.
James R. Miller	do	do	Aug. 7, 1865.
Joseph Meads	do	do	Aug. 5, 1865.
John G. Meem	do		June 26, 1865.
E. H. Murrell	do		June 26, 1865.
W. D. Miller	do		June 26, 1865.
J. B. McPhail	do	Governor Peirpoint	July 29, 1865.
W. W. Minor	do	do	Aug. 1, 1865.
Charles Mason	do	do	Sept. 23, 1865.
Thomas W. McCance	do		June 24, 1865.
N. C. Miller	do	Governor Peirpoint	July 25, 1865.
J. F. McIlwaine	do	do	July 11, 1865.
Peter McEnery	do	do	July 11, 1865.
Richard G. Morris	do	Governor Peirpoint, C. H. Lewis, secretary Commonwealth of Va., and C. L. Mosby	July 11, 1865.
Robert F. Morris	do	do	July 11, 1865.
Charles Y. Morris	do	do	July 11, 1865.
Joseph W. Morris	do	Governor Peirpoint	Aug. 19, 1865.
N. H. Maple	do	Governor Peirpoint and Lewis C. Hunt	Aug. 19, 1865.

Moses Milchisa	do.	Governor Peirpoint	Aug. 10, 1865.
E. G. McClanahan	do.	do.	Aug. 1, 1865.
C. J. Meriweather, sr.	do.	do.	Oct. 5, 1865.
John Marshall	do.	do.	Oct. 5, 1865.
I. A. Marshall	do.	do.	Oct. 5, 1865.
E. C. Marshall	do.	do.	Oct. 5, 1865.
F. A. Morgan	do.	do.	July 24, 1865.
John F. Moses	do.	do.	Sept. 29, 1865.
Samuel H. Moses	do.	do.	Sept. 29, 1865.
C. J. Meriweather, jr.	do.	do.	Oct. 6, 1865.
Christopher McIver	do.	do.	July 26, 1865.
William J. Martin	do.	do.	Aug. 10, 1865.
A. McDaniel	do.	do.	Aug. 16, 1865.
J. W. Martin	do.	Governor Peirpoint and Lewis C. Hunt, lieutenant colonel and provost marshal	Aug. 31, 1865.
John M. Miller	do.	Governor Peirpoint	Aug. 14, 1865.
David May	do.	Governor Peirpoint and L. H. Chandler, esq., United States district attorney, Va.	July 25, 1865.
William Morton	do.	Governor Peirpoint	July 13, 1865.
George M. Murrell	do.	do.	July 3, 1865.
J. W. Murrell	do.	Governor Peirpoint, John F. Baugh, and George M. Rusher	July 3, 1865.
John McClure	do.	Governor Peirpoint	Nov. 3, 1865.
John J. McBride	do.	do.	Oct. 9, 1865.
Mrs. Maria C. Massie	do.	do.	Nov. 3, 1865.
R. C. Mitchell	do.	do.	Aug. 2, 1865.
M. M. Millner	do.	do.	Sept. 9, 1865.
Thomas G. Marshall	do.	do.	Sept. 9, 1865.
S. C. Murrell	do.	do.	July 3, 1865.
Samuel Miller	do.		June 26, 1865.
Thomas McCormick	do.	Governor Peirpoint	Oct. 5, 1865.
Mrs. M. C. Morris	do.	do.	Sept. 9, 1865.
Robert H. Moss	do.	do.	Sept. 16, 1865.
Thomas K. Miller	do.	do.	July 5, 1865.
Richard C. Mason	do.	do.	July 25, 1865.
H. M. Marshal	do.	do.	Aug. 5, 1865.
Benjamin Morgan	do.	do.	July 31, 1865.
Reuben Maury	do.	Governor Peirpoint and Lewis C. Hunt, lieutenant colonel and provost marshal	Aug. 24, 1865.
R. D. McIlwaine	do.	Governor Peirpoint	July 11, 1865.
William Meredith	do.	do.	July 31, 1865.
David F. Morton	do.	do.	Aug. 16, 1865.
Thomas Moore	do.	do.	July 25, 1865.
John J. Mitchell	do.	do.	July 29, 1865.
J. J. McBride	do.	do.	Aug. 19, 1865.
William R. Mallory	do.	do.	Aug. 1, 1865.
Ed. McMahon	do.	do.	Aug. 1, 1865.
S. A. Myers	do.	Governor Peirpoint and Charles Palmer	July 5, 1865.
John W. McKinsey	do.	Governor Peirpoint	July 18, 1865.
John M. Maury	do.	do.	Oct. 27, 1865.
Samuel O. Moon	do.	do.	Aug. 19, 1865.
Dr. William S. McChesney	do.	do.	July 25, 1865.
T. G. McConnell	do.	do.	Nov. 6, 1865.
Jacob Mohler	do.	do.	Aug. 1, 1865.
G. Mosley	do.	do.	Aug. 14, 1865.
B. W. Marshal	do.	do.	July 14, 1865.

Virginia—Continued.

Name.	Exemption under amnesty proclamation of May 29, 1865.	By whom recommended.	Date of pardon.
Mrs. Anne F. Mansfield	Worth over $20,000	Governor Pierpoint	Nov. 7, 1865.
Francis McCormick	do	Governor Peirpoint and Hon. James Speed, Attorney General United States	Aug. 16, 1865.
William H. Mayo	do	Governor Peirpoint	July 31, 1865.
Samuel P. Mitchell	do	do	July 29, 1865.
Patrick C. Massie	do	do	July 29, 1865.
Charles H. Massie	do	do	Aug. 24, 1865.
J. C. C. Moore	do	do	July 17, 1865.
A. A. McCormick	do	do	July 17, 1865.
H. A. McCormick	do	do	July 17, 1865.
Charles J. Manning	do	do	July 17, 1866.
R. M. Marshall	do	do	Sept. 14, 1865.
Thomas P. Mitchell	do	do	Aug. 7, 1865.
B. H. Magruder	do	do	July 29, 1865.
John Miller	do	do	Aug. 7, 1865.
Jacob Morton	do	do	July 13, 1865.
D. F. Morton	do	do	July 13, 1865.
Martin McFerran	do	do	Sept. 26, 1865.
Samuel B. Major	do	do	Sept. 27, 1865.
John H. Montague	do	do	June 24, 1865.
Thomas E. Murrell	do	do	July 5, 1866.
John F. Moses	do	do	July 5, 1866.
Samuel H. Moses	do	do	July 5, 1866.
R. O. Morris	do	do	July 29, 1866.
T. B. Massie	do	Governor Peirpoint and C. H. Lewis, secretary of Commonwealth of Virginia	Sept. 4, 1866.
Joseph McKay	do	Governor Peirpoint	Sept. 4, 1866.
H. W. Maseley	do	do	Aug. 5, 1866.
Littlebery Moon	do	do	Aug. 14, 1866.
John Miller	do	do	June 26, 1866.
John W. Minor	do	Governor Peirpoint and Lewis McKenzie	Sept. 23, 1866.
T. McIllister	do	Governor Peirpoint	Sept. 4, 1866.
P. McCormick	do	do	Aug. 19, 1866.
J. A. Michie	do	do	Aug. 4, 1866.
James Miller	do	Governor Peirpoint, Francis J. Smith, and Franklin Stearns	July 3, 1866.
A. Mosley	do	Governor Peirpoint	July 29, 1866.
Benjamin Marable	do	do	July 18, 1866.
J. Lewis Maury	do	Governor Peirpoint and Lewis C. Hunt, lieutenant colonel and provost marshal	Aug. 24, 1866.
Thomas T. Munford	do	Governor Peirpoint	Sept. 9, 1866.
Charles P. Moncure	do	Governor Peirpoint, Philip P. Nalle, W. S. Payton, and P. B. Jones	July 5, 1866.
George Mayse	do	Governor Peirpoint	Aug. 24, 1865.
Jesse Mundy	do	do	Dec. 16, 1865.
J. J. Moorman	do	do	July 17, 1865.
Abner W. Moore	do	do	July 17, 1865.
Franklin McCue	do	do	July 28, 1865.
Dr. J. McChesney	do	do	July 28, 1865.

S. B. Morrison	do	do	July 17, 1865.
John L. Marye, sr	do	do	July 14, 1865.
John Merritt	do	do	Aug. 1, 1865.
William W. Michaux	do	do	Aug. 1, 1865.
William H. Mosby	do	do	Aug. 14, 1865.
Middlton Miller	do	do	July 31, 1865.
William W. Major	do	do	July 17, 1865.
Alfred Moses	do	do	July 11, 1865.
Samuel McCorkle	do	do	July 6, 1865.
C. T. Mitchell	do	Governor Peirpoint, Horace L. Kent, and Charles Palmer	July 7, 1865.
Lewis Marshall	do	Governor Peirpoint, W. W. Gaines, Joseph Jeffries, W. T. S. Payne, W. C. Norris, and Lewis McKenzie.	------
Charles Moore	do	Hon. James Speed, U. S. Attorney General, and Colonel T. W. Butterfield	Aug. 14, 1865.
E. W. Morris	do		July 5, 1865.
Hugh McMackey	do	Governor Peirpoint	July 17, 1865.
E. H. Montevio	do	do	July 21, 1865.
Edward Mayo	do	do	Aug. 7, 1865.
Z. J. McChesney	do	do	Aug. 24, 1865.
Eliza Preston McDowell	do	do	Aug. 7, 1865.
B. C. Megginson	do	do	Aug. 24, 1865.
A. G. Mathews	do	do	July 14, 1865.
John Maben	do	do	July 17, 1865.
J. P. Marshal	do	do	July 22, 1865.
R. D. Montague	do	do	Aug. 25, 1865.
William M. Montague	do	do	Aug. 25, 1865.
J. C. McGavock	do	do	Aug. 25, 1865.
A. F. Menefee	do	do	July 25, 1865.
Stephen McGavock	do	do	Aug. 25, 1865.
Hugh McClure	do	do	Aug. 4, 1865.
James S. Moss	do	do	Aug. 4, 1865.
Benjamin F. Miller	do	do	July 25, 1865.
James Medley	do	do	Sept. 6, 1865.
James T. Mason	do	do	Oct. 9, 1865.
Joseph Milhiser	do	do	July 3, 1865.
Jacob Michaux	do	do	Nov. 17, 1865.
William H. Macon	do	do	July 3, 1865.
Nath. Mathews	do	do	Aug. 31, 1865.
G. W. Martin	do	do	Nov. 20, 1865.
William McComb	do	do	Aug. 16, 1865.
Thomas C. Maddox	do	do	July 15, 1865.
C. Miller	do	do	Aug. 14, 1865.
R. D. Martin	do	do	Aug. 10, 1865.
Perham Moon	do	do	Aug. 16, 1865.
James Marshall	do	do	Aug. 16, 1865.
Samuel Moore	do	do	Aug. 14, 1865.
James W. Morgan	do	do	July 14, 1865.
Samuel J. Morrison	do	do	Aug. 10, 1865.
James B. McCulloch	do	do	Aug. 5, 1865.
John A. Meredith	do	do	Aug. 31, 1865.
John G. Miller	do	do	Aug. 31, 1865.
J. E. Marshall	do	do	Aug. 5, 1865.
James A. Merriwether	do	do	July 14, 1865.

Virginia—Continued.

Name.	Exemption under amnesty proclamation of May 29, 1865.	By whom recommended.	Date of pardon.
G. A. Myers	Worth over $20,000	Governor Peirpoint	July 18, 1865.
Eliza L. S. Marshall	do	do	Sept. 25, 1865.
T. C. Mayo	do	do	Aug. 1, 1865.
Mrs. Ann E. Mayben	do	do	Nov. 6, 1865.
W. J. Morgan	do	do	Sept. 29, 1865.
Dr James May	do	do	Aug. 4, 1865.
William McClintic	do	do	Aug. 25, 1865.
H. W. Massie	do	do	Aug. 25, 1865.
Hope W. Massie	do	do	Aug. 25, 1865.
A. H. McClintic	do	do	Aug. 25, 1865.
Miss Minerva R. Murrell	do	do	July 3, 1865.
L. T. Moore	do	Governor Peirpoint, G. A. Tavenner, and Lewis McKenzie	Aug. 16, 1865.
James W. Mason	do	Governor Peirpoint	July 29, 1865.
James M. Morris	do	do	July 29, 1865.
Henry B. Miller	do	do	July 31, 1865.
A. J. Michie	do	Governor Peirpoint, John R. Woods, and E. R. Watson	
W. G. T. Nelson	Member of the rebel house of delegates, and worth over $20,000.	Governor Peirpoint	July 5, 1866.
William B. Nutt	Acting treasurer of the rebel government	do	Sept. 4, 1865.
A. R. Neal	Ex-United States and rebel postmaster	do	Sept. 4, 1865.
Samuel H. Nash	do	do	Aug. 29, 1865.
Benjamin P. Newman	Rebel postmaster	do	Aug. 14, 1865.
Richard Nesbitt	do	do	Aug. 4, 1865.
Abraham Neff	do	do	Aug. 24, 1865.
C. J. Noel	do	do	Sept. 11, 1865.
William H. Nickels	do	do	July 5, 1866.
James W. Neal	do	do	Aug. 16, 1865.
A. W. C. Nowlin	Rebel tax collector	do	Aug. 24, 1865.
B. F. Nall	Rebel clerk	do	Sept. 4, 1865.
Nathan Neer	Property seized for confiscation, and worth over $20,000.	Governor Peirpoint and Lewis McKenzie	—— —, 1865.
John M. Nelson	Left a loyal State	Governor Peirpoint	July 17, 1865.
William Norwood	Left District of Columbia, and worth over $20,000	Governor Peirpoint and Charles Palmer	Aug. 10, 1865.
N. Nash	Left military lines, and property seized	Governor Peirpoint and J. M. Botts	July 1, 1865.
Cincinnatus W. Newton	Rebel presidential elector	Major General B. F. Butler	Mar. 3, 1865.
A. M. Newman	Worth over $20,000	Governor Peirpoint	July 5, 1865.
Elisha Norfleet	do	do	Aug. 24, 1865.
Burr P. Noland	do	do	July 31, 1865.
John S. Nicholas	do	do	Aug. 1, 1865.
E. F. Noel	do	do	Sept. 9, 1865.
R. N. Neblett	do	do	Aug. 1, 1865.
Sterling Neblett	do	do	Aug. 19, 1865.
J. O. A. Nadenbousch	do	do	Sept. 14, 1865.
H. A. Newberry	do	do	Aug. 25, 1865.

Albert G. Nalle	do	do	Dec. 15, 1865.
J. B. Norfleets	do	do	Aug. 24, 1865.
J. L. Nichols	do	do	Mar. 14, 1866.
Lawson Nuonally	do	Governor Peirpoint, Francis J. Smith, Benjamin H. Nash, W. F. Taylor, H. J. Miller, and William H. Macfarland.	July 3, 1865.
Lewis P. Nelson	do	Governor Peirpoint and Charles Palmer	July 17, 1865.
A. H. Nash	do	Governor Peirpoint	Sept. 26, 1865.
James B. Newman	do	do	Aug. 14, 1865.
Benjamin H. Nowlin	do		July 14, 1865.
Joseph Naff	do	Governor Peirpoint	Sept. 13, 1865.
A. B. Nichols	do	do	Aug. 11, 1865.
R. W. N. Noland	do	do	Aug. 3, 1865.
John Newton	do	do	July 25, 1865.
R. E. Nelson	do	do	July 5, 1866.
James Newman	do	do	Oct. 12, 1865.
Robert Ould	Commissioner for exchange of prisoners	Hon. Montgomery Blair	Oct. 31, 1865.
William P. Oliver	Assessor of war tax	Governor Peirpoint and Brevet Major General Smith	Aug. 1, 1865.
John M. Orr	Property seized and condemned	Governor Peirpoint and Lewis McKenzie	Sept. 14, 1865.
Thomas J. Owen	Worth over $20,000	Governor Peirpoint	Sept. 20, 1865.
N. M. Osborne	do	Governor Peirpoint and Hon. James Speed, Attorney General United States	Feb. 10, 1866.
I. H. Overall	do	Hon. Henry Stanbery, Attorney General United States	Dec. 19, 1866.
Robert L. Owen	do		July 27, 1866.
E. H. Osborne	do	Governor Peirpoint	July 29, 1866.
Dr. Thomas J. Owen	do	do	Aug. 11, 1866.
R. F. Omohundro	do	do	Aug. 24, 1866.
John Ogler	do	do	Oct. 9, 1866.
A. G. Oneale	do	do	Aug. 10, 1866.
C. E. Oliver	do	do	Sept. 4, 1866.
William Overton	do	do	Aug. 5, 1866.
John B. Oliver	do	do	July 22, 1866.
J. M. Overton	do	do	Aug. 3, 1866.
Isaac Overbey	do	do	Aug. 1, 1866.
Robert Y. Overbey	do	do	Aug. 1, 1866.
George C. Omohundros	do	do	Aug. 24, 1866.
William W. Oliver	do	do	Aug. 4, 1865.
Miss Matilda Oliver	do	do	Nov. 7, 1865.
C. H. Ogburn	do	do	Aug. 4, 1865.
John M. Overton	do	do	Aug. 31, 1865.
Richard Payne	Member of rebel legislature, and worth over $20,000	do	July 29, 1865.
Andrew Patterson	Member of rebel legislature and collector of taxes	do	Aug. 7, 1865.
Bernard Pitzer	Rebel depositary, and worth over $20,000	do	Aug. 16, 1865.
W. M. Peyton	Left loyal State, and worth over $20,000	do	Sept. 4, 1865.
William Pannill	Rebel provost marshal	do	July 11, 1865.
Thomas J. Pretlow	Agent to purchase clothing, &c.		July 6, 1865.
G. L. Pierce	Agent to commissary, and worth over $20,000	Governor Peirpoint	Aug. 25, 1865.
D. Pulley	Ex-United States and rebel mail contractor	do	Aug. 5, 1865.
G. W. Palmer	Ex-United States and rebel postmaster	do	May 27, 1865.
W. W. Perry	do	do	Aug. 7, 1865.
R. W. Pegram	do	do	Jan. 18, 1866.
S. Putzel	do	do	July 20, 1865.
G. A. Pruner	do	do	July 5, 1866.
William E. Proctor	do	do	Aug. 11, 1865.

Virginia—Continued.

Name.	Exemption under amnesty proclamation of May 29, 1865.	By whom recommended.	Date of pardon.
John Poague	Ex-United States and rebel postmaster, and worth over $20,000.	Governor Peirpoint	Aug. 19, 1865.
John O. Perdue	Rebel postmaster	Governor Peirpoint, A. E. Cogbill, John W. Howard, P. H. Wilkinson, L. O. Duval, Daniel Adkins, H. K. Graves, T. J. Cheatham, E. S. Gregory, and L. Wells.	July 29, 1865.
William A. Perry	do	Governor Peirpoint	Nov. 13, 1865.
J. F. Powell	do	do	July 29, 1865.
Charles T. Palmer	do	do	Aug. 19, 1865.
S. B. Prestlow	do	do	Aug. 14, 1865.
A. G. Pritchett	do	do	Oct. 25, 1865.
John Phillips	do	do	Oct. 5, 1865.
Daniel E. Price	do	do	Oct. 5, 1865.
John F. Palmore	do	do	Aug. 11, 1865.
William Pannill	do	do	Oct. 5, 1865.
John R. Palmore, jr	do	do	Aug. 11, 1865.
Joseph H. Prince	Rebel tax assessor	do	Aug. 16, 1865.
Henry H. Peck	Rebel collector of tax in kind	do	July 25, 1865.
I. W. Pleasants	Deputy collector of war tax	do	Aug. 2, 1865.
John Priddy	Clerk in rebel auditor's office, and worth over $20,000	do	July 1, 1865.
F. W. Pleasants	Rebel clerk	do	June 9, 1865.
W. H. Perkins	County magistrate	do	Aug. 1, 1865.
James G. Paxton	Proceedings instituted for confiscation	S. Patrick, J. H. Brown, and B. H. Smith	Aug. 3, 1865.
Jacob Potterfield	do	Governor Peirpoint	Sept. 4, 1865.
W. H. Peters	Property libelled for confiscation	L. H. Chandler, esq., United States district attorney, Virginia	July 3, 1865.
Stephen Putney	Aided rebellion	Governor Peirpoint	Aug. 24, 1865.
J. N. Powell	do	do	July 6, 1865.
J. C. Phillips	do	do	Sept. 20, 1865.
Lewis Porter	Worth over $20,000	do	Aug. 11, 1865.
Thomas M. Powers	do	do	Aug. 14, 1865.
J. E. Perkinson	do	do	July 17, 1865.
George Pannill	do	do	Oct. 12, 1865.
Benjamin Pollard	do	do	July 7, 1865.
T. M. C. Paxon	do	Governor Peirpoint and L. McKenzie	Sept. 19, 1865.
R. E. Peyton	do	Governor Peirpoint	Aug. 4, 1865.
B. M. Payne	do	Governor Peirpoint and C. L. Mosby	Aug. 14, 1865.
George J. Palmer	do	Governor Peirpoint	June 24, 1865.
J. K. Pendleton	do	do	Aug. 7, 1865.
J. W. Patterson	do	do	Aug. 11, 1865.
John Purcell	do	Attorney General Speed	June 24, 1865.
W. B. Paris	do	Governor Peirpoint	Aug. 16, 1865.
T. E. Perkinson	do	do	Aug. 14, 1865.
Howe Y. Peyton	do	do	Aug. 16, 1865.
James Priest	do	Governor Peirpoint and Lewis McKenzie; C. A. Ware, mayor of Alexandria, Virginia, and R. Johnston.	Aug. 7, 1865.
Samuel Pate	do	Governor Peirpoint	Sept. 4, 1865.

James Payne	do	do	Aug. 10, 1865.
P. F. Patton	do	do	Oct. 26, 1865.
William J. Pendleton	do	do	Sept. 4, 1865.
Charles Pickett	do	do	Aug. 5, 1865.
Benjamin E. Pope	do	do	Aug. 5, 1865.
Harrison P. Pope	do	do	Aug. 5, 1865.
Thomas J. Patrick	do	do	Aug. 5, 1865.
J. S. Persinger	do	do	Aug. 7, 1865.
John D. Priddy	do	do	Aug. 16, 1865.
Sampson Pelter	do	do	Aug. 16, 1865.
Mann R. Page	do	do	Sept. 4, 1865.
Robert S. Payne	do	Hon. Attorney General Speed	July 14, 1865.
David B. Payne	do	do	July 14, 1865.
Francis Preston	do	Governor Peirpoint	July 21, 1865.
Peter P. Penn	do	do	July 5, 1865.
J. T. L. Preston	do	Hon. Attorney General Speed	June 24, 1865.
T. P. Pendleton	do	Governor Peirpoint	June 14, 1865.
Mathew Pilson	do	do	Aug. 16, 1865.
George Pannil, sr	do	Hon. Attorney General Speed	Oct. 9, 1865.
John M. Preston	do	Governor Peirpoint	July 29, 1865.
William F. Poague	do	do	July 17, 1865.
Thomas A. Proctor	do	do	Sept. 16, 1865.
F. G. Peters	do	do	Aug. 24, 1865.
G. F. Pleasants	do	do	Oct. 9, 1865.
Joseph A. Peck	do	do	Aug. 31, 1865.
Isaac Paul	do	Governor Peirpoint, J. F. Lewis, and Charles H. Lewis, secretary Commonwealth of Virginia.	July 5, 1865.
Robert S. Payne	do	C. L. Mosby	July 6, 1865.
James H. Paxton	do	Governor Peirpoint	Aug. 9, 1865.
John E. Powell	do	do	Aug. 11, 1865.
F. W. Page	do	do	Nov. 6, 1865.
Jerman W. Pace	do	do	July 18, 1865.
William C. Pratt	do	do	Nov. 17, 1865.
Henry Preston	do	do	July 21, 1865.
Thomas L. Preston	do	do	Oct. 9, 1865.
Joseph F. Powell	do	do	July 21, 1865.
J. F. Preston	do	do	July 21, 1865.
W. A. Poe	do	do	July 14, 1865.
S. T. Pulliam	do	do	July 20, 1865.
Samuel Putney	do	do	July 20, 1865.
A. K. Phillips	do	do	Sept. 29, 1865.
George Price	do	do	Nov. 13, 1865.
Stephen Porter	do	do	Sept. 11, 1865.
T. J. Penn	do	do	Aug. 14, 1865.
William Palmer	do	do	July 17, 1865.
Andrew Pizzini	do	do	July 11, 1865.
Dempsey Padgett	do	do	Oct. 9, 1865.
C. W. Purcell	do	do	July 13, 1865.
R. W. Payne	do	Hon. Thomas Corwin, Ohio; Hon. Richard Wallach, mayor of Washington, D. C.; John H. Semmes, and Joseph H. Bradley.	July 11, 1865.
Robert T. Preston	do	Governor Peirpoint	Sept. 11, 1865.
William Persinger	do	do	Aug. 7, 1865.

Virginia—Continued.

Name.	Exemption under amnesty proclamation of May 29, 1865.	By whom recommended.	Date of pardon.
Colin C. Porter	Worth over $20,000	Governor Peirpoint	Aug. 14, 1865.
William G. Paine	do	do	June 24, 1865.
Thomas Pollard	do	do	July 29, 1865.
R. A. Paine	do	Hon. Attorney General Speed	June 24, 1865.
John J. Pace	do	Governor Peirpoint and Lewis C. Hunt, lieutenant colonel	Aug. 11, 1865.
R. W. Powers	do	Governor Peirpoint	July 31, 1865.
James B. Pace	do	do	July 13, 1865.
Mathew W. Pettigrew	do	do	Sept. 26, 1865.
John Pence	do	do	Sept. 26, 1865.
W. C. Parry	do	do	July 25, 1865.
Thomas R. Price	do	Governor Peirpoint and Charles Palmer; S. B. Chittenden & Co.; E. S. Jaffrayt & Co.; George Bliss & Co.; W. B. Clefient & Co.; Wilmerdings & Mount; Hoyt, Sprague & Co., and Halstead, Haines & Co., New York city.	July 21, 1865.
John Pannill	do	Governor Peirpoint and C. L. Mosby, esq	Aug. 4, 1865.
Thomas M. Powers	do	Governor Peirpoint	Aug. 4, 1865.
Rufus Pitzer	do	do	Aug. 12, 1865.
R. H. Phillips	do	do	Aug. 12, 1865.
L. B. Price	do	do	Aug. 12, 1865.
T. F. Perkins	do	do	Aug. 2, 1865.
Louisa S. Payne	do	do	Sept. 16, 1865.
William A. Poore	do	Governor Peirpoint and C. L. Mosby	July 31, 1865.
W. B. Pleasants	do	Governor Peirpoint	Aug. 1, 1865.
Christopher Proctor	do	do	Oct. 5, 1865.
William K. Perrin	do	do	Aug. 24, 1865.
John L. Pendleton	do	Attorney General Speed	Aug. 7, 1865.
C. G. Paleske	do	Governor Peirpoint and W. Goddin	Aug. 4, 1865.
Juan Pizzini	do	Governor Peirpoint	Aug. 10, 1865.
Mundley Pierce	do	do	Sept. 9, 1865.
Philip M. Payne	do	Attorney General Speed	July 6, 1865.
Lemuel Peebles	do	Governor Peirpoint	Aug. 7, 1865.
John F. Preston	do	do	Aug. 16, 1865.
A. J. Paxton	do	do	July 17, 1865.
C. H. C. Preston	do	do	Aug. 16, 1865.
W. H. Parrish	do	Governor Peirpoint and C. L. Mosby	July 31, 1865.
Alexander R. Preston	do	Governor Peirpoint	Aug. 16, 1865.
George W. Pettyjohn	do	Attorney General Speed	June 26, 1865.
William L. Pannill	do	Governor Peirpoint	July 11, 1865.
J. H. Poindexter	do	Governor Peirpoint, H. A. Claiborne, Wm. H. Macfarland, Abraham Warwick, and other names too badly written to be made out.	July 6, 1865.
Inman H. Payne	do	Governor Peirpoint	Aug 25, 1865.
W. W. Payne	do	Attorney General Speed and F. P. Blair	July 11, 1865.
Sarah Ann Payne	do	Governor Peirpoint	Aug. 25, 1865.
A. Painter	do	Robert Sayers, jr., James Trucks, Robert Gibboney, and Governor Peirpoint	July 25, 1865.
James Paxton	do	Governor Peirpoint	Aug. 25, 1865.

Edward L. Pettyjohn	do	do	July 3, 1865.
William H. Payne	Rebel brigadier general	Attorney General Speed, Governor Peirpoint, and F. P. Blair	Oct. 28, 1865.
James M. Quillin	Ex-United States and rebel postmaster	Governor Peirpoint	Nov. 13, 1865.
Charles L. Quillin	Rebel postmaster	do	Nov. 13, 1865.
Charles Quarles	Worth over $20,000	do	Sept. 13, 1865.
John R. Quarles	do	do	Sept. 13, 1865.
Wyndham Robertson	Member of the legislature	Attorney General Speed	July 13, 1865.
L. G. Rucker	Ex-United States and rebel postmaster	Governor Peirpoint	Sept. 19, 1865.
W. A. Rogers	do	do	Sept. 16, 1865.
D. V. Ruckman	Ex-United States and rebel postmaster, and worth over $20,000.	do	July 11, 1865.
Wm. H. Robinson	Rebel postmaster	do	Sept. 9, 1865.
Wm. O. Ross	do	do	Aug. 4, 1865.
Wm. P. Rawlings	do	Governor Peirpoint and G. H. McKibbin, brigadier general	Aug. 2, 1865.
Andrew H. Ross	do	Governor Peirpoint	Aug. 4, 1865.
J. S. Reeve	do	do	Sept. 20, 1865.
M. D. Richmond	Rebel deputy postmaster	do	Nov. 9, 1865.
V. C. Ryals	Rebel assessor of tax in kind	do	Aug. 4, 1865.
W. W. Raney	Rebel tax collector	Attorney General Speed	Aug. 12, 1865.
George M. Raney	Rebel mail contractor	Governor Peirpoint and Major W. J. Bailey	July 29, 1865.
John J. Rawlings	do	Governor Peirpoint and Brigadier General McKibbin	July 29, 1865.
J. H. Renick	Rebel mail contractor, and worth over $20,000	Governor Peirpoint	Aug. 7, 1865.
E. F. Ragland	do	Governor Peirpoint and Charles Palmer	Aug. 24, 1865.
Valentine H. Rucker	do	Governor Peirpoint	July 5, 1866.
Samuel Rinker	Commissioner of revenue	do	Aug. 4, 1865.
S. B. Ragland	Rebel clerk to provost marshal	do	Oct. 12, 1865.
C. A. Rose	Rebel clerk, and worth over $20,000	Governor Peirpoint and H. L. Kent	July 3, 1865.
S. V. Reid	Left a loyal State	Governor Peirpoint	Aug. 24, 1865.
John M. Royall	do	do	Aug. 1, 1865.
John A. Rosson	Left United States military lines	do	Oct. 5, 1865.
Washington Reed	Proceedings instituted for confiscation	Hon. L. H. Chandler, United States district attorney, Virginia	July 3, 1865.
Alexander H. Rogers	do	Governor Peirpoint	Aug. 10, 1865.
Nathaniel Raines	Worth over $20,000	do	Aug. 24, 1865.
Mrs. Maria M. Robertson	do	do	Aug. 4, 1865.
George T. Rust	do	Governor Peirpoint and Lewis McKenzie	Aug. 24, 1865.
George Rivers	do	Governor Peirpoint	Aug. 2, 1865.
Richard Russell	do	do	Aug. 1, 1865.
William Russell	do	do	Aug. 1, 1865.
J. P. Rayall	do	do	Aug. 29, 1865.
W. B. Richards, jr	do	do	Aug. 29, 1865.
Bartlett Roper	do	do	Aug. 1, 1865.
C. H. Rhodes	do	do	Oct. 5, 1865.
A. B. Rucker	do	do	June 26, 1865.
O. T. Rogers	do	do	Aug. 25, 1865.
George T. Rust	do	Attorney General Speed	Sept. 9, 1865.
J. B. Radford	do	Governor Peirpoint	Aug. 1, 1865.
Dr. B. F. Randolph	do	do	Oct. 9, 1865.
Wm. R. Robinson	do	Governor Peirpoint and H. L. Kent	July 11, 1865.
J. D. Richardson	do	Attorney General Speed	July 5, 1865.
George M. Rucker	do	Governor Peirpoint	July 3, 1865.
A. J. Rahm	do	Governor Peirpoint, Charles Palmer, and Franklin Stearns	July 15, 1865.
F. G. Ruffin	do	Governor Peirpoint, Hon. J. M. Botts, M. F. Pleasants, F. Stearns and F. J. Smith	June 24, 1865.

Virginia—Continued.

Name.	Exemption under amnesty proclamation of May 29, 1865.	By whom recommended.	Date of pardon.
Mrs. C. A. Rowland	Worth over $20,000	Governor Peirpoint	July 5, 1866.
W. D. Reynolds	do	do	Nov. 20, 1865.
Samuel Rixey, jr	do	Governor Peirpoint and Hon. J. M. Botts	Sept. 16, 1865.
R. H. Riddick	do	Governor Peirpoint	July 21, 1865.
William Roades	do	do	Aug. 24, 1865.
R. T. Riddicks	do	do	Aug. 24, 1865.
R. Raper	do	do	Aug. 7, 1865.
Robert Rosbaugh	do	do	Aug. 5, 1865.
Edmund Ruffin	do	do	July 25, 1865.
James R. Richards	do	do	Sept. 4, 1865.
John C. Redd	do	do	Aug. 31, 1865.
H. Robertson	do	do	July 13, 1865.
N. F. Rivers	do	do	July 29, 1865.
S. C. Robinson	do	do	July 14, 1865.
Charles H. Rucker	do	do	Oct. 6, 1865.
W. W. Read	do	do	July 13, 1865.
Thomas J. Randolph, jr	do	do	Aug. 19, 1865.
Valentine Ripley	do	Governor Peirpoint and F. W. Butterfield, colonel 192d O. V. I., commanding	Aug. 14, 1865.
A. P. Rowe	do	Governor Peirpoint	Aug. 14, 1865.
Ferd. Rover	do	do	Aug 25, 1865.
James Russell	do	do	July 29, 1865.
William Daniel, jr	do	do	July 14, 1865.
Samuel Rector	do	Governor Peirpoint and Attorney General Speed	Sept. 13, 1865.
John A. Robinson	do	Governor Peirpoint	July 11, 1865.
John Rutherford	do	Governor Peirpoint, Chas. Palmer, R. W. Hughes & J. M. Taylor, and Robert King Stone, M. D., Washington, D. C.	July 25, 1865.
A. T. M. Rust	do	Thomas A. Clagett, W. W. Williams, W. H. Gray, Charles Douglass, and F. P. Blair	Sept. 6, 1865.
P. S. Roller	do	Governor Peirpoint	July 13, 1865.
T. J. Randolph	do	do	Aug. 19, 1865.
G. W. Robinson	do	do	Sept. 19, 1865.
Peter Roller	do	do	Aug. 19, 1865.
E. C. Robinson	do	do	July 5, 1866.
John S. Rodgers	do	do	Sept. 27, 1865.
Casper Rodenhizer	do	do	July 13, 1865.
Z. Raines	do	Governor Peirpoint and Charles Palmer, esq	Aug. 11, 1865.
Powhatan Robertson	do	Governor Peirpoint and C. L. Mosley, esq	Aug. 11, 1865.
James A. Reid	do	Governor Peirpoint	Sept. 13, 1865.
Joseph T. Redd	do	do	Aug. 14, 1865.
Thomas Ridley	do	do	Nov. 17, 1865.
H. W. Reynolds	do	do	Aug. 25, 1865.
William Robinson	do	do	July 25, 1865.
John N. Ryland	do	do	Sept. 16, 1865.
J. B. Rice	do	do	July 13, 1865.
Abraham Rindsburg	do	Governor Peirpoint and Lewis E. McKenzie	July 26, 1865.

E. A. Rawlins	do	Governor Peirpoint, —— Campbell, and E. Chambers	
J. H. Ruckman	do	Governor Peirpoint	
Henry Raines	do	do	Aug. 12, 1865.
M. W. Robertson	do	Governor Peirpoint, P. J. Wright, and R. A. Lancaster	July 22, 1865.
Asa Rogers	do	Governor Peirpoint	Aug. 29, 1865.
Alexander H. Rutherford	do	Governor Peirpoint, Charles Palmer, and Charles A. Rose	July 21, 1865.
W. B. Randolph	do	Governor Peirpoint, Charles Palmer, and H. L. Kent	July 17, 1865.
B. F. Rixey	do	Governor Peirpoint	Nov. 17, 1865.
F. T. Ridley	do	do	Nov. 17, 1865.
R. B. Rennolds	do	do	July 26, 1865.
William Rutherfood	do	Governor Peirpoint, and H. L. Kent, W. H. Macfarland, and Lawson Nunnally	July 3, 1865.
Samuel J. Rutherford	do	Governor Peirpoint, Hon. J. M. Botts, and H. L. Kent	July 3, 1865.
Josiah Ryland	do	Governor Peirpoint	Sept. 20, 1865.
M. Rosenbaum	do	Governor Peirpoint, J. L. Apperson, W. H. Lyons, John A. Meridith, and H. W. Thomas	July 20, 1865.
R. Rives	do	Governor Peirpoint	July 29, 1865.
A. B. Rucker	do	Attorney General	
George W. Redd	do	Governor Peirpoint	Aug. 14, 1865.
F. D. Redd	do	do	Aug. 14, 1865.
W. A. Richasen	do	do	Oct. 6, 1865.
John Robertson	do	do	July 25, 1865.
Levi Renker	do	do	Aug. 10, 1865.
David S. Reed	do	Governor Peirpoint and C. L. Mosby	Aug. 11, 1865.
D. S. Redd	do	do	Aug. 11, 1865.
G. W. Rocke	do	Governor Peirpoint and H. T. Cox	Oct. 25, 1865.
J. T. Randolph	do	do	July 20, 1865.
W. H. Rose	do	Attorney General	July 14, 1865.
John Rowlett	do	Governor Peirpoint	Oct. 2, 1865.
T. A. Rector	do	do	Aug. 19, 1865.
Leroy Roper	do	do	July 11, 1865.
Reuben Ragland	do	do	July 11, 1865.
John H. Ruckman	do	do	Oct. 6, 1865.
William N. Radford	do	Governor Peirpoint and C. L. Mosby	Aug. 24, 1865.
Samuel McD. Reid	do	Governor Peirpoint	July 17, 1865.
Walter Staples	Member of rebel congress	do	Nov. 11, 1865.
Peter Saunders, jr.	Member of rebel legislature	do	Aug. 16, 1865.
C. H. Smith	Rebel mail agent	do	Oct. 14, 1865.
J. F. Shields	Ex-United States and rebel postmaster	do	Sept. 26, 1865.
George Sandoe	do	do	July 21, 1865.
L. L. Stevenson	do	Governor Peirpoint and Brigadier General J. D. Stevenson	July 11, 1865.
R. H. Spindle	do	Governor Peirpoint	Aug. 16, 1865.
T. M. Scott	do	Governor Peirpoint and D. H. Hoge	Nov. 3, 1865.
David Stratton	do		
P. Schmucker	do	Governor Peirpoint	July 25, 1865.
F. K. Sear	do	do	Aug. 29, 1865.
Wm. Sandige	do	do	Oct. 12, 1865.
J. W. Seiver	do	do	July 5, 1866.
J. L. Scott	Rebel postmaster	do	July 5, 1866.
J. O. Steger	do	Attorney General	June 26, 1865.
R. H. Sharp	do	C. H. McKibbin, brevet brigadier general, and Major Wm. S. Bailey	July 17, 1865.
F. H. Spotts	do	Governor Peirpoint	July 5, 1866.
W. Sutherland	do	do	Aug. 4, 1865.
J. R. Seward	do	do	Aug. 10, 1865.

Virginia—Continued.

Name.	Exemption under amnesty proclamation of May 29, 1865.	By whom recommended.	Date of pardon.
T. G. Stout	Rebel postmaster	Governor Peirpoint	Aug. 4, 1865.
R. M. Stafford	do	do	Aug. 31, 1865.
Wm. Swadley	do	do	Aug. 24, 1865.
J. R. Sanders	do	do	July 17, 1865.
Lafayette Sehorn	do	do	July 17, 1865.
Wm. C. Staples	do	do	Nov. 3, 1865.
Wm. O. Spencer	do	Governor Peirpoint and Brevet Major General Smith	Aug. 5, 1865.
L. P. Sale	do	Governor Peirpoint	Aug. 10, 1865.
Bettie M. Shart	Rebel postmistress	do	Aug. 10, 1865.
John F. Smith	Rebel tax assessor	do	Aug. 16, 1865.
John G. Stover	do	do	July 25, 1865.
Abraham Saum	Assistant tax assessor	do	Aug. 2, 1865.
James B. Sener	Rebel tax collector	do	Sept. 9, 1865.
Wm. P. Shepherd	Rebel tax collector, and worth over $20,000	do	Aug. 11, 1865.
S. G. Stewart	Worth over $20,000	do	Aug. 5, 1865.
Wm. F. Small	Rebel deputy tax collector	do	July 3, 1865.
C. J. Sinton	District collector	Governor Peirpoint, Weed, Becker & Co., T. Otis Le Roy & Co., R. Hoe & Co., J. Macy's Sons, Hilger & Sons, P. G. Taylor, C. V. Wright, and Bogert & Oakley, all of New York city.	Sept. 15, 1865.
A. Y. Stokes	Agent to collect tithe, and worth over $20,000	Governor Peirpoint	July 6, 1865.
James A. Scott	Collector of tobacco taxes	do	July 11, 1865.
J. G. Spotts	Commissary sergeant	do	July 5, 1865.
W. H. Sims	County commissary for collection of provisions	do	Aug. 2, 1865.
R. M. Stevenson	Rebel clerk, and worth over $20,000	do	July 29, 1865.
J. G. Steele	Rebel clerk	do	July 17, 1865.
Francis L. Smith	Petty civil officer	Hon. James Speed, Attorney General United States	June 26, 1865.
James M. Stuart	Left loyal State	Governor Peirpoint	May 3, 1866.
C. D. Smith	do	do	July 5, 1866.
Robert Swan	do	do	June 16, 1865.
W. L. Shooter	Left loyal State, and proceedings instituted for confiscation.	do	Aug. 7, 1865.
L. R. Smoot	Left loyal State, and rebel foreign agent	do	Oct. 26, 1865.
Samuel Sheppard	Left loyal district	do	Aug. 7, 1865.
A. A. Smith	Left District of Columbia	do	Sept. 9, 1865.
W. T. Smith	Proceedings instituted for confiscation	do	Sept. 11, 1865.
A. J. C. Sigourney	do	do	Aug. 11, 1865.
Daniel T. Shreve	do	Governor Peirpoint, Lewis McKenzie, and W. F. Mercier	Sept. 19, 1865.
J. W. N. Smith	do	Governor Peirpoint and W. B. Downey	Sept. 14, 1865.
John F. Simpson	Property seized and confiscated	Governor Peirpoint	Sept. 9, 1865.
George W. Semple	Property libelled for confiscation	Governor Peirpoint and Brevet Major General Dyer	Dec. 16, 1865.
William Selden	do	Governor Peirpoint, L. H. Chandler, esq., United States district attorney, Virginia, and Hon. J. H. Millson	July 11, 1865.
G. A. Schwarzman	Petty civil officer	B. B. French	June 12, 1865.
Catharine M. Slaughter	Worth over $20,000	Governor Peirpoint	June 26, 1865.

George Stillman	do	do	June 29, 1865.
John Scott	do	do	Aug. 1, 1865.
Robert Smith	do	do	Aug. 4, 1865.
Dr. Henry E. Shore	do	do	Aug. 2, 1865.
John L. Stanbery	do	do	Sept. 9, 1865.
Wm. F. Smith	do	do	Sept. 9, 1865.
Franklin Stearns	do	Hon. John M. Botts, Chas. H. Lewis, and Horace L. Kent	July 18, 1865.
Champ Shepherd	do	Governor Peirpoint	Aug. 24, 1865.
J. W. Sowers	do	do	Aug. 24, 1865.
Fred. Schultz	do	do	Aug. 24, 1865.
P. B. Snapp	do	do	Sept. 9, 1865.
E. J. Smith	do	do	Sept. 9, 1865.
W. A. Stuart	do	do	July 21, 1865.
D. H. Skipwith	do	do	July 31, 1865.
J. W. Shields	do	Attorney General	July 13, 1865.
J. W. Sheffey	do	Governor Brownlow, Tenn	July 5, 1865.
W. T. Scott	do	Governor Peirpoint	July 13, 1865.
George Seawright	do	do	Nov. 17, 1865.
J. T. Subett	do	do	July 11, 1865.
George B. Sloan	do	Hon. James Speed, Attorney General United States, and Governor Peirpoint	Aug. 12, 1865.
W. B. Stanard	do	Governor Peirpoint	July 3, 1865.
W. F. Smith	do	do	Aug. 25, 1865.
William Steen	do	do	Aug. 25, 1865.
William Simms	do	do	Aug. 25, 1865.
William Scott	do	do	Aug. 25, 1865.
R. H. Stuart	do	do	June 12, 1865.
S. T. Stuart	do	do	Sept. 13, 1865.
G. W. Sutherland	do	do	July 29, 1865.
W. M. Sibert	do	Governor Peirpoint and S. R. Sterling	July 25, 1865.
F. Skipwith	do	Governor Peirpoint	July 25, 1865.
C. A. Smith	do	Governor Peirpoint and C. L. Mosby	Aug. 14, 1865.
B. H. Shakelford	do	Governor Peirpoint and L. C. Hunt	Aug. 19, 1865.
Dandridge Sale	do	Governor Peirpoint	Aug. 10, 1865.
John W. Stone	do	do	July 14, 1865.
R. H. Spencer	do	do	July 5, 1866.
G. W. F. Smith	do	do	Sept. 18, 1865.
E. H. Skinker	do	do	July 3, 1865.
J. C. Shelton	do	do	July 5, 1866.
James Smith	do	do	Aug. 18, 1865.
C. W. Statham	do	Hon. Attorney General United States	June 26, 1865.
John W. Stone	do	Governor Peirpoint	July 17, 1865.
J. M. Suthelin	do	do	Oct. 2, 1865.
Edward Sears	do	do	Aug. 24, 1865.
James M. Spiller	do	do	July 17, 1865.
D. W. Shanks	do	do	July 5, 1866.
James P. Scott	do	do	July 26, 1865.
F. A. Schmely	do	Governor Peirpoint and T. Taylor	July 11, 1865.
T. Stringfellow	do	Governor Peirpoint and J. M. Botts	July 31, 1865.
William Slater	do	Hon. John Minor Botts	June 30, 1865.
H. W. Sheffey	do	John M. Speed, esq	June 28, 1865.
Asa Snyder	do		June 12, 1865.
R. H. Smith	do	Governor Peirpoint	Aug. 24, 1865.

Virginia—Continued.

Name.	Exemption under amnesty proclamation of May 29, 1865.	By whom recommended.	Date of pardon.
Benj. Sutton	Worth over $20,000	Governor Peirpoint	Aug. 2, 1865.
W. P. Strother	do	do	Aug. 2, 1865.
John J. Scott	do	do	Sept. 9, 1865.
Wm. Ira Smith	do	do	Nov. 7, 1865.
Robert C. Sale	do	do	Aug. 9 1865.
Robert Saunders	do	Governor Peirpoint and L. H. Chandler, United States district attorney, Virginia	July 26, 1865.
D. C. Shanks	do	Governor Peirpoint	July 17, 1865
John Shuey	do	do	Sept. 16, 1865.
G. B. Stephens	do	do	Aug. 24, 1865.
H. M. Stanard	do	do	July 18, 1865.
William Sigler	do	Governor Peirpoint and Hon. James Speed, Attorney General United States	Aug. 14, 1865.
Mrs. E. J. Steptoe	do	Governor Peirpoint	July 3, 1865.
H. O. Schoolfield	do	Hon. James Speed, Attorney General United States	June 26, 1865.
James Sanders	do	Governor Peirpoint	July 5, 1866.
John Stewart	do	do	Nov. 6, 1865.
S. R. Shield	do	Governor Peirpoint and Hon. Joseph Segar	Sept. 5, 1865.
Adam Shuey	do	Governor Peirpoint	May 31, 1866.
J. B. Stinker	do	do	Sept. 14, 1865.
Edward Scott, sr	do	do	July 25, 1865.
M. L. Straus	do	do	July 21, 1865.
S. M. Simpson	do	do	Nov. 20, 1865.
Thomas Shannon	do	do	Aug. 31, 1865.
D. J. Saunders	do	do	July 17, 1865.
Charles Stebbins	do	do	July 11, 1865.
P. B. Starke	do	do	Nov. 7, 1865.
J. A. Scott	do	do	July 22, 1865.
E. H. Stokes	do	do	July 22, 1865.
Treadwell Smith	do	do	Sept. 19, 1865.
John M. Savage	do	do	July 2, 1866.
S. G. Staples	do	do	Oct. 12, 1865.
Jeff. B. Sinclair	do	Governor Peirpoint and Hon. Joseph Segar	Oct. 12, 1865.
Joseph H. Snead	do	do	Aug. 10, 1865.
Francis A. Schmelz	do	do	Aug. 10, 1865.
G. W. Shanks	do	Governor Peirpoint and C. L. Mosby	Aug. 11, 1865.
Joseph Schultz	do	Governor Peirpoint	Aug. 11, 1865.
John Shumate	do	do	Aug. 9, 1865.
R. H. Spencer	do	do	Aug. 19, 1865.
Washington Swinks	do	do	Aug. 19, 1866.
W. M. Sterrett	do	do	Aug. 19, 1865.
John D. Sterrett	do	do	Aug. 19, 1865.
H. G. Shackelford	do	do	Aug. 14, 1865.
W. H. Southall	do	Governor Peirpoint and B. J. Barbour	Aug. 14, 1865.
J. W. Slaughter	do	Governor Peirpoint	Aug. 19, 1865.
W. H. Sanford	do	do	Sept. 23, 1865.

F. Saunders	do	do	Oct. 26, 1865.
W. P. Smith	do	do	Sept. 13, 1865.
John Southan	do	do	Sept. 13, 1865.
John Seawright	do	do	Oct. 24, 1865.
Lewis Shumate	do	do	Aug. 11, 1865.
Mrs. Susan Spiller	do	do	Aug. 11, 1865.
Benj. F. Smoot	do	do	Sept. 23, 1865.
S. G. Snead	do	do	Sept. 23, 1865.
Henry Stokes	do	do	July 20, 1865.
C. M. Sublett	do	do	July 13, 1865.
J. R. Sterrett	do	do	Aug. 19, 1865.
John A. Scott	do	do	July 20, 1865.
R. Semmerson	do	do	July 25, 1865.
Fred. Sheffer	do	do	Aug. 2, 1865.
D. G. Smith	do	do	Aug. 4, 1865
Zachariah Shirley	do	do	Jan. 18, 1866.
Montgomery Slaughter	do	do	Aug. 1, 1865.
Mrs. C. M. Stribley	do	do	Oct. 9, 1865.
W. J. Shumate	do	do	Aug. 1, 1865.
A. A. Sproul	do	do	July 25, 1865.
Thomas Scott	do	do	Aug. 1, 1865.
J. M. Stout	do	do	July 25, 1865.
Grey Skipwith	do	do	Aug. 1, 1865.
C. J. Stovin	do	do	Aug. 1, 1865.
J. B. Strayer	do	do	July 5, 1865.
J. C. Shields	do	do	Oct. 6, 1865.
W. T. Sutherlin	do	do	July 14, 1865.
H. A. Sydnor	do	do	Aug. 16, 1865.
Richard Stokes	do	do	July 29, 1865.
George Shuey	do	do	July 5, 1865.
F. W. Scott	do	do	Sept. 26, 1865.
Thomas Street	do	do	Sept. 26, 1865.
James Stinson	do	do	Oct. 9, 1865.
George J. Sumner	do	do	July 25, 1865.
James Scott	do	do	July 13, 1865.
John C. Shafer	do	do	July 13, 1865.
William Saltiee	do	do	Aug. 22, 1865.
J. F. Slaughter	do	do	Sept. 20, 1865.
L. T. Slater	do	do	July 20, 1865.
M. P. Scott	do	do	July 31, 1865.
John T. Sayers	do	do	Aug. 7, 1865.
Ann M. Saunders	do	Governor Peirpoint, H. Latham, and C. W. Britton	Aug. 7, 1865.
David Sexton	do	Governor Peirpoint	Aug. 7, 1865.
J. W. Sheffey	do	do	Aug. 7, 1865.
Robert Sayers, sr	do	do	Aug. 7, 1865.
J. P. M. Simmerman	do	do	Aug. 7, 1865.
J. B. Smith	do	do	Aug. 7, 1865.
Wm. R. Snyder	do	do	Aug. 7, 1865.
Cornelius Smith	do	do	Aug. 7, 1865.
George W. Stark	do	do	Aug. 7, 1865.
E. J. Simberlake	do	Governor Peirpoint and L. W. Hunt	Aug. 7, 1865.
J. S. Spengler	do	Governor Peirpoint	Sept. 4, 1865.

Virginia—Continued.

Name.	Exemption under amnesty proclamation of May 29, 1865.	By whom recommended.	Date of pardon.
F. B. Smith	Worth over $20,000	Governor Peirpoint	Sept. 4, 1865.
Miles G. Selden	do	do	Sept. 4, 1865.
Benj. Shoemaker	do	do	Sept. 4, 1865.
George C. Scott	do	do	Sept. 4, 1865.
W. E. Taylor	Member of State senate, clerk in rebel war department, and worth over $20,000.	Governor Peirpoint and L. H. Chandler, esq., U. S. district attorney	Sept. 1, 1865.
Thomas T. Treadway	Member of rebel house of delegates, and worth over $20,000.	Governor Peirpoint	July 20, 1865.
George P. Taylor	Member of rebel State convention, and worth over $20,000.	do	July 29, 1865.
H. W. Thomas	Rebel auditor	do	Aug. 29, 1865.
P. M. Thompson	Rebel agent, and worth over $20,000	Attorney General U. S	June 6, 1865.
Paris Taylor	Ex-United States and rebel postmaster	Governor Peirpoint	July 5, 1865.
Evans Tanner	do	do	Aug. 29, 1865.
J. H. Turner	do	do	July 29, 1865.
I. H. Trotter	do	do	
Isaac N. Turner	do	do	Aug. 4, 1865.
W. C. Tate	do	do	Aug. 29, 1865.
R. T. Thorn	Rebel postmaster	do	
Nathan Thompson	do	do	Oct. 5, 1865.
R. T. Thorn	do	Governor Peirpoint and George Wood	Aug. 24, 1865.
Archibald Thompson	do	Governor Peirpoint	Aug. 26, 1865.
P. G. Talley	do	do	Aug. 24, 1865.
J. W. Taylor	do	do	July 13, 1865.
Thomas Tinsley	Member of rebel examining board	do	July 22, 1865.
A. D. Townes	Clerk in rebel treasury department, and worth over $20,000.	do	Aug. 4, 1865.
W. A. Thorn	Rebel telegraph manager	C. L. Mosby and H. H. Marshal	June 27, 1865.
Alexander Tinsley	Clerk in rebel treasury department	Governor Peirpoint	July 22, 1865.
S. G. Tinsley	do	do	July 22, 1865.
E. M. Tidball	Rebel clerk	do	Aug. 29, 1865.
C. R. Taylor	Left a loyal State	Hon. James Speed, Attorney General of the United States	Dec. 29, 1865.
A. S. Tebbs	do	Governor Peirpoint and Thomas Ewing, jr	June 23, 1866.
C. E. Thorn	do	Attorney General U. S	June 27, 1865.
Robert Tyler	Resigned clerkship of supreme court of Pennsylvania, went south, and accepted clerkship in rebel treasury department.	Governor Peirpoint, Ro. Tyler, Charles Palmer, J. Allison, and M. Blair	July 13, 1865.
W. W. Thornton	Proceedings instituted for confiscation	Governor Peirpoint	Aug. 29, 1865.
John H. Thompson	do	do	Aug. 16, 1865.
C. B. Tebbs	do	do	Sept. 13, 1865.
Sanderson Thrift	do	do	Aug. 24, 1865.
Henry Tabb	Abandoned property; proceedings begun	do	Sept. 13, 1865.
Edward P. Tayloe	Aided the rebellion	do	Oct. 12, 1865.
Alexander Trent	Worth over $20,000	do	

Samuel Tyree	do	do	Aug. 4, 1865.
William C. Terry	do	do	Sept. 4, 1865.
W. G. Thompson	do	do	July 25, 1865.
John Terrell	do	do	Aug. 3, 1865.
A. Thomas	do	do	Sept. 9, 1865.
C. J. Terrell	do	do	Aug. 16, 1865.
J. O. Taylor	do	do	Jan. 18, 1866.
John L. Tate	do	Governor Peirpoint and Charles Palmer	Sept. 23, 1865.
George Tyler	do	Governor Peirpoint, R. H. Coleman, and Hugh R. White	Aug. 31, 1865.
George Turner	do	Governor Peirpoint	Sept. 9, 1865.
M. P. Todd	do	do	Sept. 9, 1865.
John R. Tongue	do	do	Aug. 29, 1865.
W. P. Tate	do	do	July 25, 1865.
Charles C. Taylor	do	do	Sept. 9, 1865.
William W. Tally	do	do	Aug. 1, 1865.
John W. Taylor	do	do	Sept. 9, 1865.
William M. Tate	do	do	Aug. 16, 1865.
George Terry, sr	do	do	July 3, 1865.
R. H. Turner	do	do	Nov. 13, 1865.
Thomas M. Tate	do	do	Oct. 16, 1865.
William H. Taylor	do	do	Sept. 29, 1865.
A. G. Taliaferro	do	do	Sept. 25, 1865.
J. E. Tackett	do	do	July 5, 1865.
W. A. Turner	do	do	July 21, 1865.
Benjamin Temple	do	do	Sept. 9, 1865.
Miles Turpin	do	do	July 21, 1865.
E. T. Taylor	do	do	Aug. 24, 1865.
G. W. Tinsley	do	do	July 5, 1866.
Dr. C. Thomas	do	do	July 25, 1865.
James Taylor	do	do	July 21, 1865.
Joseph Taylor	do	do	July 29, 1865.
David G. Thomas	do	do	Nov. 6, 1865.
John H. Tyler	do	do	July 29, 1865.
W. C. Thomas	do	do	July 21, 1865.
William Tyler	do	do	July 17, 1865.
S. J. Tibb	do	do	Sept. 25, 1865.
Mrs. S. J. Tuggle	do	do	July 22, 1865.
John F. Tanner	do	William Macfarland, P. V. Daniel, Charles Ellis, J. Garritt, J. J. Fry, James L. Davis, and T. H. Ellis.	Sept. 22, 1865.
J. B. Trimble	do	Governor Peirpoint	July 5, 1866.
William H. Twyman	do	do	Aug. 3, 1865.
S. B. Thurman	do	do	July 5, 1866.
Bacon Tait	do	do	July 27, 1865.
J. S. Twyman	do	do	Aug. 3, 1865.
A. H. Taylor	do	do	July 25, 1865.
John Trimble	do	do	July 25, 1865.
J. J. A. Trotter	do	do	July 25, 1865.
N. K. Trout	do	do	July 25, 1865.
James B. Taylor	do	do	July 29, 1865.
T. G. Turner	do	do	Aug. 19, 1865.
John W. Toney	do	do	Aug. 19, 1865.
William R. Trent	do	do	Aug. 19, 1865.

Virginia—Continued.

Name.	Exemption under amnesty proclamation of May 29, 1865.	By whom recommended.	Date of pardon.
Carolinus Turner	Worth over $20,000	Governor Peirpoint	Aug. 19, 1865.
Benjamin T. Tinsley	do	Governor Peirpoint and C. L. Mosby	Aug. 11, 1865.
C. H. Tate	do	Governor Peirpoint	Aug. 25, 1865.
Samuel C. Tardy	do	do	July 15, 1865.
D. G. Thomas	do	do	Sept. 13, 1865.
Edward Thurman	do	do	Sept. 16, 1865.
George Taylor	do	Governor Peirpoint and Hon. James Speed, Attorney General U. S	Feb. 17, 1866.
T. Talliafferro	do	do	Feb. 14, 1866.
Henry Taylor	do	Mrs. Ann G. Thomas	Aug. 23, 1866.
John M. Trevillian	do	Governor Peirpoint	Aug. 4, 1865.
Henry L. Tynes	do	do	Aug. 24, 1865.
John R. Taylor	do		July 29, 1865.
R. M. Taylor	do	Governor Peirpoint	July 26, 1865.
Zachariah Talby	do	do	
John Taylor	do	do	Nov. 4, 1865.
Edward C. Turner	do	General Augur	July 22, 1865.
James Thomas, jr	do	Attorney General U. S	June 26, 1865.
John E. Thomas	do	Governor Peirpoint	Sept. 20, 1865.
C. W. Turley	do	do	Aug. 25, 1865.
James M. Taylor	do	do	July 3, 1865.
James Thompson	do	do	Aug. 19, 1865.
W. H. Tappy	do	do	Aug. 1, 1865.
Rudolph Turk	do	do	Aug. 1, 1865.
John Trout	do	do	Aug. 1, 1865.
B. F. Tinsley	do	do	Aug. 1, 1865.
Dr. Z. Talley	do	do	Aug. 14, 1865.
E. T. Taylor	do	do	Aug. 1, 1865.
J. H. Tyree	do	do	Oct. 19, 1865.
J. F. Trayhorn	do	do	Aug. 16, 1865.
O. H. P. Terrell	do	do	Aug. 19, 1865.
C. Turner	do	do	Oct. 9, 1865.
James W. Twyman	do	do	July 25, 1865.
Thornton Thomas	do	do	July 25, 1865.
Tazewell Thomson	do	do	Aug. 24, 1865.
Henry Taylor	do	Hon. James Speed, Attorney General U. S	Aug. 23, 1865.
Lemuel Turner	do	Governor Peirpoint	Aug. 24, 1865.
William Towers	do	do	July 3, 1865.
Nathan Taliafferro	do	Governor Peirpoint and C. L. Mosby	Aug. 11, 1865.
John P. Tabb	do	Governor Peirpoint	Aug. 31, 1865.
James Thomas	do	do	July 5, 1865.
Charles Talbott	do	do	Aug. 10, 1865.
Robert Thompson	do	do	Aug. 10, 1865.
W. N. M. Taylor	do	do	Aug. 10, 1865.
John H. Tyree	do	do	July 14, 1865.

E. M. Taylor	do	do	Oct. 6, 18[illegible]
James M. Talbott	do	do	Aug. 10, 1865.
J. W. Taylor	do	do	Oct. 9, 1865.
R. H. Timberlake	do	do	Sept. 4, 1865.
E. B. Tucker	do	do	July 5, 1866.
Peterfield Trent	do	do	July 29, 1865.
John H. Timberlake	do	do	Aug. 5, 1865.
Preston Trotter	do	do	Aug. 7, 1865.
David B. Tennant	do	do	July 11, 1865.
Alex. Trent	do	do	Aug. 4, 1865.
William Terry	do	do	Nov. 19, 1866.
C. F. Urguhart	Rebel postmaster, and worth over $20,000	Governor Peirpoint and L. H. Chandler, esq., U. S. district attorney, Virginia	Sept. 11, 1865.
Abraham Umbarger	Rebel tax collector	Governor Peirpoint	Sept. 23, 1865.
J. B. Urguhart	Worth over $20,000	Governor Peirpoint and L. H. Chandler, esq., United States attorney, Virginia	Sept. 11, 1865.
William P. Underwood	do	Governor Peirpoint	Aug. 10, 1865.
William G. Venable	Rebel depositary	do	Sept. 4, 1865.
A. M. Vandewarter	Rebel collector of war tax	Governor Peirpoint and Lewis McKenzie	Sept. 19, 1865.
Lavinia C. Vaughan	Property confiscated		Aug. 29, 1865.
B. F. Vaughan	Rebel	Governor Peirpoint	Aug. 29, 1865.
J. A. Venable	Worth over $20,000	do	July 11, 1865.
G. Woodson Venable	do	do	July 5, 1866.
W. W. Vest	do	do	Oct. 2, 1865.
James Venable	do	do	Aug. 10, 1865.
George C. Venable	do	do	Aug. 1, 1865.
Joseph E. Venable	do	do	July 29, 1865.
James M. Vest	do	do	Aug. 24, 1865.
W. W. Vest	do	do	July 3, 1865.
John Richard Vest	do	do	July 5, 1866.
Samuel Varner	do	do	Aug. 3, 1865.
J. C. Voss	do	do	July 13, 1865.
James A. Walker	Rebel brigadier general	do	Aug. 10, 1865.
Thomas H. Wynne	Member of the rebel legislature	do	Aug. 31, 1865.
John C. Williams	Rebel mail contractor, and worth over $20,000	do	July 29, 1865.
W. E. M. Word	Rebel agent of post office department	do	July 29, 1865.
L. O. Washington	Left District of Columbia, went south and accepted clerkship in rebel State department.	Governor Peirpoint and Hon. Richard Wallach, mayor of Washington, D. C	July 5, 1865.
William Wertenbaker	Ex-United States and rebel postmaster	Governor Peirpoint	Aug. 24, 1865.
J. W. Womack	do	do	Aug. 29, 1865.
Levi L. Watterman	do	do	Aug 16, 1865.
John W. Worley	do	do	Sept. 23, 1865.
J. G. Wall	do	do	Sept. 4, 1865.
John B. Williams	Rebel postmaster	do	Aug. 29, 1865.
William M. White	do	do	Aug. 7, 1865.
E. F. Williamson	do	do	Aug. 26, 1865.
J. T. White	do	do	July 18, 1865.
H. T. Wattermann	do	Governor Peirpoint and S. R. Sterling	July 25, 1865.
John W. Williamson	do	Governor Peirpoint	July 3, 1865.
John M. Wright	do	do	Sept. 26, 1865.
Isaac Whisser	do	do	July 13, 1865.
E. B. Walthall	do	do	Aug. 31, 1865.
James Waugh	do	do	Sept. 16, 1865.
William M. White	do	do	Aug. 24, 1865.

Virginia—Continued.

Name.	Exemption under amnesty proclamation of May 29, 1865.	By whom recommended.	Date of pardon.
James M. Webb	Rebel postmaster	Governor Peirpoint	Aug. 24, 1865.
N. A. Whitelaw	do	do	Sept. 9, 1865.
Samuel A. Wilson	do	do	Aug. 1, 1865.
Thomas M. Wilson	do	do	Aug. 16, 1865.
D. C. Willis	Rebel deputy postmaster	do	Nov. 9, 1865.
Sarah A. Wilkes	Rebel postmistress	Governor Peirpoint, William S. Bailey, major and provost marshal, and Brevet Brigadier G. H. McKibbin.	Aug. 2, 1865.
Thomas P. Wilson	Rebel tax assessor	Governor Peirpoint	July 25, 1865.
J. R. Wilson	do	do	Aug. 14, 1865.
J. H. Wood	do	do	Oct. 5, 1865.
W. R. Weaver	do	do	Aug. 16, 1865.
W. H. Waller	do	do	Aug. 29, 1865.
J. B. Watkins	Rebel tax assessor, and worth over $20,000	do	June 26, 1865.
John R. Wilson	Assessor of tax in kind	do	Aug. 4, 1865.
J. K. Woods	Assessor of war tax	Hon. Robert C. Grier, associate justice Supreme Court United States	July 25, 1865.
L. B. Williams	Tax collector	Governor Peirpoint	July 20, 1865.
John W. Wilson	Tax collector, and worth over $20,000	do	Aug. 14, 1865.
J. B. Williams	Rebel collector of war tax	Governor Peirpoint and Major C. H. Palmer	July 22, 1865.
C. W. Wyatt	Left a loyal State	Governor Peirpoint	July 14, 1865.
W. B. Williams	do	do	Sept. 4, 1865.
James H. Williams	do	do	Aug. 9, 1865.
James C. White	Left United States military lines	L. H. Chandler, esq., United States attorney, Virginia	June 7, 1865.
E. V. White	Proceedings instituted for confiscation	Governor Peirpoint and Lewis McKenzie	Sept. 19, 1865.
J. B. Winston	do	Governor Peirpoint	Oct. 26, 1865.
L. T. Winder	do	do	Aug. 16, 1865.
John R. White	do	Hon. James Speed, Attorney General of the United States	Sept. 4, 1865.
J. F. Wheeler	do	Governor Peirpoint	Aug. 31, 1865.
J. T. White	do	do	Sept. 19, 1865.
Hezekiah Wilson	Property libelled for confiscation	Governor Peirpoint, Hon. James Speed, Attorney General United States	Nov. 22, 1865.
Elizabeth R. White and T. W. White.	Property confiscated	Governor Peirpoint	Sept. 14, 1865.
F. A. Walke	Proceedings instituted for confiscation	L. H. Chandler	Oct. 6, 1865.
William H. Wilson	Abandoned property; proceedings instituted	Hon. L. H. Chandler, United States attorney, Virginia	Nov. 10, 1865.
Edgar Whitehead	Worth over $20,000	Governor Peirpoint	July 14, 1865.
A. R. Woodroof	do	Hon. Attorney General United States	July 14, 1865.
T. W. Wooding	do	Governor Peirpoint	Aug. 10, 1865.
W. L. Waring	do	do	Aug. 10, 1865.
W. G. C. White	do	do	Aug. 14, 1865.
John S. Walker	do	do	Aug. 3, 1865.
J. Andrew White	do	do	Oct. 6, 1865.
Edwin Watson	do	do	June 28, 1866.
William N. Worthington	do	do	Oct. 18, 1865.
William J. Watkins	do	do	July 5, 1866.
F. T. Wootton	do	do	Sept. 26, 1865.

W. W. Willingham	do	do	June 27, 1865.
John Washington	do	do	July 7, 1865.
R. W. Wingfield	do	do	Aug. 24, 1865.
William Watts	do	Governor Peirpoint and C. L. Mosby	Aug. 14, 1865
P. E. Waugh	do	Governor Peirpoint	Oct. 9, 1865.
Andrew White	do	do	July 13, 1865.
John R. Woods	do	Governor Peirpoint and Hon. J. M. Botts	Aug. 14, 1865.
Abraham Warwick	do	Governor Peirpoint	July 29, 1865.
J. N. Woodfin	do	do	July 29, 1865.
R. A. Wilson	do	do	July 25, 1865.
W. W. Wesson	do	do	Oct. 26, 1865.
C. H. Wynne	do	do	June 24, 1865.
N. C. Wilson	do	do	Nov. 24, 1865.
R. W. Wheeler	do	do	Oct. 24, 1865.
Thomas Wallace	do	Governor Peirpoint and L. H. Chandler, United States district attorney	July 29, 1865.
W. M. Watkins	do	Governor Peirpoint	Aug. 1, 1865.
Lucy R. Waring	do	do	Sept. 9, 1865.
R. A. Willis	do	do	Aug. 4, 1865.
Thomas R. Waring	do	do	Sept. 9, 1865.
L. W. T. Wickham	do	do	July 3, 1865.
Curtis Wilhoit	do	do	Aug. 5, 1865.
W. M. Willcox	do	do	Aug. 1, 1865.
Luke Woodward	do	do	Aug. 5, 1865.
William W. Womack	do	do	Aug. 25, 1865.
W. E. Walkup	do	do	Aug. 25, 1865.
Joseph S. Wilson	do	do	Aug. 19, 1865.
Wilson Williams	do	do	Aug. 4, 1865.
Edwin Wortham	do	do	June 26, 1865.
Anderson Wade	do	do	July 11, 1865.
Wesley Wright	do	do	July 14, 1865.
James Warwick	do	do	Oct. 9, 1865.
W. H. Wilson	do	do	Sept. 22, 1865.
Holt Wilson	do	Governor Peirpoint and L. H. Chandler, United States attorney	July 1, 1865.
F. T. West	do	Governor Peirpoint	Aug. 24, 1865.
John White	do	do	Aug. 24, 1865.
J. E. Wadsworth	do	Governor Peirpoint and William H. Macfarland	Aug. 24, 1865.
S. G. White	do	Governor Peirpoint	Aug. 24, 1865.
Benjamin Wood	do	do	Aug. 24, 1865.
J. W. Warwick	do	do	Aug. 24, 1865.
Edward Wilcox	do	do	Sept. 9, 1865.
W. F. Ward	do	do	July 22, 1865.
Thomas Watkins	do	do	Aug. 5, 1865.
A. G. Wortham	do	do	Sept. 20, 1865.
B. F. Walker	do	do	Sept. 29, 1865.
R. Wallace	do	do	July 20, 1865.
J. W. Woods	do	do	Sept. 25, 1865.
J. M. Wolff	do	do	July 21, 1865.
Edmund Winston	do	do	July 25, 1865.
Jourdan Woolfolk	do	Governor Peirpoint and F. J. Smith	July 22, 1865.
D. T. Williams	do	Governor Peirpoint	July 21, 1865.
J. T. Williams	do	do	July 15, 1865.
Daniel E. Watson	do	Governor Peirpoint and Colonel L. C. Hunt	Aug. 31, 1865.

Virginia—Continued.

Name.	Exemption under amnesty proclamation of May 29, 1865.	By whom recommended.	Date of pardon.
T. N. Welch	Worth over $20,000	Governor Peirpoint	Aug. 31, 1865.
W. J. Weirs	do	do	Sept. 20, 1865.
Benjamin Wilkes	do	do	Sept. 20, 1865.
Thomas Withers	do	do	July 11, 1865.
Corbin Warwick	do	do	Aug. 2, 1865.
D. F. Womack	do	do	Aug. 31, 1865.
J. M. Warwick	do	do	July 14, 1865.
Isaac Wenger	do	do	July 13, 1865.
W. W. Wallace	do	do	Oct. 9, 1865.
Thomas Wiley	do	do	Oct. 9, 1865.
Isaac H. Watson	do	do	July 5, 1866.
C. D. Whittle	do	do	July 5, 1866.
James O. Williams	do	do	July 5, 1866.
James W. Walker	do	do	Aug. 3, 1866.
John E. White	do	do	July 29, 1866.
J. L. Woodville	do	do	Oct. 26, 1866.
Isaac Willis	do	do	Aug. 3, 1866.
Thomas C. Williams	do	do	July 13, 1866.
Gustavis A. White	do	do	July 17, 1866.
D. S. Woodridge	do	do	Sept. 4, 1866.
A. N. Wellford	do	do	Sept. 4, 1866.
Dr. Samuel Webb	do	do	Sept. 4, 1866.
Mrs. Sallie J. Willis	do	do	Aug. 19, 1866.
R. V. Watkins	do	do	Aug. 19, 1866.
John Willis	do	do	Aug. 19, 1866.
Edward D. Withers	do	do	July 25, 1866.
A. W. Womack	do	do	July 25, 1866.
Robert Wilson	do	do	July 25, 1866.
J. H. Wilson	do	do	July 6, 1866.
Samuel Wilson	do	do	Aug. 2, 1866.
Edwin White	do	Governor Peirpoint, B. F. Winger, lieutenant colonel Pennsylvania artillery, and Brevet Major General G. H. McKibbin.	Aug. 2, 1866.
H. W. Wood	do	Governor Peirpoint	Aug. 5, 1866.
T. E. Williamson	do	do	Aug. 19, 1866.
John Wickham	do	Governor Peirpoint and Hon. James Speed, Attorney General United States	June 26, 1866.
C. W. Wormeley	do	Governor Peirpoint	Aug. 29, 1866.
C. T. Wortham	do	do	June 26, 1866.
R. P. Waller	do	do	June 26, 1866.
William Waller	do	do	June 26, 1866.
Garrett F. Watson	do	do	July 5, 1866.
J. D. Williamson	do	Governor Peirpoint and Hon. C. H. Lewis	July 5, 1866.
J. W. Walker	do	Governor Peirpoint	Aug. 14, 1866.
James Willis	do	do	Aug. 3, 1866.
Dr. John U. Wilson	do	do	July 13, 1866.

John R. Wilson	do	do	July 13, 1866.
George Wilson	do	do	July 13, 1866.
James Wood	do	do	Aug. 11, 1866.
James Woodard	do	do	Sept. 23, 1866.
John B. Winfree	do	do	Sept. 23, 1866.
Lawrence Washington	do	do	Aug. 25, 1866.
James Williamson	do	do	Aug. 4, 1866.
Drury Wood	do	do	July 29, 1866.
Maclurg Wickham	do	do	July 26, 1866.
John Walker	do	do	Oct. 12, 1866.
Edwin Watson	do	do	July 14, 1866.
William Wirt	do	Governor Peirpoint, Hon. Richard Wallach mayor of Washington, D. C., and W. B. Webb, esq.	Oct. 5, 1866.
F. C. Williams	do	Governor Peirpoint	July 22, 1865.
A. M. Woodroff	do	do	July 5, 1866.
John A. Worsham	do	L. H. Chandler, esq., United States attorney, Virginia	Nov. 10, 1865.
C. E. Whitlock	do	Hon. Attorney General United States	June 24, 1865.
Coleman Wortham	do	do	June 26, 1865.
J. Warner	do	Governor Peirpoint and W. W. Wing	July 20, 1865.
J. P. Winston	do	Governor Peirpoint, Charles Palmer, Hon. J. M. Botts, F. J. Smith, and Franklin Stearns.	July 3, 1865.
Lewis W. Washington	do	Order of President	July 17, 1865.
Parker West	do	Governor Peirpoint	Sept. 16, 1865.
Richard P. Walker	do	do	July 5, 1866.
A. G. Walters	do	do	July 18, 1865.
George Whitmore	do	do	Aug. 2, 1865.
B. P. Walter	do	Governor Peirpoint and C. L. Mosby	July 31, 1865.
John F. Whitfield	do	Governor Peirpoint	July 29, 1865.
William F. Wickham	do	do	Aug. 7, 1865.
J. W. Ware	do	do	Oct. 2, 1865.
James Wyson	do	do	Sept. 4, 1865.
John Walden	do	do	Sept. 9, 1865.
Seth Woodroof	do	do	July 14, 1865.
J. P. Williamson	do	do	Aug. 7, 1865.
Daniel Wilson	do	do	Aug. 16, 1865.
R. T. Wallace	do	do	Aug. 16, 1865.
R. Wood	do	do	Aug. 16, 1865.
Alexander W. Weddell	do	do	Aug. 16, 1865.
T. S. Watson	do	do	Aug. 10, 1865.
R. C. Waring	do	do	Aug. 10, 1865.
Alexander White	do	Governor Peirpoint and C. L. Mosby	Aug. 11, 1865.
John W. Witt	do	Governor Peirpoint	Aug. 11, 1865.
Newton K. White	do	do	Aug. 11, 1865.
S. Woods	do	do	Aug. 11, 1865.
Susan D. Watson	do	do	Aug. 19, 1865.
A. D. Williams	do	do	July 29, 1865.
Jesse Williams	do	do	July 29, 1865.
Thomas Wood	do	do	July 29, 1865.
James W. Watts	do	do	Sept. 19, 1865.
Lawrence Washington	do	do	Aug. 24, 1865.
Allen Williams	do	do	Aug. 29, 1865.
John C. Wilson	do	Governor Peirpoint and L. H. Chandler, United States district attorney, Virginia	July 26, 1865.

Virginia—Continued.

Name.	Exemption under amnesty proclamation of May 29, 1865.	By whom recommended.	Date of pardon.
Francis N. Watkins	Worth over $20,000	Governor Peirpoint	Aug. 14, 1865.
W. T. Walker	do	do	July 3, 1865.
G. R. Wilson	do	C. R. Sinneren and Colonel Browning	July 26, 1865.
James M. Wilcox	do	Governor Peirpoint	July 15, 1865.
Samuel P. Wilson	do	do	July 15, 1865.
William B. Whitehead	do	Tazwell Taylor	July 3, 1865.
W. W. Watkins	do	Governor Peirpoint	Aug. 16, 1865.
H. C. Warsham	do	do	July 29, 1865.
John Wood, jr	do	do	July 29, 1865.
W. A. Woods	do	do	July 13, 1865.
Joel Watkins	do	do	July 13, 1865.
Isaac R. Watkins	do	do	July 13, 1865.
Thomas Walker	do	do	Aug. 7, 1865.
William White	do	do	July 17, 1865.
James Walker	do	do	Aug. 1, 1865.
R. H. Whitfield	Member of rebel congress	Governor Peirpoint, Hon. J. H. Ashton, assistant attorney general United States; Hon. Joseph Segar; L. H. Chandler, U. S. district attorney, Va., and L. C. P. Cowper.	Aug. 14, 1865.
John B. Young	Member of the rebel State convention, and worth over $20,000.	Governor Peirpoint	July 31, 1865.
Samuel W. Young	Rebel postmaster	do	Nov. 6, 1865.
R. A. Young	Army contractor, and worth over $20,000	do	Aug. 1, 1865.
W. Yellott	Left a loyal State	L. H. Chandler, esq., United States district attorney	Aug. 7, 1865.
William G. Young	Property libelled and seized for confiscation	do	July 14, 1865.
N. P. Young	Worth over $20,000	Leopold C. V. Cowper, lieutenant governor of Virginia	Aug. 3, 1865.
G. W. Yancey	do	Governor Peirpoint	Aug. 2, 1865.
William T. Yancey	do	do	July 3, 1865.
Nicholls W. Yager	do	do	Aug. 16, 1865.
William B. Young	do	do	Aug. 10, 1865.
John James Young	do	do	Sept. 2, 1865.
F. M. Young	do	do	Aug. 12, 1865.
A. D. Zion	Rebel deputy postmaster	do	Nov. 9, 1865.
Lewis Zirkle	Worth over $20,000	do	Aug. 7, 1865.
John R. Zentemeyer	do	do	Aug. 4, 1865.
Moses Zirkel	do	do	July 25, 1865.

WEST VIRGINIA.

Name.	Exemption under amnesty proclamation of May 29, 1865.	By whom recommended.	Date of pardon.
William Adair	Worth over $20,000	W. C. Hutchison, G. C. Landcraft, James Bartin, Joel Burtin, John Graham, Jos. W. Graham, Samuel Allen, and John H. Dunn.	July 5, 1866.
John Argabright	do	Governor Boreman, Joel McPherson, clerk of the court, and Judge Harrison	Nov. 6, 1865.
Andrew Aldridge	do	Governor Boreman, Henry Berry, State's attorney; William Rush, sheriff; William A. Chapline, clerk of circuit court, and L. P. W. Balch, judge, &c.	Nov. 6, 1865.

M. Byrnside	Rebel funding agent	Judge Harrison and Benjamin H. Smith, United States district attorney	Sept. 25, 1865.
Thomas Bray	Rebel tax assessor	do	Oct. 4, 1865.
Wm. J. Blund	Proceedings instituted for confiscation	Governor Boreman	Oct. 17, 1865.
James Bennett	do	Governor Boreman and Hon. John S. Carlile	Dec. 19, 1865.
William B. Buster	do	Hon. J. J. Jackson and Benjamin H. Smith, United States district attorney	Sept. 27, 1865.
Oliver Beirne	Worth over $20,000	Attorney General Speed	Oct. 28, 1865.
C. J. Beirne	do	Governor Boreman	Feb. 17, 1865.
Patrick Beirne	do	Governor Boreman, Judge Harrison, and Joel McPherson, clerk of the court	Nov. 6, 1865.
Joseph Beard	do	Governor Boreman	Sept. 29, 1865.
Wolf Crotchen	Rebel postmaster	Judge Harrison and Benjamin H. Smith, United States district attorney	Aug. 12, 1865.
Lewis E. Caperton	Rebel tax assessor	Attorney General United States	Mar. 12, 1866.
Lewis E. Caperton	Rebel tax collector	do	July 6, 1866.
Alexander Campbell, jr.	Indicted for treason	L. M. Sherley and W. R. Thompson	Sept. 19, 1865.
James L. Carr	Proceedings instituted for confiscation	J. J. Jackson, jr., Judge Harrison, and Benj H. Smith, United States district attorney	July 12, 1865.
W. B. Calwell	Aid and comfort to rebels	Judge Harrison and Benjamin H. Smith, United States district attorney	Aug. 5, 1865.
A. A. Chapman	Worth over $20,000	Judge Harrison and J. McPherson, clerk of court	Aug. 26, 1865.
Andrew Campbell	do	Attorney General United States	July 5, 1866.
Sheldon Clark	do	Governor Boreman	Nov. 6, 1865.
Caperton Campbell	do	Attorney General United States	July 5, 1866.
W. S. Cunningham	do	A. J. Greenfield, lieutenant colonel commanding	Sept. 8, 1865.
H. W. Castleman	do	Henry Berry, States attorney; William Rush, sheriff; William A. Chapline, clerk of court, and L. P. W. Balch, judge, &c.	Nov. 6, 1865.
J. P. Donaldson	Information filed for confiscation	Samuel Kobb, 230 South Fourth street, Philadelphia	July 7, 1865.
John Duffy	Worth over $20,000	E. B. Tyler, brigadier general commanding	July 25, 1865.
H. B. Davenport	do	Governor Boreman	Oct. 21, 1865.
John W. Dunn	do	Governor Boreman and George W. Summers	Sept. 29, 1865.
Philip Duffey	do	By order of the President	Mar. 12, 1866.
George N. Fitzhugh	Proceedings commenced for confiscation	Governor Boreman and P. G. Van Winkle, U. S. S	Jan. 30, 1866.
John A. Fearnster	Worth over $20,000	Governor Boreman	Sept. 29, 1865.
John W. Garvin	Ex-United States and rebel postmaster	do	Nov. 6, 1865.
John F. Garing	Rebel postmaster	do	July 6, 1866.
David Gibson	Worth over $20,000	do	Aug. 29, 1865.
Henry F. Hunter	Rebel agent to collect taxes in kind	Judge Harrison and J. McPherson, clerk of the court	Aug. 26, 1865.
M. H. Houston	Proceedings instituted for confiscation	Governor Peirpoint and Benjamin H. Smith, United States district attorney, and Hon. C. D. Hubbard, M. C.	Aug. 5, 1865.
John H. Hansburger	Worth over $20,000	Judge Harrison, J. McPherson, clerk of the court; Benjamin H. Smith, United States district attorney.	Aug. 12, 1865.
A. C. Hammond	do	Governor Peirpoint and John E. Norris	July 29, 1865.
Uriah Hevener	do	By order of the President	Nov. 14, 1866.
John G. Harness	do	Wm. F. Speer, captain and provost marshal; Wm. Champion, and John W. Duffey	Sept. 8, 1865.
Hampton Hider	do	do	Sept. 8, 1865.
J. H. L. Hunter	do	Governor Boreman, A. McIntire, John J. Sanborn, W. H. Simpson, James D. Fayman, United States assistant assessor; L. P. W. Balch, judge of thirteenth judicial district.	Nov. 6, 1865.
James A. Hurst	do	Governor Boreman	July 5, 1866.
Alexander R. Humphreys	do	do	July 5, 1866.
J. R. Heiskell	do	do	Oct. 21, 1865.
A. A. Inskeep	do	do	Sept. 8, 1865.
B. H. Jones	Under bonds to the United States authorities	do	Aug. 29, 1865.
G. W. Kniseley	Proceedings instituted for confiscation	do	Jan. 6, 1866.
Alexander Kearns	Worth over $20,000	do	Sept. 29, 1865.
James Kingkendall	do	W. F. Speer, captain and provost marshal; Wm. Champion, and Wm. M. Randolph	Sept. 8, 1865.
S. C. Luddington	do	Attorney General Speed and B. H. Smith, United States district attorney	June 29, 1865.

West Virginia—Continued.

Name.	Exemption under amnesty proclamation of May 29, 1865.	By whom recommended.	Date of pardon.
James F. Lewis	Worth over $20,000	Governor Boreman	Sept. 13, 1865.
W. A. Lewis	do	do	Sept. 13, 1865.
Edward Lewis	do	do	Sept. 13, 1865.
John C. McDonald	Ex-United States and rebel postmaster	do	Nov. 6, 1865.
Thomas Masin	Member of seces'n convention; worth over $20,000	W. F. Speer, captain and provost marshal; John W. Duffey, and Wm. M. Randolph	Oct. 12, 1865.
Paul McNeel	Worth over $20,000	Governor Boreman	Sept. 23, 1865.
Samuel B. McClintock	do	do	Sept. 29, 1865.
Daniel R. McNeill	do	A. J. Greenfield, lieutenant colonel commanding; William M. Randolph, John W. Duffey, and William Champion.	Sept. 8, 1865.
Benjamin S. McNeill	do	do	Sept. 8, 1865.
S. A. McMechen	do	do	Sept. 8, 1865.
William L. McNeill	do	Attorney General Speed and J. McPherson	Aug. 26, 1865.
John Maddy	do	Governor Boreman, John Ballard, sr., William McDaniel, William Mann, sr., J. Ballard, Baldwin Ballard.	Oct. 21, 1865.
W. W. Newman	Proceedings instituted for confiscation	Governor Boreman, J. J. Jackson, United States judge; G. B. Thomas, G. W. Setzer, C. Sehon, John Hall, L. C. George, and M. H. Hale.	Sept. 14, 1865.
Samuel Price	Lieutenant Governor of Virginia, and worth over $20,000.	Governor Boreman	Sept. 29, 1865.
John T. Peirce	Worth over $20,000	George Crook, brevet brigadier general United States army; A. J. Watkins, A. Reed, D. Wolford, Sanford Carder, Amos Poland, James Pepper, Peter Haines, David Holt, George Wolf, D. C. Sabb, Asa Cline, Hugh McKever, James French, George W. Arnold, James Parker, J. W. Duffey, William Champion, James Brooks, William Randolph, Thomas Smith, R. W. Swift, H. Homan, John A. Vest, E. C. Rinehart, John Keller, Henry Baker, and John W. Lease.	A p
Jacob Reinhart	do	Governor Boreman	Oct. 9, 1865.
K. B. Stephenson	Left a loyal district, proceedings commenced for confiscation, and worth over $20,000.	do	June 26, 1865.
A. J. Smith	Proceedings instituted for confiscation	Governor Boreman and C. D. Hubbard, M. C. first district West Virginia	Mar. 17, 1866.
B. M. Smith	do	do	Mar. 17, 1866.
D. B. Smith	do	do	Mar. 17
R. J. Smith	do	do	Mar. 17, 1866.
W. T. Smith	do	do	Mar. 17, 1866.
Washington Summers	do	Governor Boreman, H. Simpson, Edward J. Colerider, and Nathan H. Taft	April 25, 1866.
Isaac Strider	Worth over $20,000	Governor Boreman	Nov. 6, 1865.
Jonathan Seymour	do	A. J. Greenfield, lieutenant colonel commanding; W. M. Randolph, John W. Duffey, and William Champion.	Sept. 8, 1865.
P. H. Thommasson	Proceedings instituted for confiscation, and worth over $20,000.	Governor Boreman and Benjamin H. Smith, United States district attorney	July 6, 1866.
Charles C. Tompkins	Worth over $20,000	Benjamin H. Smith, United States district attorney, and N. Harrison	Sept. 25, 1865.
William H. Tompkins	do	do	Sept. 25, 1865.
Elliott Vawter	Rebel tax collector	K. V. Whaley, M. C., and J. J. Jackson, jr	
David Vanmeter	Worth over $20,000	W. F. Speer, captain and provost marshal; John W. Duffey, and William Champion	Sept. 8, 1865.
Solomon C. Vanmeter	do	do	Sept. 8, 1865.
Wm. C. Vanmeter	do	do	Sept. 8, 1865.

John Withrow	Rebel depositary	Judge Harrison, Benj. H. Smith, United States district attorney; and Joel McPherson, clerk of court.	Aug. 5, 1865.
Wilson Watts	Rebel postmaster	do	Aug. 12, 1865.
B. C. Washington	Left a loyal district	Governor Boreman	July 6, 1866.
Felix B. Welton	Worth over $20,000	W.F. Speer, captain and provost marshal; William M. Randolph, William Champion, and John W. Duffey.	Sept. 8, 1865.
Edward Williams	do	do	Sept. 8, 1865.
James Withrow	do	Governor Boreman, Judge Summers, and Dr. Patrick	Sept. 29, 1865.
Cyrus Welton	do	A. J. Greenfield, lieutenant colonel commanding; William M. Randolph, John W. Duffey, and William Champion.	Sept. 8, 1865.
George T. Williams	do	William F. Speer, captain and provost marshal; John W. Duffey, William Champion, and William M. Randolph.	Sept. 8, 1865.
A. B. Young	Proceedings instituted for confiscation	Governor Boreman	Oct. 9, 1865.
Francis Yates	Worth over $20,000	do	Oct. 4, 1865.

GEORGIA.

*Charles D. Anderson	Brigadier general of Georgia militia	Governor Johnson	Sept. 25, 1865.
*George T. Anderson	Rebel brigadier general	do	Aug. 25, 1865.
Obadiah Arnold	Rebel enrolling officer	do	Sept. 4, 1865.
Thompson Allen	Clerk in rebel treasury department, and tax commissioner.	Governor Jenkins	July 5, 1866.
George W. Archer	Left a loyal State	do	July 5, 1866.
Abram B. Adams	Rebel collector of wool	Governor Johnson	Oct. 6, 1865.
G. W. Arnold	Rebel tax assessor	Governor Jenkins	July 5, 1865.
George S. Avery	do	Governor Johnson	Oct. 2, 1865.
George W. Awtrey	do	do	Sept. 16, 1865.
James H. Anderson	do	do	Oct. 10, 1865.
Isaac M. Aiken	Rebel tax collector	do	Sept. 4, 1865.
Allison Allen	do	do	Oct. 10, 1865.
Nathan L. Atkinson	do	do	Aug. 31, 1865.
John G. Addison	Rebel mail contractor	do	Sept. 16, 1865.
E. H. Abercombie	do	do	Sept. 11, 1865.
O. D. Anderson	Rebel postmaster	do	July 5, 1866.
M. C. Awtry	do	do	Oct. 2, 1865.
Charles W. Avery	do	do	Nov. 8, 1865.
Rufus R. Asbury	do	do	Nov. 8, 1865.
A. H. Arnold	do	do	Nov. 8, 1865.
Gideon H. Allen	do	do	Oct. 18, 1865.
John L. Anderson	Rebel postmaster, and worth over $20,000	Governor Johnson and Judge Reese	Oct. 2, 1865.
Andrew P. Allgood	do	Governor Johnson	Oct. 2, 1865.
James M. Anderson	Ex-United States and rebel postmaster	do	Oct. 10, 1865.
Henry Asbury	do	do	Sept. 16, 1865.
George W. Anderson	do	do	Nov. 8, 1865.
Edward C. Anderson	Paroled prisoner	Hon. James M. Wayne, associate justice of the Supreme Court of the United States.	July 18, 1865.
John Adams	Worth over $20,000	Governor Johnson	July 5, 1866.
William D. Allen	do	do	July 5, 1866.
Andrew W. Ard	do	do	July 5, 1866.
Robert A. Allen	do	do	July 5, 1866.

Georgia—Continued.

Name.	Exemption under amnesty proclamation of May 29, 1865.	By whom recommended.	Date of pardon.
James Arnold	Worth over $20,000	Governor Johnson	Oct. 2, 1865.
George W. Anderson	do	Hon. James M. Wayne, associate justice of the Supreme Court of the United States	July 18, 1865.
R. D. Arnold	do	By order of the President	June 16, 1865.
Park E. Arnold	do	Governor Johnson	Aug. 28, 1865.
Thomas C. Arnold	do	Attorney General Speed and Governor Johnson	Oct. 2, 1865.
William W. Anderson	do	Governor Johnson	Sept. 15 1865.
John W. Anderson	do	Attorney General Speed	July 6, 1865.
William D. Alexander	do	Governor Johnson	Sept. 11, 1865.
John P. Atkinson	do	do	Sept. 11, 1865.
Martin T. Alexander	do	do	Aug. 21, 1865.
Alfred Austell	do	P. F. Winslow, brevet brigadier general United States volunteers, and John Erskine, judge of United States district court for Georgia.	Aug. 31, 1865.
James W. Armstrong	do	Governor Johnson	Sept. 16, 1865.
Thomas C. Ayer	do	do	Sept. 25, 1865.
Jesse A. Ausley	do	do	Sept. 28, 1865.
Cornelius K. Ayer	do	do	Sept. 25, 1865.
Willis Allen	do	do	Sept. 25, 1865.
B. A. Arnett	do	do	Oct. 13, 1865.
Asher Ayers	do	do	Sept. 20, 1865.
Asbury A. Adams	do	do	Sept. 25, 1865.
Moses Arnold	do	do	Sept. 20, 1865.
Willis Arnold	do	do	Oct. 18, 1865.
Edmund B. Atwater	do	do	Oct. 6, 1865.
William E. Alexander	do	do	Sept. 20, 1865.
William P. Anderson	do	do	Oct. 2, 1865.
William P. Anderson	do	do	Oct. 2, 1865.
James Arnold	do	do	Oct. 2, 1865.
Mrs. Mary W. Anderson	do	do	Oct. 2, 1865.
Adam L. Alexander	do	do	Oct. 2, 1865.
David R. Adams	do	do	Sept. 28, 1865.
B. F. Adams	do	do	Sept. 28, 1865.
William Amis	do	do	Oct. 2, 1865.
William G. Andrews	do	do	Oct. 2, 1865.
James N. Armor	do	do	Oct. 2, 1865.
*William M. Browne	Rebel assistant secretary of state and brigadier general.	Governor Johnson and M. S. Ewen, major 156th New York volunteers	July 5, 1866.
Nathan Bass	Member of rebel provisional congress and worth over $20,000.	Hon. James M. Wayne, associate justice of the Supreme Court United States	Aug. 4, 1865.
Hiram P. Bell	Member of rebel congress	Governor Johnson and John Simpkins, ordinary of Jackson county, Georgia	Sept. 11, 1865.
A. V. Brumby	Educated at West Point, colonel in rebel army, and worth over $20,000.	Governor Johnson	Aug. 28, 1865.
E. H. Bacon	Rebel purchasing agent	do	Aug. 28, 1865.
Joel Britt	do	Governor Johnson, J. C. Shugart, and D. M. Young	Oct. 2, 1865.
B. D. Brantly	do	Governor Johnson and C. H. Hopkins	Oct. 18, 1865.

C. O. Brooks	Rebel mail agent	Governor Johnson	Nov. 15, 1865.
L. E. Bleckley	Rebel agent of nitre bureau	do	Oct. 10 1865.
L. G. Bowers	Rebel commercial agent for a line of "blockade runners."	Isaac Scott and R. L. Mott	Aug. 26, 1865.
Thomas C. Broddus	Member of rebel advisory board, and worth over $20,000.	Governor Johnson	Sept. 2, 1865.
T. C. Brown	Indicted for treason	Governor Jenkins	July 5, 1866.
James H. Burton	Superintendent of rebel armories and worth over $20,000.	Isaac Scott	Oct. 3, 1865.
William M. Browne	Petty civil officer	By order of the President	Dec. 12, 1865.
William A. Beck	Rebel postmaster and tax collector	Governor Johnson	Oct. 18, 1865.
James Buchanon	Rebel tax collector and worth over $20,000	do	Aug. 21, 1865.
John B. Beall	Rebel tax assessor	do	Oct. 18, 1865.
H. T. Brysey	do	do	Oct. 6, 1865.
E. H. Bloodworth	do	do	Oct. 6, 1865.
William W. Brooks	do	do	Sept. 23, 1865.
Joel C. Barnett	do	do	Sept. 20, 1865.
William M. Ball	do	do	Oct. 10, 1865.
Warren L. Battle	do	Governor Jenkins	July 5, 1865.
Wilson M. Barton	do	Governor Johnson	Oct. 25, 1865.
Nathan Berry	do	do	July 5, 1865.
James H. Blackwell	do	Governor Jenkins	July 5, 1865.
Thomas Barnes	do	Governor Johnson	Oct. 25, 1865.
William B. Bell	do	do	Nov. 8, 1865.
William L. Brown	Rebel tax collector	do	Nov. 8, 1865.
Asa R. Brown	do	do	Nov. 8, 1865.
Thomas P. Blount	do	do	Oct. 6, 1865.
B. F. Bruton	do	do	Oct. 2, 1865.
J. Madison Bagwell	do	do	Sept. 16, 1865.
Isaac E. Bartlett	do	do	Sept. 4, 1865.
William Barton	do	do	Oct. 10, 1865.
Baxter B. Brown	do	do	Oct. 10, 1865.
William D. Bently	Ex-United States and rebel postmaster	do	Sept. 16, 1865.
Haywood Brookins	do	do	Sept. 4, 1865.
William F. Brown	do	do	July 5, 1866.
William Barry	do	do	Oct. 2, 1865.
M. L. Barron	do	do	July 5, 1866.
Job Bowers	do	do	Oct. 2, 1865.
William Bowers	do	do	Oct. 2, 1865.
Peter Bennett	do	do	Oct. 28, 1865.
J. M. Bennett	do	do	Oct. 28, 1865.
James Baskins	do	do	Nov. 15, 1865.
William Burt	do	do	Oct. 25, 1865.
John C. Bowden	do	do	Nov. 8, 1865.
James Boyd	do	do	Oct. 18, 1865.
William A. Banks	do	do	Aug. 28, 1865.
William H. Byrom	Rebel postmaster and worth over $20,000	do	Oct. 6, 1865.
Marshall P. Brown	Rebel postmaster	do	Oct. 2, 1865.
David S. Butler	do	do	Sept. 25, 1865.
Asa W. Bruner	do	do	Sept. 16, 1865.
Martin E. Buckner	do	do	Sept. 16, 1865.
Isaac Burlison	do	do	Oct. 28, 1865.

Georgia—Continued.

Name.	Exemption under amnesty proclamation of May 29, 1865.	By whom recommended.	Date of pardon.
James C. Blackstock	Rebel postmaster	Governor Johnson	Oct. 10, 1865.
Eli E. Boyett	do	do	Oct. 10, 1865.
John A. Boon	do	do	Oct. 10, 1865.
David N. Buckhalter	do	By order of the President	July 5, 1866.
James F. Butler	do	Governor Johnson	July 5, 1866.
Eli Barrett	do	do	July 5, 1866.
Benjamin J. Boynton	do	do	Oct. 2, 1865.
Lemuel Bennett	do	do	Oct. 2, 1865.
L. W. Burtz	do	Governor Jenkins	July 5, 1866.
Ezekiel Burns	do	do	July 5, 1866.
William A. Ballard	do	do	July 5, 1866.
Samuel Brown	do	Governor Johnson	Nov. 8, 1865.
John W. Black	do	do	Nov. 8, 1865.
George T. Boroughs	do	do	Nov. 8, 1865.
C. A. Barrett	do	do	Nov. 8, 1865.
Silas Beavers	do	do	Nov. 8, 1865.
Green B. Bently	do	do	Nov. 8, 1865.
Barnabus Barron	do	do	Oct. 18, 1865.
William Bryan	Worth over $20,000	do	Oct. 6, 1865.
A. C. Brown	do	do	Sept. 23, 1865.
George H. Bryan	do	do	Oct. 2, 1865.
B. T. Bowdre	do	do	Oct. 2, 1865.
Horace I. Bates	do	do	Oct. 2, 1865.
James Baggs	do	do	Oct. 25, 1865.
Needham Bullard	do	do	Sept. 20, 1865.
Marcus A. Bell	do	do	Aug. 25, 1865.
J. R. Browne	do	do	Aug. 28, 1865.
J. A. Barclay	do	do	Aug. 25, 1865.
James E. Butler	do	do	Aug. 25, 1865.
James Bond	do	do	Jan. 6, 1866.
James T. Bothwell	do	do	Sept. 19, 1865.
Andrew F. Bird	do	do	Sept. 20, 1865.
Mrs. C. C. Barnes	do	Governor Jenkins	Mar. 2, 1866.
Thomas J. Burney	do	Governor Johnson	Oct. 2, 1865.
William Battersby	do	do	Oct. 2, 1865.
John A. Broughton	do	Governor Johnson and Joshua Hill	Oct. 2, 1865.
Edwin F. Birdsong	do	Governor Johnson	Oct. 2, 1865.
James N. Brown	do	do	Oct. 2, 1865.
N. K. Butter	do	do	Oct. 2, 1865.
Green B. Burney	do	do	Oct. 2, 1865.
George T. Bartlett	do	do	Oct. 2, 1865.
Gustavus H. Bates	do	do	Oct. 2, 1865.
Frank W. Bivins	do	do	Sept. 28, 1865.
William Barber	do	do	Sept. 28, 1865.

E. E. Brown	do	do	Oct. 6, 1865.
C. Bateman	do	do	Oct. 12, 1865.
Edward M. Bayward	do	do	Oct. 10, 1865.
Simeon N. Brown	do	Governor Johnson and Joshua Hill	Oct. 10, 1865.
William M. Brown	do	Governor Johnson	Oct. 28, 1865.
Amos Brown	do	do	Oct. 28, 1865.
W. H. Barrett	do	do	Oct. 28, 1865.
Mary Savannah Barrett	do	do	Oct. 28, 1865.
Thomas G. Barrett	do	do	Oct. 28, 1865.
Joseph Brown	do	do	Oct. 2, 1865.
Jacob W. Bason	do	do	Sept. 28, 1865.
William Brown	do	do	Sept. 28, 1865.
James W. Belvin	do	do	Sept. 28, 1865.
S. C. Bryan	do	do	Sept. 28, 1865.
Robert H. Bryan	do	do	Sept. 28, 1865.
Robert W. Baskin	do	do	Sept. 28, 1865.
John W. Burney	do	do	Sept. 20, 1865.
David C. Barron	do	do	Sept. 20, 1865.
Elijah Bond	do	Governor Johnson and Major General Wilson	Aug. 25, 1865.
D. L. Boober	do	Governor Johnson	Aug. 21, 1865.
J. J. Boswell	do	do	Mar. 3, 1865.
James H. Born	do	do	Nov. 15, 1865.
Moody Burt	do	do	Oct. 25, 1865.
John Billups	do	do	Nov. 15, 1865.
Erasmus T. Beall	do	do	Aug. 25, 1865.
Joseph G. Blount	do	do	Aug. 28, 1865.
Samuel B. Brown	do	do	Aug. 28, 1865.
Thomas W. Battle	do	do	Aug. 25, 1865.
Willard Boynton	do	do	Aug. 25, 1865.
Samuel Beall	do	do	Aug. 25, 1865.
Loverd Bryan	do	do	Aug. 25, 1865.
Alfred Baker	do	do	Aug. 25, 1865.
John L. Burkhalter	do	do	Sept. 15, 1865.
Marcus H. Bunn	do	do	Aug. 28, 1865.
John Bowes	do	do	Aug. 28, 1865.
John Billingslea	do	do	Aug. 31, 1865.
John T. Boykin	do	do	Aug. 31, 1865.
Wm. T. Bousley	do	do	Aug. 31, 1865.
John Banks	do	do	Sept. 11, 1865.
P. J. Biggers	do	do	Sept. 11, 1865.
S. T. Bridges	do	do	Sept. 11, 1865.
N. H. Beal	do	do	Sept. 11, 1865.
Nathan Bryall	do	do	Aug. 28, 1865.
W. C. Battle	do	do	Aug. 28, 1865.
John H. Bass	do	do	Aug. 28, 1865.
Robert J. Bacon	do	do	Aug. 28, 1865.
Joseph M. Boardman	do	do	Aug. 28, 1865.
Benson Blake	do	do	Aug. 28, 1865.
Stephen S. Boon	do	do	Sept. 25, 1865.
Thomas P. Burdett	do	do	Sept. 25, 1865.
Robert C. Black	do	do	Sept. 25, 1865.
George W. Bivins	do	do	Sept. 25, 1865.

Georgia—Continued.

Name.	Exemption under amnesty proclamation of May 29, 1865.	By whom recommended.	Date of pardon.
John Batts	Worth over $20,000	Governor Johnson	Sept. 25, 1865.
Wright Brady	do	do	Sept. 25, 1865.
William W. Barbow	do	do	Sept. 25, 1865.
Henry Bunn	do	do	Sept. 25, 1865.
Sampson Bell	do	do	Sept. 25, 1865.
Wm. B. Berry	do	do	Sept. 16, 1865.
Andrew J. Berry	do	do	Sept. 16, 1865.
Zadock Bonner	do	do	Sept. 16, 1865.
Green Brantley	do	do	Sept. 16, 1865.
Benjamin Barron	do	do	Sept. 16, 1865.
Milton C. Balls	do	do	Sept. 16, 1865.
Wm. R. Brown	do	do	Sept. 16, 1865.
Harris Brantley	do	do	Sept. 16, 1865.
John W. Bacon	do	do	Sept. 16, 1865.
R. J. Blount	do	do	Sept. 16, 1865.
T. S. M. Bloodworth	do	Governor Johnson, A. J. Murray, M. G. Dobbins, D. H. Johnson, H. C. Roberts, and John C. Neal.	Sept. 4, 1865.
Thurston R. Bloom	do	Hon. James M. Wayne, associate justice of the Supreme Court of the United States	Aug. 4, 1865.
John T. Brown	do	Governor Johnson	Sept. 2, 1865.
Wm. Bennett	do	do	Aug. 28, 1865.
Robert L. Bass	do	do	Sept. 25, 1865.
Alexander Bryan	do	do	Sept. 16, 1865.
A. P. Bailey	do	do	Sept. 13, 1865.
John N. Barnett	do	do	Sept. 25, 1865.
Samuel A. Billing	do	do	Aug. 29, 1855.
Wm. H. Brantley	do	do	Sept. 4, 1865.
James A. Beeks	do	do	Sept. 4, 1865.
James Brown	do	do	Sept. 4, 1865.
G. J. Blake	do	do	Sept. 4, 1865.
David J. Bothwell	do	do	Oct. 6, 1865.
Elijah Butts	do	do	Oct. 6, 1865.
Vienus Brinson	do	do	July 5, 1866.
John M. Boyd	do	Governor Jenkins	July 5, 1866
Madison Baker	do	do	July 5, 1866.
John G. Barnwell	do	do	July 5, 1866.
Edward Broughton	do	do	July 5, 1866.
Henry Banks	do	Governor Johnson	July 5, 1866.
Willis Benham	do	Governor Jenkins, Judge Milner, J. R. Parrott, and J. A. Howard	Nov. 16, 1866.
H. Bingham	do	Edward Padelford and J. G. Mills	June 16, 1865.
N. J. Bussey	do	Governor Johnson	Aug. 2, 1865.
James R. Butts	do	do	Nov. 1, 1865.
Wm. Battersby	do	Attorney General Speed and Hon. James M. Wayne, associate justice of the Supreme Court of the United States.	July 25, 1865.
John W. Burney	do	Governor Johnson	Sept. 20, 1865.

D. H. Baldwin	do	Attorney General Speed, L. E. Chittenden, and Isaac Scott, of New York	June 29, 1865.
Walker R. Branham	do	Governor Johnson	Oct. 25, 1865.
Henry Banks	do	do	July 5, 1866.
F. A. Billingslea	do	do	Oct. 18, 1865.
Wm. T. Burge	do	Governor Jenkins and William T. Wofford	July 5, 1866.
Lawrence Battle	do	Governor Johnson	May 12, 1866.
Moses H. Baldwin	do	do	Oct. 18, 1865.
Jacob Barrett	do	do	Oct. 18, 1865.
M. L. Bivins	do	do	Sept. 23, 1865.
Edmund Bradley	do	do	Nov. 8, 1865.
E. W. Baynes	do	do	Nov. 8, 1865.
James B. Bishop	do	do	Nov. 8, 1865.
Thomas Blackshear	do	do	Nov. 8, 1865.
Jeremiah Beall	do	do	Nov. 8, 1865.
John S. Byne	do	do	Nov. 8, 1865.
Thomas T. Buttrell	do	do	Oct. 18, 1865.
Lorenzo M. Biggers	do	do	Sept. 23, 1865.
James Bunckley	do	do	Nov. 15, 1865.
Alfred Cummings	Graduate of West Point and rebel brigadier gen'l.	Attorney General Stanbery	Nov. 2, 1866.
M. J. Crawford	Ex-United States and rebel member of Congress	John Sherman, United States senator, and Governor Johnson	July 14, 1866.
Joseph P. Carr	Left a loyal State	Governor Johnson	Aug. 28, 1865.
Wm. W. Cato	Rebel collecting agent	do	Aug. 31, 1865.
Lewis Cruger	Comptroller of rebel treasury	Governor Jenkins, and Governor Perry, of South Carolina	Sept. 27, 1865.
L. C. Coppedge	Rebel mail contractor	Governor Johnson	Oct. 6, 1865.
Philip A. Clayton	Rebel States marshal	do	Nov. 8, 1865.
Eleazar H. Cohen	Member of rebel examining board	do	Oct. 10, 1865.
James L. F. Cottrell	Rebel commissioner of prizes	do	Sept. 2, 1865.
Charter Campbell	Rebel depositary, and worth over $20,000	do	Sept. 19, 1865.
Solomon Cohen	Civil officer, and worth over $20,000	Hon. M. Blair	July 13, 1865.
Wm. P. Carmichael	Rebel clerk, special agent of treasury at Augusta, and worth over $20,000.	Governor Johnson	Sept. 4, 1865.
John A. Crawford	Rebel clerk	do	Oct. 18, 1865.
Joseph S. Claghorn	Paroled prisoner	Stewart L. Woodford, brevet brigadier general commanding post	July 3, 1865.
John Cunningham	do	do	July 14, 1865.
James L. Clark	Rebel purchasing agent	Governor Johnson	Oct. 2, 1865.
Bradford T. Chapman	Rebel purchasing agent, and worth over $20,000	do	Sept. 11, 1865.
Elias B. Carr	do	do	Aug. 28, 1865.
James M. Cantrell	Rebel postmaster and worth over $20,000	do	Nov. 8, 1865.
James Castelberry	Rebel postmaster and tax collector	do	Oct. 2, 1865.
Elbridge G. Cabaniss	Rebel chief collector of taxes for the State of Ga.	do	Oct. 6, 1865.
Samuel W. Callaway	Rebel tax collector	do	Sept. 16, 1865.
Isaac S. Clement	do	do	Oct. 2, 1865.
Thomas W. Cobb	do	do	Oct. 10, 1865.
James Cantrell	do	do	Nov. 8, 1865.
D. G. Cotting	do	Joshua Hill	July 13, 1865.
Henry D. Chapman	Rebel tax assessor	Governor Johnson	Oct. 6, 1865.
Jacob M. Cleveland	do	do	Oct. 2, 1865.
Wm. J. Chambers	do	do	Sept. 16, 1865.
James J. Colt	do	do	Nov. 8, 1865.
Webster Coffey	do	do	Oct. 18, 1865.
Wm. P. Campbell	do	do	Oct. 18, 1865.
Noah L. Cloud	Ex-United States and rebel postmaster	do	Oct. 2, 1865.

Georgia—Continued.

Name.	Exemption under amnesty proclamation of May 29, 1865.	By whom recommended.	Date of pardon.
John H. H. Colquitt	Ex-United States and rebel postmaster	Governor Johnson	Aug. 31, 1865.
A. B. Croft	do	do	Aug. 31, 1865.
James A. Chaffin	do	do	Aug. 29, 1865.
Wm. M. Cleveland	do	do	July 5, 1866.
W. P. Chester	do	do	Oct. 10, 1865.
E. S. Candler	do	do	Nov. 8, 1865.
Bryan W. Collier	do	do	Oct. 6, 1865.
George H. Camp	Ex-U. S. and rebel postmaster; worth over $20,000	do	Nov. 15, 1865.
J. M. Chamblee	Rebel postmaster	do	Oct. 28, 1865.
Thomas Collins	do	do	Oct. 25, 1865.
James Collier	do	do	Oct. 6, 1865.
Thomas Callahan	do	do	Oct. 2, 1865.
James M. Culpepper	do	do	Oct. 2, 1865.
Thomas Crawford	do	do	Sept. 28, 1865.
Samuel G. Chandler	do	do	Sept. 4, 1865.
William G. Crain	do	do	Aug. 31, 1865.
Wm. J. Conley	do	do	July 5, 1866.
James C. Cutchin	do	do	July 5, 1866.
Wm. J. Cushing	do	do	Oct. 2, 1865.
Joseph J. Chappell	do	do	Oct. 10, 1865.
William Carter	do	do	Oct. 10, 1865.
B. G. N. Chandler	do	do	Nov. 8, 1865.
Andrew J. Corner	do	do	Nov. 8, 1865.
Archibald Campbell	do	do	Oct. 18, 1865.
Henry C. Christian	do	do	Oct. 18, 1865.
John P. Cobb	do	do	Oct. 18, 1865.
Eginardus R. Carswell	Worth over $20,000	do	Oct. 13, 1865.
Joseph J. Carson	do	do	Aug. 28, 1865.
Stephen Collins	do	do	Sept. 11, 1865.
Wm. B. Carter	do	Governor Jenkins	July 5, 1866.
Daniel B. Cunyus	do	Governor Jenkins and Wm. T. Woffard	July 5, 1866.
Virgil N. Childers	do	Governor Johnson	Aug. 31, 1865.
Green P. Cozart	do	do	May 12, 1866.
James C. Cook	do	do	Aug. 25, 1865.
G. A. Clower	do	do	Aug. 25, 1865.
P. L. Clower	do	do	Aug. 25, 1865.
W. W. Chapman	do	do	Sept. 2, 1865.
Daniel Callahan	do	By order of the President	July 27, 1866.
R. J. Castelbury	do	General U. S. Grant	Apr. 4, 1866.
O. L. Cloud	do	Governor Johnson	Sept. 11, 1865.
George L. Cope	do	do	Oct. 12, 1865.
B. F. Coleman	do	do	Oct. 6, 1865.
Hamlin J. Cook	do	do	Oct. 6, 1865.
Henry F. Campbell	do	do	Sept. 20, 1865.

Joseph Catching	do	B. S. Dartt, major and post commander	Sept. 20, 1865.
Jesse Carter	do	Governor Johnson	Sept. 23, 1865.
James A. Chapman	do	do	Sept. 23, 1865.
John Chambless	do	do	Oct. 2, 1865.
B. H. Crawford	do	do	Oct. 2, 1865.
Wiley Cobb	do	do	Oct. 2, 1865.
Joel T. Coney	do	do	Oct. 2, 1865.
George W. Camp	do	do	Oct. 2, 1865.
Isaac G. Cheeves	do	do	Sept. 28, 1865.
Franklin Cherry	do	do	Oct. 2, 1865.
George L. Carswell	do	do	Oct. 2, 1865.
Edward J. Coates	do	do	Oct. 2, 1865.
Josepq J. Collier	do	do	Oct. 6, 1865.
Joseph J. Cohen	do	do	Oct. 6, 1865.
Jacob Carreker	do	do	Oct. 6, 1865.
M. B. Clarke	do	do	Sept. 16, 1865.
William A. Carr	do	do	Sept. 16, 1865.
William Cline	do	do	Sept. 28, 1865.
J. H. Clarke	do	do	Sept. 28, 1865.
W. P. Chisolm	do	do	Sept. 28, 1865.
Henry E. A. Candler	do	do	Sept. 28, 1865.
Adam Cason	do	do	Sept. 15, 1865.
Samuel M. Carter	do	do	Sept. 11, 1865.
William A. Cheny	do	do	Sept. 11, 1865.
William Carithers	do	do	Sept. 11, 1865.
Isaac Cheney	do	do	Sept. 11, 1865.
C. W. Charlton	do	do	Oct. 30, 1865.
James M. Chambers	do	do	Sept. 28, 1865.
Seymore Catching	do	do	Aug. 28, 1865.
Samuel Clayton	do	do	Aug. 28, 1865.
Robert A. Crawford	do	do	Aug. 28, 1865.
George Cornwell	do	do	Oct. 28, 1865.
T. W. Chichester	do	do	Sept. 28, 1865.
J. R. Coombs	do	Hon. James M. Wayne, associate justice of the Supreme Court of the United States	Aug. 4, 1865.
Augustus W. Callaway	do	Governor Johnson	Aug. 25, 1865.
William A. Cooke	do	do	Aug. 25, 1865.
George W. Collier	do	do	Sept. 16, 1865.
George Cooper	do	do	Sept. 16, 1865.
J. M. Calhoun	do	do	Sept. 16, 1865.
Merrill P. Callaway	do	do	Oct. 18, 1865.
A. H. Chappell	do	do	Oct. 25, 1865.
William Cox	do	do	Nov. 13, 1865.
Nelson Clements	do	do	Aug. 25, 1865.
Julius A. Cade	do	do	Aug. 25, 1865.
James H. Callaway	do	do	Aug. 31, 1865.
John P. Cubburson	do	do	Aug. 31, 1865.
John M. Clark	do	do	Aug. 28, 1865.
William Carswell, sen	do	do	Aug. 25, 1865.
Julius R. Clapp	do	do	Oct. 2, 1865.
Mrs. Mary Colt	do	do	Oct. 2, 1865.
D. B. Cade	do	do	Oct. 2, 1865.
John Collier	do	do	Sept. 4, 1865.

Georgia—Continued.

Name.	Exemption under amnesty proclamation of May 29, 1865.	By whom recommended.	Date of pardon.
John Craig	Worth over $20,000	Governor Johnson	Sept. 4, 1865.
Zachariah H. Clark	do	do	Sept. 4, 1865.
James Clarke	do	do	Aug. 28, 1865.
Francis H. Cook	do	do	Aug. 28, 1865.
George W. Crawford	do	do	Aug. 28, 1865.
P. M. Compton	do	do	Aug. 28, 1865.
Wade C. Cothran	do	do	Aug. 28, 1865.
M. J. Carswell	do	do	Sept. 4, 1865.
John B. Campbell	do	do	Aug. 25, 1865.
James D. Carhart	do	do	Aug. 25, 1865.
W. C. Cleveland	do	do	Aug. 28, 1865.
John M. Cutliff	do	do	Aug. 25, 1865.
George W. Cheek	do	Hon. James M. Wayne, associate justice of the Supreme Court of the United States	Aug. 4, 1865.
Joseph W. Clarke	do	do	Aug. 4, 1865.
Henry W. Coleman	do	Governor Johnson	Sept. 16, 1865.
S. H. Cox	do	do	Sept. 4, 1865.
Anderson Corner	do	do	Sept. 4, 1865.
John Chapman	do	do	Sept. 25, 1865.
William N. L. Crocker	do	do	Sept. 25, 1865.
J. R. Cheves	do	do	Sept. 25, 1865.
Allen S. Cutts	do	do	Oct. 6, 1865.
Robert M. Clarke	do	do	Sept. 25, 1865.
Henry H. Cumming	do	do	Sept. 19, 1865.
A. B. Calhoun	do	do	Sept. 28, 1865.
John M. Cooper	do	do	Oct. 18, 1865.
David L. Curtis	do	do	Oct. 18, 1865.
N. Cruger	do	do	Oct. 18, 1865.
Parker Callaway	do	do	Oct. 18, 1865.
Robert Craig	do	do	Oct. 18, 1865.
Robert M. Cleveland	do	do	Oct. 18, 1865.
Sanders Coalson	do	do	Oct. 18, 1865.
Seabourn Callaway	do	do	Nov. 8, 1865.
John Cunningham	do	do	Nov. 8, 1865.
Richard G. Carlton	do	do	Nov. 8, 1865.
Lorenzo D. Carlton	do	do	Nov. 8, 1865.
J. H. N. Clinch	do	do	Nov. 8, 1865.
Mrs. Julia A. Cumming	do	Attorney General Speed	Oct. 25, 1865.
F. L. Cook	do	Governor Jenkins	Jan. 15, 1866.
William Copeland	do	By order of the President	Dec. 10, 1865.
Jerry Cowles	do	Governor Johnson	Sept. 16, 1865.
George L. Cope	do	United States Senators Nye and Morgan, and Hon. S. Draper	July 21, 1865.
James M. Calhoun	do	Stewart L. Woodford, brevet brigadier general commanding	July 24, 1865.
Mrs. Charlotte L. Cheves	do	Attorney General Speed	July 24, 1865.
Enoch J. Collins	do	By order of the President	Sept. 9, 1865.
	Rebel postmaster and worth over $20,000	Governor Johnson	Aug. 25, 1865

E. P. Clayton	Rebel agent for the purchase of cotton	Major General Humphreys	July 14, 1865.
B. F. De Bow	Rebel clerk	Governor Johnson	Sept. 16, 1865.
John W. Duncan	Rebel depositary	do	June 19, 1865.
William C. Daniell	Rebel commissioner, under bonds to the United States military authorities and worth over $20,000.	do	July 5, 1865.
William C. Duke	Rebel purchasing agent	do	Aug. 31, 1865.
J. W. Darracott	do	do	Nov. 15, 1865.
John S. Dickinson	Rebel mail contractor	do	Oct. 10, 1865.
Joseph W. Dickerson	do	do	Oct. 2, 1865.
C. E. Dopson	do	do	Oct. 20, 1865.
Alexander Deas	Rebel tax collector	do	Oct. 7, 1865.
A. P. Dearing	do	do	Aug. 28, 1865.
Alfred B. Davis	do	do	Oct. 10, 1865.
E. Douglass	do	do	Nov. 8, 1865.
John T. Duncan	do	do	Oct. 18, 1865.
Joseph E. Dent	Rebel tax assessor and worth over $20,000	do	Aug. 25, 1865.
William Doyle	Rebel tax assessor	do	Sept. 28, 1865.
Thomas J. Darling	do	do	Oct. 18, 1865.
John R. Dyer	do	do	Nov. 15, 1865.
Marshall Douglass	do	do	Oct. 10, 1865.
M. S. Durham	Rebel postmaster	do	Oct. 2, 1865.
John B. Davis	do	do	Sept. 16, 1865.
Benjamin B. Dykes	do	do	Sept. 25, 1865.
James B. Dell	do	do	Sept. 4, 1865.
W. L. Dean	do	do	Oct. 25, 1865.
Henry K. Downs	do	do	Oct. 2, 1865.
Samuel P. Dobbins	do	do	Oct. 10, 1865.
D. F. Dickinson	do	do	Oct. 10, 1865.
James J. Deese	do	do	Oct. 10, 1865.
George W. Donaldson	do	do	Oct. 10, 1865.
John Durden	Ex-United States and rebel postmaster and worth over $20,000.	do	Oct. 28, 1865.
William Dicken	Ex-United States and rebel postmaster	do	Oct. 2, 1865.
Young Davis	do	do	Oct. 25, 1865.
S. H. Dickinson	do	do	July 5, 1866.
John A. Davis	Worth over $20,000	Hon. James M. Wayne, associate Justice of the Supreme Court of the United States, and Attorney General Speed.	July 20, 1865.
William H. Dunning	do	Governor Johnson	Oct. 2, 1865.
Jonathan Donalson	do	do	Oct. 2, 1865.
Archibald Davis	do	do	Oct. 2, 1865.
Thomas C. Dempsey	do	do	Oct. 2, 1865.
Thomas E. Dickey	do	do	Oct. 2, 1865.
Robert Darriell	do	do	Oct. 2, 1865.
J. M. Daniels	do	do	Oct. 2, 1865.
Charles A. Davis	do	do	Oct. 2, 1865.
J. W. Dent	do	do	Oct. 2, 1865.
Joseph A. Davis	do	do	Oct. 2, 1865.
James C. Davis	do	do	Sept. 20, 1865.
Richard R. Davis	do	do	Oct. 2, 1865.
Alfred L. Dearing	do	do	Sept. 28, 1865.
Lewis J. Dewpree	do	do	Sept. 20, 1865.
Samuel A. Durand	do	do	Sept. 20, 1865.

Georgia—Continued.

Name.	Exemption under amnesty proclamation of May 29, 1865.	By whom recommended.	Date of pardon.
O. P. Daniel	Worth over $20,000	Governor Johnson	Sept. 20, 1865.
William W. Davenport	do	do	Sept. 16, 1865.
Andrew Dominick	do	do	Sept. 16, 1865.
Samuel Davis	do	do	Sept. 16, 1865.
Samuel F. Dickinson	do	do	Sept. 16, 1865.
George Dent	do	do	Sept. 16, 1865.
John G. Davis	do	do	Sept. 16, 1865.
Samuel P. Davis	do	do	Sept. 16, 1865.
William H. Dabney	do	do	Sept. 16, 1865.
John P. Davis	do	do	Sept. 16, 1865.
Mrs. Mary E. Deas	do	Attorney General Speed	Sept. 21, 1865.
Perry E. Duncan	do	Governor Johnson	Sept. 16, 1865.
William M. Davis	do	do	Sept. 16, 1865.
Larkin Davidson	do	do	Sept. 23, 1865.
James Doyle	do	do	Oct. 18, 1865.
Charles Delaigle	do	do	Sept. 20, 1865.
J. R. Dubose	do	do	Aug. 25, 1865.
James Dent	do	do	Aug. 25, 1865.
Thomas Dewberry	do	do	Aug. 25, 1865.
Louis A. Dugas	do	do	Aug. 25, 1865.
Edgar G. Dawson	do	do	Aug. 25, 1865.
Gustavus Delaney	do	do	Aug. 25, 1865
Charles Du Bignon	do	do	Sept. 25, 1865.
John H. Deuson	do	do	Sept. 25, 1865.
James M. Dye	do	do	Sept. 4, 1865.
David Dickson	do	do	Sept. 4, 1865.
L. T. Downing	do	do	Sept. 11, 1865.
Charles M. Davis	do	do	Oct. 2, 1865.
E. L. Douglass	do	do	Sept. 4, 1865.
Jackson De Loache	do	do	Sept. 4, 1865.
John Douglass	do	do	Aug. 31, 1865.
Joseph Day	do	do	Sept. 28, 1865.
Hugh L. Dennard	do	do	Sept. 28, 1865.
Thomas J. Dickson	do	do	Sept. 4, 1865.
Jacob Danforth	do	do	Aug. 28, 1865.
B. S. Dunbar	do	do	Aug. 28, 1865.
William M. Davidson	do	do	Aug. 28, 1865.
W. P. Drumright	do	do	Aug. 25, 1865.
Michael Dennis	do	do	Aug. 25, 1865.
John B. Dozier	do	do	Aug. 25, 1865.
Joseph Donaldson	do	do	Oct. 18, 1865.
Davis Dawson	do	do	Oct. 18, 1865.
B. B. Dykes	do	do	Oct. 18, 1865.
William E. Dubose	do	do	Oct. 18, 1865.

Charles C. Dupont	do	do	Oct. 18, 1865.
John C. Drake	do	do	Oct. 18, 1865.
Samuel E. Daniel	do	do	May 12, 1866.
Henry J. Dickerson	do	do	Oct. 25, 1865.
Edward Deumead	do	do	Aug. 28, 1865.
Ira E. Dupree	do	do	Aug. 28, 1865.
Charles Day	do	do	Aug. 28, 1865.
Elisha Davis	do	do	Aug. 28, 1865.
George W. Dye	do	do	Nov. 8, 1865.
G. L. Dening	do	do	Sept. 13, 1865.
James B. Dunwoody	do	do	July 5, 1866.
Thomas H. Dawson	do	do	July 5, 1866.
Mrs. A Damour	do	Governor Johnson and Major General Wilson	July 5. 1866.
Lemuel Dean	do	Governor Johnson	July 5, 1866.
Robert S. Dunlap	do	do	July 5, 1866.
John A. Douglass	do	do	Nov. 13, 1865.
W. Duncan	do	By order of the President	July 18, 1865.
Thomas H. Dawson	do	do	Mar. 1, 1866.
James C. Dunham	do	Governor Jenkins	April 25, 1866.
Henry J. Dickson	do	do	July 5. 1866.
Talbot Davidson	do	Governor Johnson	Nov. 8, 1865.
G. T. Dortic	dc	do	Nov. 8, 1865.
Israel P. Davis	dc	Governor Jenkins	Sept. 4, 1865.
William Daugherty	do	Governor Johnson and Joshua Hill	Sept. 26, 1866.
James F. Deven	do	Governor Johnson	Aug. 28, 1865.
B. F. Edwards	Ex-United States and rebel route agent	do	Oct. 25, 1865.
Charles E. Earnest	Rebel route agent	do	July 5, 1866.
W. H. Edwards	Rebel mail contractor	do	Oct. 2, 1865.
James T. Evans	do	do	Nov. 8, 1865.
Drury P. Evans	Rebel tax collector	do	Sept. 20, 1865.
Thomas S. Elliott	do	do	Nov. 8, 1865.
Charles H. Everett	Rebel postmaster and tithing agent	do	Oct. 18, 1865.
John Eberhart	Rebel postmaster and worth over $20,000	do	Nov. 8, 1865.
W. B. Ellington	Rebel postmaster	do	Oct. 18, 1865.
W. W. Everett	do	do	Oct. 10, 1865.
Alexander Erwin	Ex-United States and rebel postmaster	do	Oct. 25, 1865.
N. N. Edge	do	do	Oct. 2, 1865.
G. W. Emerson	Worth over $20,000	do	Oct. 6, 1865.
Josiah J. Everett	do	do	Oct. 18, 1865.
John Edmundson	do	do	Oct. 18, 1865.
Philoclea E. Eve	do	do	Oct. 28, 1865.
Mrs. Sarah G. Early	do	do	Oct. 2, 1865.
Simeon C. Ellington	do	do	Oct. 2, 1865.
Joseph A. Eve	do	do	Sept. 28, 1865.
Charles A. Ells	do	do	Sept. 16, 1865.
Henderson S. Estes	do	do	Sept. 23, 1865.
James Ennis	do	do	Sept. 23, 1865.
James R. Elliott	do	do	Sept. 25, 1865.
James A. Everett	do	do	Sept. 28, 1865.
William Ezzard	do	do	Sept. 4, 1865.
John C. Epps	do	do	Sept. 25, 1865.
E. C. Ellington	do	do	Aug. 28, 1865.

Georgia—Continued.

Name.	Exemption under amnesty proclamation of May 29, 1865.	By whom recommended.	Date of pardon.
Henry H. Epping	Worth over $20,000	Governor Johnson	Aug. 28, 1865.
J. W. B. Edwards	do	do	Aug. 31, 1865.
Joel M. Estes	do	do	Sept. 11, 1865.
Charles Estes	do	Joshua Hill, William H. Stark, (president of Union Club, Savannah, Ga.,) W. R. Kenney, and H. E. McPrince, of New York.	June 27, 1865.
J. A. Everett	do	Governor Jenkins	May 1, 1866.
Carl Epping	do	Hon. James M. Wayne, associate justice of the Supreme Court of the United States, and Attorney General Speed.	Oct. 16, 1865.
Thomas W. Fleming	Ex-United States and rebel surveyor of the port of Augusta.	Governor Johnson, W. E. Jackson, W. J. Owens, S. D. Heard, Plumb & Leitner, W. C. Jones, Robert H. May, J. M. Newby, Edward Thomas, George T. Jackson & Co., D. L. Adams, Charles J. Jenkins, Henry Moore, E. Starnes, George Schley, John Schley, and Henry H. Cumming.	Sept. 25, 1865.
Francis M. Fuller	Rebel quartermaster's agent	Governor Johnson	Oct. 25, 1865.
Leroy Fleetwood	Rebel tithing agent	do	Oct. 2, 1865.
John J. Floyd	Rebel commissioner, and worth over $20,000	do	Sept. 28, 1865.
John C. Ferrill	Rebel depositary, and worth over $20,000	do	Apr. 30, 1866.
James W. Furlow	Rebel tax collector, and worth over $20,000	do	Sept. 25, 1865.
Timothy M. Furlow	do	do	Sept. 25, 1865.
John M. Freeman	Rebel tax collector	do	Sept. 16, 1865.
Henry A. Fuller	Rebel tax assessor	do	Aug. 28, 1865.
Samuel T. Feagin	do	do	Sept. 25, 1865.
Albert Fuller	Rebel mail contractor	do	Oct. 18, 1865.
Francis M. Fielder	do	do	Oct. 18, 1865.
F. A. Finch	Rebel postmaster	do	Sept. 25, 1865.
Thomas Fleming	do	do	Sept. 16, 1865.
John Fale	do	do	Oct. 25, 1865.
James Farrilea	do	do	Oct. 28, 1865.
Benjamin Fordham, jr	do	do	Oct. 18, 1865.
John C. Fudge	do	do	July 5, 1866.
Andrew F. Fraser	do	do	July 5, 1866.
Mercer Fain	do	do	Nov. 8, 1865.
S. H. Freeman	do	Governor Jenkins	May 9, 1866.
Hugh Farrier	Worth over $20,000	Governor Johnson	Sept. 25, 1865.
George W. Faulk	do	do	Sept. 25, 1865.
John Faulk	do	do	Sept. 25, 1865.
Calvin W. Felder	do	do	Sept. 25, 1865.
Francis W. Forth	do	do	Sept. 25, 1865.
David Flanders	do	do	Sept. 4, 1865.
John Fitzpatrick	do	do	Sept. 4, 1865.
William Fraley	do	do	Sept. 4, 1865.
O. P. Fitzsimmons	do	do	Aug. 25, 1865.
Lewis D. Ford	do	do	Aug. 25, 1865.
Francis A. Frost	do	do	Aug. 31, 1865.
James H. Fannin	do	do	Aug. 31, 1865.

James M. Flowers	do	do	Aug. 31, 1865.
Blount C. Ferrell	do	do	Aug. 31, 1865.
James A. Fort	do	do	Aug. 25, 1865.
James Fitzgerald	do	do	Aug. 25, 1865.
F. M. Fisk	do	Attorney General Speed	Aug. 25, 1865.
M. C. Fulton	do	Governor Johnson	Aug. 28, 1865.
John Foster	do	do	Aug. 28, 1865.
J. C. Fargo	do	do	Aug. 28, 1865.
Leroy M. Felton	do	do	Aug. 28, 1865.
James Freeman	do	do	Aug. 28, 1865.
John R. Freeman	do	do	Aug. 28, 1865.
W. H. Felton	do	do	Aug. 28, 1865.
James. C. Freeman	do	do	Aug. 28, 1865.
Mrs. V. F. Fulton	do	Attorney General Speed	Oct. 2, 1865.
Welcome Fanning	do	Governor Johnson	Sept. 25, 1865.
Josiah Freeman	do	do	Oct. 6, 1865.
James M. Field	do	do	Oct. 6, 1865.
B. W. Fortson	do	do	Oct. 2, 1865.
Abner C. Flewellen	do	do	Oct. 2, 1865.
Zeno Fitzpatrick	do	do	Oct. 2, 1865.
G. M. T. Feagin	do	do	Oct. 2, 1865.
William Faulk	do	Hon. James M. Wayne, associate justice of the Supreme Court of the United States	Aug. 4, 1865.
F. Ficklen	do	Governor Johnson	Sept. 28, 1865.
Stephen Felker	do	do	Sept. 28, 1865.
Charles Fisher	do	do	Sept. 20, 1865.
N. G. Foster	do	do	Sept. 20, 1865.
Isham S. Fannin	do	Governor Johnson and Joshua Hill	Sept. 20, 1865.
Mrs. Martha L. Fort	do	Governor Johnson	Sept. 20, 1865.
George W. Fort	do	do	Sept. 20, 1865.
John Faver	do	do	Sept. 28, 1865.
Elias E. Field	do	do	Sept. 23, 1865.
Daniel Frederick	do	do	Sept. 28, 1865.
Samuel Felder	do	do	Sept. 28, 1865.
George W. Fish	do	do	Sept. 16, 1865.
William A. Fort	do	do	Sept. 16, 1865.
J. W. Fears	do	do	Sept. 16, 1865.
Edward L. Felder	do	do	Sept. 28, 1865.
T. S. Fonlaine	do	do	Sept. 11, 1865.
Charles R. Faulk	do	Hon. James M. Wayne, associate justice of the Supreme Court of the United States	Aug. 4, 1865.
James H. Flynt	do	Governor Johnson	Oct. 28, 1865.
Porter Fleming	do	do	Aug. 26, 1865.
Ira R. Foster	do	Governor Jenkins	July 5, 1866.
John H. Fitten	do	Governor Johnson	July 5, 1866.
Benjamin B. Fontaine	do	do	Nov. 8, 1865.
G. R. Fairbanks	do	Governor Marvin, of Florida	Dec. 22, 1865.
C. E. Groover	Member of rebel legislature, and worth over $20,000	Captain Burdett, post commander	July 5, 1866.
Daniel Griffin	Ex-United States and rebel mail contractor, and worth over $20,000.	Governor Johnson	Aug. 25, 1865.
A. Guyton	Rebel mail contractor	do	July 5, 1866.
Thomas A. Grace	Rebel tax assessor	do	Oct. 2, 1865.
N. J. Garrison	do	do	Oct. 18, 1865.
James W. Green	Rebel tax collector	do	Oct. 6, 1865.

Georgia—Continued.

Name.	Exemption under amnesty proclamation of May 29, 1865.	By whom recommended.	Date of pardon.
Isaac M. Griffin	Rebel tax collector	Governor Johnson	Oct. 2, 1865.
William H. Gilbert	do	do	Sept. 4, 1865.
Joseph F. Garner	do	do	Sept. 4, 1865.
Joel L. Galt	do	do	Oct. 18, 1865.
P. G. Garrison	do	do	Oct. 18, 1865.
L. H. Griffith	Rebel postmaster	do	Oct. 2, 1865.
James W. Godkin	do	do	Sept. 28, 1865.
W. H. Griffith	do	do	Sept. 16, 1865.
William H. Gilliam	do	do	Sept. 16, 1865.
William Goldsberry	do	do	Sept. 11, 1865.
Luther H. Greenleaf	do	Governor Johnson and C. H. Hopkins	Oct. 18, 1865.
David Gay	do	Governor Johnson	Oct. 18, 1865.
William F. Groves	do	do	Oct. 2, 1865.
Charles W. Gee	do	do	Oct. 10, 1865.
Nathan Gunnels	Ex-United States and rebel postmaster, and rebel tax assessor.	do	Sept. 16, 1865.
T. S. Garrison	Ex-United States and rebel postmaster	do	Sept. 16, 1865.
Ansalam Graham	do	do	Oct. 28, 1865.
Lucius Goddard	do	do	Oct. 18, 1865.
E. H. Growby	do	do	Nov. 15, 1865.
Robert T. Gray	do	do	Oct. 10, 1865.
W. R. Gignilliat	Worth over $20,000	Governor Johnson and Senator Dixon	Nov. 15, 1865.
Norman P. Gignilliat	do	Governor Johnson	Oct. 2, 1865.
Edmund B. Gresham	do	do	Oct. 13, 1865.
James Grubbs	do	do	Oct. 13, 1865.
Samuel A. Grier	do	do	Oct. 6, 1865.
Springer Gibson	do	Governor Johnson and Augustus R. Wright	Oct. 6, 1865.
Thomas M. Gordon	do	Governor Johnson	Oct. 2, 1865.
Leonard Greer	do	do	Oct. 2, 1865.
J. T. Gray	do	do	Oct. 2, 1865.
Moses Guyton	do	do	Oct. 2, 1865.
John H. Graves	do	do	Oct. 2, 1865.
Thomas S. Gresham	do	do	Oct. 2, 1865.
George W. Gresham	do	do	Oct. 2, 1865.
Henry Glover	do	do	Oct. 2, 1865.
John O. Gartrell	do	do	Oct. 2, 1865.
J. McK. Gunn	do	do	Oct. 2, 1865.
Jackson Graham	do	do	Sept. 28, 1865.
Alfred M. George	do	do	Sept. 28, 1865.
Cincinnatus S. Guyton	do	do	Sept. 28, 1865.
P. A. Guttinger	do	do	Sept. 28, 1865.
William W. Garrard	do	do	Sept. 23, 1865.
George Gibbon	do	do	Sept. 16, 1865.
Samuel Griswold	do	do	Sept. 16, 1865.

Myles L. Green	do	do	Sept. 16, 1865.
James L. Grant	do	do	Sept. 16, 1865.
R. M. Gunby	do	do	Sept. 11, 1865.
William D. Grant	do	do	Sept. 11, 1865.
William Gray	do	do	Sept. 11, 1865.
Thomas Glover	do	do	Sept. 25, 1865.
William H. Green	do	do	Sept. 25, 1865.
Levi Gallemore	do	do	Sept. 25, 1865.
Nathaniel S. Glover	do	do	Sept. 4, 1865.
John T. Grant	do	do	Sept. 4, 1865.
L. P. Grant	do	do	Sept. 4, 1865.
Roger L. Gamble	do	do	Oct. 7, 1865.
Cardin Goolsby	do	do	Sept. 4, 1865.
John Gorham	do	do	Aug. 31, 1865.
Charles S. Gaulden	do	Governor Johnson and Major Hastings, commanding post	Aug. 28, 1865.
John G. Gilmer	do	Governor Johnson	Aug. 28, 1865.
Richard P. Glem	do	do	Aug. 28, 1865.
John J. Gresham	do	Hon. James M. Wayne, associate justice of the Supreme Court of the United States	Aug. 4, 1865.
R. J. F. Grist	do	do	Aug. 4, 1865.
Taylor F. Gibson	do	do	Aug. 4, 1865.
A. Gould	do	Governor Johnson	Aug. 28, 1865.
William H. Goodrich	do	do	Aug. 28, 1865.
Harriet G. Gould	do	do	Oct. 28, 1865.
John R. Greer	do	do	Oct. 28, 1865.
William B. Griffin	do	do	Oct. 28, 1865.
James S. Green	do	do	Oct. 25, 1865.
Nathaniel E. Gardner	do	do	Oct. 25, 1865.
G. W. Garmany	do	do	Nov. 17, 1865.
Etheldred Griffin	do	do	July 5, 1866.
Barnard E. Guerard	do	Governor Jenkins	July 5, 1866.
Hill Gowdy	do	do	July 5, 1866.
J. A. Gray	do	Governor Johnson	July 5, 1866.
William W. Gerrard	do	do	Mar. 8, 1866.
James M. Green	do	do	Nov. 8, 1865.
Sarah V. Green	do	do	Nov. 8, 1865.
Moses P. Green	do	do	Nov. 8, 1865.
William E. Green	do	do	Nov. 8, 1865.
John D. Gray	do	do	Nov. 8, 1865.
Joseph Gartrell	do	do	Sept. 25, 1865.
Z. H. Gordon	do	do	Sept. 20, 1865.
Charles Green	do	J. D. Webster, brigadier general of volunteers, and A. Mawyer, lieutenant colonel, assistant adjutant general military division of Mississippi.	July 29, 1865.
F. L. Gué	Member of rebel State legislature, and worth over $20,000.	Attorney General Speed	July 18, 1865.
Duff Green	Worth over $20,000	Hon. Robert J. Walker, Hon. Thomas Corwin, and J. H. R. Washington	
Hugh F. Grant	do	Governor Jenkins	May 2, 1866.
William H. Gibbons	do	F. S. Lathrop, New York; William Marvin, Charles T. Baker	July 6, 1865.
Riley Garrett	do	Governor Johnson	Oct. 2, 1865.
Hines Holt	Member of rebel congress, and worth over $20,000	do	Aug. 29, 1865.
Thomas Hardeman	Left seat in United States Congress to aid rebellion	Governor Johnson and Frank White, lieutenant colonel commanding	Aug. 28, 1865.
Elijah Hawkins	Left a loyal district	Hon. James M. Wayne, associate justice of the Supreme Court of the United States	Aug 4, 1865.
James U. Horne	Rebel depositary and worth over $20,000	Governor Johnson	Sept. 2, 1865.

Georgia—Continued.

Name.	Exemption under amnesty proclamation of May 29, 1865.	By whom recommended.	Date of pardon.
R. L. Harris	Rebel depositary of the treasury	Governor Johnson	Oct. 18, 1865.
Henry Hull, jr	do	Hon. James M. Wayne, associate justice of the Supreme Court of the United States	Aug. 4, 1865.
W. H. Hunt	Rebel clerk of district court	Governor Johnson	Sept. 11, 1865.
James M. Hamilton	Rebel purchasing agent	do	Oct. 6, 1865.
S. B. Hoyt	Rebel commissioner	do	Sept. 13, 1865.
Robert H. Hardaway	Rebel funding agent	Governor Jenkins	Nov. 26, 1866.
Daniel P. Hill	Member of rebel house of representatives, and worth over $20,000.	Governor Johnson	Oct. 2 1865.
Robert Holland	Left a loyal district and worth over $20,000	Attorney General Speed	Sept. 11, 1865.
Henry Hull, jr.	Rebel depositary, and worth over $20,000	Governor Johnson	Oct. 2, 1865.
D. F. Hammond	Rebel commissioner for the northern district of Ga.	do	Oct. 2, 1865.
William Hope Hull	Commissioner of rebel district court	Hon. James M. Wayne, associate justice of the Supreme Court of the United States	Aug. 4, 1865.
Edward J. Harden	Rebel judge for the district of Georgia and under bonds to the United States military authorities.	Governor Johnson	Oct. 28, 1865.
Henry E. Hyman	Rebel purchasing agent and postmaster	do	Sept. 16, 1865.
George G. Hillyer	Rebel auditor	do	Sept. 4, 1865.
F. M. Hernden	Rebel mail contractor	do	Oct. 10, 1865.
George W. Humphrey	do	do	Aug. 31, 1865.
Frederick S. Hunt	Ex-United States and rebel route agent	do	Oct. 18, 1865.
S. P. Harris	do	do	Nov 15, 1865.
T. A. Hammond	Rebel route agent	do	Sept. 20, 1865.
James S. Hamilton	Rebel tax assessor and worth over $20,000	do	Aug. 31, 1865.
Francis A. Huson	do	do	Sept. 15, 1865.
T. W. Hutchison	do	do	Sept. 16, 1865.
William J. Hudson	Rebel tax assessor	do	Sept. 23, 1865.
C. Howell	do	do	Sept. 16, 1865.
J. W. Hancock	do	do	Oct. 28, 1865.
Cuyler W. Hilliard	do	do	Oct. 18, 1865.
J. D. Hammock	do	do	Nov. 15, 1865.
William M. Harlett	do	do	Oct. 10, 1865.
P. F. Hoyle	Rebel tax collector	do	Sept. 4, 1865.
Jordan L. Howell	do	do	Sept. 16, 1865.
F. G. Hughs	do	do	Nov. 8, 1865.
Thomas J. Haralson	Rebel tax assessor and postmaster	do	Nov. 8, 1865.
David Howard	Rebel postmaster and tax collector	do	Oct. 10, 1865.
Daniel B. Hack	Rebel postmaster and worth over $20,000	do	Sept. 4, 1865.
James Hutcheson	do	do	Sept. 16, 1865.
J. H. Hatcher	Rebel postmaster	do	Sept. 11, 1865.
Robert T. Hames	do	do	Sept. 25, 1865.
Benjamin F. Hall	do	do	Aug. 25, 1865.
Thomas W. Hollaway	do	do	Oct. 6, 1865.
S. D. Henderson	do	do	Oct. 28, 1865.
Henry Harrison	do	do	Oct. 18, 1865.
Arthur Hain	do	do	Oct. 18, 1865.

Nathan Howard	do	do	Oct. 18, 1865.
James H. Heidt	do	do	Oct. 18, 1865.
David W. Humphreys	do	do	Nov. 15, 1865.
Richard A. Henderson	do	do	Nov. 8, 1865.
Benjamin W. Holt	do	do	Nov. 8, 1865.
Thomas C. Howard	do	do	Nov. 8, 1865.
Charles Hargrove	do	do	Oct. 18, 1865.
S. B. Henderson	do	do	Oct. 18, 1865.
Daniel S. Hopping	do	Governor Patton, of Alabama	July 5, 1866.
J. H. Harrison	do	By order of the President	July 14, 1866.
William P. Hames	Ex-United States and rebel postmaster	Governor Johnson	Sept. 25, 1865.
N. N. Howard	do	do	Sept. 11, 1865.
John J. Hamilton	do	do	Sept. 28, 1865.
William B. Hunt	do	do	Oct. 26, 1865.
James L. Harris	do	do	Sept. 16, 1865.
A. T. Hardin	do	do	Sept. 16, 1865.
Reuben Holcombe	do	do	Oct. 18, 1865.
Simeon Harrell	do	do	Oct. 18, 1865.
John B. Hattaway	do	Governor Johnson and Joshua Hill	Sept. 13, 1865.
Thomas M. Hamilton	do	Governor Johnson	July 5, 1866.
William Hassier	do	do	July 5, 1866.
William Hearn	do	do	Oct. 10, 1865.
William R. Henny	do	do	Nov. 8, 1865.
J. W. Horton	Worth over $20,000	do	Oct. 23, 1865.
John H. Hose	do	do	Sept. 28, 1865.
Julian A. Hayden	do	do	Sept. 16, 1865.
Erastus C. Hood	do	do	Sept. 16, 1865.
David H. Hill	do	do	Sept. 25, 1865.
Haywood Hughes	do	do	Sept. 25, 1865.
George G. Hull	do	do	Sept. 4, 1865.
William M. Hight	do	do	Sept. 4, 1865.
Miles G. Harris	do	do	Sept. 4, 1865.
Thomas Humphreys	do	do	Sept. 15, 1865.
Benjamin T. Harris	do	do	Sept. 4, 1865.
James M. Harris	do	do	Sept. 4, 1865.
Asbury Hull	do	Hon. James M. Wayne and Governor Johnson	Aug. 4, 1865.
W. H. Howard	do	do	Aug. 25, 1865.
John Hogg	do	do	Aug. 31, 1865.
Waid Hill	do	do	Aug. 31, 1865.
James Hines	do	do	Aug. 31, 1865.
Henry R. Harris	do	do	Aug. 31, 1865.
A. S. Harris	do	do	Aug. 31, 1865.
Charles A. Harris	do	do	Aug. 25, 1865.
James Harrison	do	do	Aug. 25, 1865.
Robert A. Hardwick	do	do	Aug. 25, 1865.
Thomas J. Hines	do	do	Aug. 25, 1865.
William Herring	do	do	Aug. 21, 1865.
Benjamin Harris	do	do	Aug. 28, 1865.
John W. Harris	do	do	Aug. 28, 1865.
James Hicks	do	do	Aug. 28, 1865.
Henry Hurt	do	do	Aug. 28, 1865.
Benjamin B. Hamilton	do	do	Aug. 28, 1865.

Georgia—Continued.

Name.	Exemption under amnesty proclamation of May 29, 1865.	By whom recommended.	Date of pardon.
John W. Hurt	Worth over $20,000	Hon. James M. Wayne and Governor Johnson	Aug. 28, 1865.
William M. Harlam	do	do	Aug. 28, 1865.
F. A. Hurt	do	do	Aug. 28, 1865.
William A. Huff	do	dc	Aug. 28, 1865.
Daniel G. Hughes	do	Hon. James M. Wayne, associate justice of the Supreme Court of the United States	Aug. 4, 1865.
Pulaski S. Holt	do	do	Aug. 4, 1865.
T. G. Holt, sr.	do	do	Aug. 4, 1865.
William S. Holt	do	do	Aug. 4, 1865.
Haydon Hughes	do	do	Aug. 4, 1865.
Nathan Hawkins	do	do	Aug. 4, 1865.
Walter B. Heyward	do	Governor Johnson	Aug. 28, 1865.
William M. Heard	do	do	Aug. 25, 1865.
Edmund C. Hardaway	do	do	Sept. 11, 1865.
Lodowick M. Hill	do	do	Sept. 4, 1865.
H. H. Hickman	do	do	Aug. 28, 1865.
Marcus D. Huson	do	do	Aug. 25, 1865.
John Hollingsworth	do	do	Sept. 4, 1865.
Nathan L. Hutchins	do	do	Oct. 6, 1865.
William H. Hughes	do	do	Oct. 6, 1865.
Mrs. Mary A. Hood	do	do	Oct. 6, 1865.
B. F. Hooper	do	do	Oct. 6, 1865.
James S. Hamilton	do	do	Oct. 6, 1865.
John W. Hinton	do	do	Oct. 2, 1865.
A. J. Hansell	do	do	Oct. 2, 1865.
William B. Hall	do	do	Oct. 2, 1865.
Daniel Hougabook	do	do	Oct. 2, 1865.
William Harris	do	do	Oct. 2, 1865.
Edward S. Harrison	do	do	Oct. 2, 1865.
James M. Harris	do	do	Oct. 2, 1865.
Louis Halman	do	do	Oct. 2, 1865.
Mason J. Huguley	do	do	Oct. 2, 1865.
Thomas C. Hogue	do	do	Oct. 2, 1865.
Thomas J. Hamilton	do	do	Oct. 2, 1865.
William J. Harley	do	dc	Oct. 2, 1865.
B. F. Hardeman	do	do	Sept. 28, 1865.
Ambrose Hunley	do	do	Sept. 28, 1865.
John F. Hollis	do	do	Sept. 28, 1865.
William W. Hughes	do	do	Oct. 13, 1865.
J. Gordon Howard	do	do	Oct. 13, 1865.
F. S. Heam, sr.	do	do	Oct. 12, 1865.
Lemuel L. Hoon	do	do	Oct. 18, 1865.
Henry T. Hall	do	do	Sept. 23, 1865.
Benjamin Harris	do	do	Sept. 20, 1865.
Robert M. Hooke	do	do	Sept. 20, 1865.

Young L. G. Harris	do	do	Sept. 16, 1865.
M. S. High	do	do	Sept. 16, 1865.
David H. Houser	do	do	Sept. 16, 1865.
William P. Head	do	do	Sept. 16, 1865.
J. R. Holliday	do	do	Sept. 16, 1865.
George J. Haslam	do	do	Oct. 28, 1865.
Isaac Holmes	do	do	Oct. 28, 1865.
George Hargroves	do	do	Sept. 11, 1865.
B. W. Heard	do	do	Sept. 25, 1865.
Mrs. S. S. Hamilton	do	Attorney General Speed	Oct. 2, 1865.
J. J. Howard	do	Governor Johnson	Nov. 17, 1865.
Juriah Harriss	do	do	Oct. 28, 1865.
John W. Harriss	do	do	Oct. 18, 1865.
Henry Horne	do	do	Oct. 18, 1865.
John M. Hill	do	do	Oct. 18, 1865.
Joseph H. Hines	do	do	Oct. 18, 1865.
Isaac J. Hartsfield	do	do	Nov. 15, 1865.
Noble A. Hardee	do	do	Nov. 13, 1865.
Robert Habersham	do	do	Nov. 13, 1865.
A. S. Hartridge	do	Major General Birge commanding	July 24, 1865.
C. B. Howard	do	Governor Jenkins	Feb. 20, 1866.
William Habersham	do	Governor Jenkins and U. S. Senator E. D. Morgan	Jan. 26, 1866.
Miss Susan J. Howard	do	Governor Johnson	Sept. 18, 1865.
Thomas H. Hodgkiss	do	do	Oct. 9, 1865.
Mrs. Sophia Harriss	do	Governor Jenkins	Jan. 15, 1866.
James Hicks	do	Governor Johnson	Nov. 8, 1865.
William B. Hodgson	do	Hon. James M. Wayne, associate justice of the Supreme Court of the United States	Sept. 16, 1865.
John T. Henderson	do	Governor Johnson	July 5, 1866.
Robert G. Harper	do	do	July 5, 1866.
James Hilliard	do	do	July 5, 1866.
Robert S. Hardaway	do	do	July 5, 1866.
Richard Huff	do	do	July 5, 1866.
Henrietta W. Hill	do	Governor Jenkins	July 5, 1866.
Henry P. Hill	do	do	July 5, 1866.
Herrman Hersh	do	do	July 5, 1866.
L. W. Hazlehurst	do	Governor Johnson	July 5, 1866.
W. M. Habersham	do	Major General Birge commanding	July 24, 1865.
Joshua Hill	do	By order of the President	June 22, 1865.
Mary G. Harrison	do	Governor Jenkins	Nov. 1, 1866.
Henry W. Hilliard	Rebel commissioner to Tennessee	A. H. Lochrane	Sept. 14, 1865.
* James Harding	Left a loyal State, and rebel brigadier general	By order of the President	Aug. 25, 1865.
John Henry	Ex-United States and rebel postmaster	Governor Johnson	Oct. 10, 1865.
David Irwin	Rebel elector	By order of the President	July 24, 1865.
Samuel D. Irwin	Rebel tax collector	Governor Johnson	Aug. 28, 1865.
Charles M. Irwin	Rebel collector of supplies, and worth over $20,000	Hon. James M. Wayne, associate justice of the Supreme Court of the United States	Aug. 4, 1865.
Wm. A. Irwin	Rebel postmaster, and worth over $20,000	Governor Johnson	Sept. 16, 1865.
R. D. Ivey	Worth over $20,000	do	Oct. 6, 1865.
Stephen M. Ingersoll	do	do	Oct. 2, 1865.
Jeremiah Inman	do	do	Oct. 18, 1865.
Jeremiah S. Inman	do	do	Sept. 20, 1865.
Mary L. Inman	do	do	Sept. 20, 1865.
Jacob P. Illges	do	do	Sept. 11, 1865.

Georgia—Continued.

Name.	Exemption under amnesty proclamation of May 29, 1865.	By whom recommended.	Date of pardon.
John Irwin	Worth over $20,000	Governor Johnson	Aug. 28, 1865.
Abraham Illges	do	do	Aug. 25, 1865.
Allen E. Izard	do	By order of the President	Nov. 8, 1865.
James Jackson	Resigned his seat in United States Congress to aid the rebellion.	United States Senators Guthrie, Saulsbury, Cowan, Buckalew, Hendricks, and Davis.	July 26, 1866.
Herschel V. Johnson	Member of secession convention	By order of the President	Aug. 10, 1865.
Richard P. Johnson	Rebel route agent	Governor Johnson	Sept. 11 1865.
Charles H. Johnson	Rebel depositary	do	Aug. 28, 1865.
Thomas C. Johnson	Left a loyal State	Hon. Edward Bates and Governor Johnson	July 5, 1865.
Calvin E. Johnston	Rebel tithe agent, and worth over $20,000	Governor Johnson	Sept. 23, 1865.
Charles J. Jenkins	Rebel judge of supreme court of Georgia, and worth over $20,000.	do	Sept. 28, 1865.
W. B. Johnston	Rebel depositary, and worth over $20,000	Hon. James M. Wayne, associate justice of the Supreme Court of the United States, and Attorney General Speed.	July 25, 1865.
Charles K. Jarrett	Rebel postmaster and purchasing agent	Governor Johnson	Sept. 28, 1865.
Joseph B. Jones	Rebel postmaster, and worth over $20,000	do	Oct. 7, 1865.
E. M. Johnston	Rebel postmaster and tax collector	do	Oct. 2, 1865.
Huell A. Joyner	Rebel postmaster	do	Sept. 16, 1865.
Wm. E. Jones	do	do	July 5, 1866.
John W. Jordan	do	do	Oct. 2, 1865.
John W. Jackson	do	do	Nov. 8, 1865.
Henry M. Jeter	Ex-United States and rebel postmaster	do	Sept. 23, 1865.
Francis S. Johnson	Rebel tax assessor, and worth over $20,000	do	Oct. 2, 1865.
Wm. A. Juhan	Rebel tax assessor	do	Oct. 6, 1865.
Edward Jackson	do	do	Sept. 28, 1865.
George J. James	do	do	Aug. 31, 1865.
Josiah W. Jessey	do	do	Oct. 11, 1865.
John J. Justice	do	do	Nov. 8, 1865.
John H. Jones	Rebel tax collector, and worth over $20,000	do	Oct. 2, 1865.
Joseph M. Johnson	Rebel tax collector	do	Oct. 18, 1865.
John S. Jobson	do	do	Sept. 28, 1865.
Thomas H. Jones	do	do	Sept. 25, 1865.
B. F. Jordan	Worth over $20,000	do	Sept. 25, 1865.
Caroline E. Jones	do	do	Oct. 13, 1865.
A. S. Jones	do	do	Oct. 25, 1865.
James M. Jones	do	do	Oct. 18, 1865.
James W. Jackson	do	do	Oct. 18, 1865.
John R. Jenkins	do	do	Oct. 6, 1865.
A. A. Jernigan	do	do	Oct. 2, 1865.
A. M. Jenkins	do	do	Oct. 2, 1865.
W. M. Jordan	do	do	Oct. 2, 1865.
Edwin J. Jones	do	do	Oct. 2, 1865.
James V. Jones	do	do	Oct. 2, 1865.
Thomas J. Jennings	do	do	Oct. 2, 1865.

John Jackson	do	do	Oct. 2, 1865.
David H. James	do	do	Oct. 2, 1865.
Wm. C. Johnston	do	do	Sept. 23, 1865.
W. B. Jones	do	do	Sept. 20, 1865.
Elijah E. Jones	do	do	Sept. 20, 1865.
Lancelot Johnson	do	do	Sept. 20, 1865.
John E. Jackson	do	do	Sept. 16, 1865.
Walter E. Johnston	do	do	Sept. 16, 1865.
O. H. Jones	do	do	Sept. 25, 1865.
Malcolm D. Jones	do	do	Sept. 25, 1865.
Wm. C. Jessup	do	do	Sept. 28, 1865.
John A. Johnson	do	do	Sept. 25, 1865.
Vinson A. Johnson	do	do	Sept. 15, 1865.
Henry R. Johnson	do	do	Sept. 25, 1865.
Thomas S. Jones	do	do	Sept. 25, 1865.
Elias Jones	do	do	Sept. 25, 1865.
John E. Jones	do	do	Sept. 4, 1865.
John Jones	do	do	Sept. 4, 1865.
Benj. O. Jones	do	do	Sept. 4, 1865.
Adam Johnston	do	do	Sept. 4, 1865.
G. W. Jones	do	do	Sept. 4, 1865.
Henry L. Jewett	do	do	Sept. 4, 1865.
Robt. C. Jenkins	do	do	Sept. 13, 1865.
Thomas M. Jordan	do	do	Sept. 11, 1865.
Henry W. Jones	do	do	Oct. 7, 1865.
J. Jackson	do	W. L. Sharkey	Sept. 28, 1866.
William Jones	do	Governor Johnson	Aug. 25, 1865
Thomas Jennings	do	do	Aug. 31, 1865.
Wm. L. Jarrell	do	do	Aug. 25, 1865.
Horace M. Jenkins	do	do	Aug. 25, 1865.
Thomas Jones, sr	do	do	Aug. 28, 1865.
John L. Jones	do	do	Aug. 28, 1865.
Asa Jolly	do	do	Aug. 28, 1865.
Edwin T. Jones	do	Hon. James M. Wayne, associate justice of the Supreme Court of the United States	Aug. 4, 1865.
Thomas P. Janes	do	Governor Johnson	Aug. 25, 1865.
Wm. A. Jarratt	do	do	Aug. 25, 1865.
George T. Jackson	do	do	Sept. 4, 1865.
Wm. E. Jackson	do	do	Sept. 28, 1865.
Aaron M. Jones	do	do	Aug. 31, 1865.
Leonidas A. Jordan	do	do	Aug 31, 1865.
John Jones	do	Governor Jenkins	Apr. 11, 1866.
G. W. Jones	do	Hon. James M. Wayne, associate justice of the Supreme Court of the United States	Aug. 29, 1865.
Seaborn Jones, jr	do	Governor Jenkins	July 5, 1866.
A. R. Jones	do	do	July 5, 1866.
Wm. F. Janes	do	do	July 5, 1866.
David H. Janes	do	do	July 5, 1866.
Mrs. Mary M. Jones	do	do	July 21, 1866.
Charles C. Jones, jr	do	By order of the President	Dec. 1, 1866.
G. N. Jones	do	Hon. James M. Wayne, associate justice of the Supreme Court of the United States	Aug. 5, 1865.
A. M. Jackson	do	Governor Johnson	Nov. 8, 1865.
E. J. Johnston	do	Major General Wilson	Aug. 15, 1865.

Georgia—Continued.

Name.	Exemption under amnesty proclamation of May 29, 1865.	By whom recommended.	Date of pardon.
George Kellogg	Superintendent and treasurer of the United States branch mint, Georgia.	Governor Johnson	July 24, 1865.
J. S. Kramer	Left a loyal State	Governor Jenkins	July 5, 1866.
George Kramer	do	Governor Johnson	Aug. 28, 1865.
John J. Kelly	Clerk in rebel depository, and worth over $20,000	do	Sept. 23, 1865.
George L. Kilpatrick	Rebel mail contractor	do	Aug. 29, 1865.
R. B. Knight	Rebel assessor and clerk of the general assembly of Georgia.	do	July 5, 1866.
Rufus L. King	Rebel tax assessor	do	Oct. 18, 1865.
John R. Kay	do	do	Sept. 28, 1865.
John H. King	Rebel tax collector	do	Nov. 13, 1865.
Elisha F. Kirksey	do	do	Aug. 25, 1865.
David Knott	Ex-United States and rebel postmaster	do	Nov. 8, 1865.
Henry J. Knight	do	do	July 5, 1866.
Samuel Knox	do	do	Sept. 16, 1865.
Lemuel Kendrick	Rebel postmaster	do	July 5, 1866.
Benj. B. Keaton	do	do	July 5, 1866.
Daniel W. Killian	do	do	July 5, 1866.
Philip Kitterer	do	do	Oct. 18, 1865.
W. J. Kiser	do	do	Oct. 25, 1865.
A. Keeter	do	do	Oct. 28, 1865.
George Kellogg	do	do	Nov. 8, 1865.
Robt. C. Kerr	Worth over $20,000	do	Sept. 4, 1865.
McMillan C. King	do	Hon. James M. Wayne, associate justice of the Supreme Court of the United States	July 11, 1865.
Noah B. Knapp	do	do	July 21, 1865.
John Kincaid	do	Governor Jenkins	July 5, 1866.
James Kirlin	do	do	July 5, 1866.
James Kirksey	do	Governor Johnson and G. A. Hastings, major 12th Maine volunteers, commanding post.	Aug. 21, 1865.
Henry King	do	Governor Johnson	Aug. 21, 1865.
John Kirkpatrick	do	do	Sept. 4, 1865.
Beloved L. Kinebrough	do	do	Aug. 25, 1865.
Erastus Kirtland	do	Governor Johnson and Major General Wilson	Aug. 25, 1865.
James R. King	do	Governor Johnson	Sept. 4, 1865.
John F. Kinsey	do	do	Sept. 15, 1865.
Allen Kennedy	do	do	Sept. 11, 1865.
Joseph Kyle	do	do	Sept. 11, 1865.
John R. King	do	do	Oct. 25, 1865.
Noah King	do	do	Oct. 25, 1865.
Wm. B. Kendrick	do	do	May 12, 1866.
John Killen	do	do	Sept. 28, 1865.
Wesley King	do	do	Sept. 16, 1865.
Thomas Kile	do	do	Sept. 20, 1865.
Daniel Kirkpatrick	do	do	Sept. 20, 1865.
Nancy Kolb	do	Governor Johnson and Joshua Hill	Sept. 20, 1865.

T. M. Kirkpatrick	do	Governor Johnson	Sept. 26, 1865.
Thomas D. Key	do	do	Oct. 13, 1865.
J. S. Key	do	do	Oct. 13, 1865.
Barrington King	do	do	Oct. 2, 1865.
Jesse B. Key	do	do	Oct. 2, 1865.
A. R. Lamar	Clerk of rebel congress	do	Oct. 28, 1865.
Joseph H. Lumpkin	Rebel judge	do	Aug. 25, 1865.
H. H. Linville	Paroled prisoner of war	John Gammell, Edward Paddleford, and George W. Wyley	July 3, 1865.
Thomas E. Lloyd	Member of rebel State legislature, and worth over $20,000.	Hon. James M. Wayne and Governor Johnson	Aug. 28, 1865.
J. C. Levy	Property in possession of agent of United States Treasury Department, and worth over $20,000.	Governor Johnson	Sept. 2, 1865.
Wm. C. Leavitt	Rebel purchasing agent, and worth over $20,000	do	Sept. 11, 1865.
Enoch Louis Lowe	Left a loyal State, and worth over $20,000	Hon. James M. Wayne, associate justice of the Supreme Court of the United States, Hon. Simon Cameron, and Governor Johnson.	Mar. 14, 1866.
Eben. E. Little	Rebel tax assessor	Governor Johnson	Oct. 10, 1865.
Edward C. Legriel	Rebel tax collector	Hon. James M. Wayne, associate justice of the Supreme Court of the United States	Aug. 4, 1865.
Joseph A. L. Lee	do	Governor Johnson	Sept. 16, 1865.
Lucius A. Luke	do	do	Sept. 16, 1865.
Edward R. Lewis	Rebel mail contractor	do	Sept. 28, 1865.
Franklin Lane	do	do	July 5, 1866.
Henry D. Leitner	Ex-United States and rebel postmaster	do	Aug. 28, 1865.
Joseph B. Long	do	do	Nov. 8, 1865.
Eliel Lockhart	do	do	Sept. 16, 1865.
Emery Lasetter	Rebel postmaster, and worth over $20,000	do	Oct. 10, 1865.
Anderson Little	Rebel postmaster and commissary agent	do	Oct. 10, 1865.
John Logan	Rebel postmaster	do	Nov. 8, 1865.
Dilmus R. Lyle	do	do	Sept. 16, 1865.
John F. Lewis	do	do	Oct. 6, 1865.
W. F. Landrum	do	do	Oct. 6, 1865.
Alfred Lanzenby	do	do	Sept. 11, 1865.
A. J. Lyon	do	do	Nov. 8, 1865.
Anderson Leslie	do	do	Oct. 25, 1865.
W. T. Loftin	do	do	Oct. 18, 1865.
Wm. H. Logan	do	do	Aug. 25, 1865.
John Logan	do	do	Aug. 25, 1865.
James Lassetter	do	do	Oct. 2, 1865.
Augustus Lamkin	Worth over $20,000	do	Sept. 4, 1865.
Mrs. Elizabeth F. Lamkin	do	do	Sept. 4, 1865.
W. T. Lightfoot	do	do	Sept. 4, 1865.
Sherwood C. Lindsay	do	do	Sept. 11, 1865.
Edward Lovell	do	do	Sept. 11, 1865.
John H. Lowe	do	do	Sept. 2, 1865.
B. B. Lewis	do	do	Sept. 2, 1865.
Robert Lachison	do	do	Sept. 4, 1865.
S. D. Linton	do	do	Aug. 25, 1865.
Andrew J. Lane	do	do	Sept. 19, 1865.
Wm. S. Lawson	do	do	Aug. 31, 1865.
Lucius Lovelace	do	do	Aug. 31, 1865.
Hugh G. Lyle	do	do	Aug. 25, 1865.
Jephtha Landrum	do	do	Aug. 28, 1865.
John Low	do	do	Aug. 28, 1865.

Georgia—Continued.

Name.	Exemption under amnesty proclamation of May 29, 1865.	By whom recommended.	Date of pardon.
M. W. Linton	Worth over $20,000	Governor Johnson	Aug. 28, 1865.
James A. Linton	do	do	Aug. 28, 1865.
Benj. G. Lockett	do	do	Aug. 28, 1865.
John P. Lamar	do	do	Aug. 28, 1865.
Henry J. Lamar	do	do	Aug. 28, 1865.
Wm. J. Lawton	do	do	Aug. 28, 1865.
F. Lamback	do	do	Aug. 28, 1865.
John B. Lewis	do	do	Aug. 28, 1865.
Seaborn J. Lawrence	do	do	Oct. 6, 1865.
S. H. Lockett	do	do	Oct. 2, 1865.
Henry R. J. Long	do	do	Oct. 2, 1865.
Crawford W. Long	do	do	Oct. 2, 1865.
Richard A. Lane	do	do	Oct. 2, 1865.
Benj. G. Lockett	do	do	Oct. 2, 1865.
John S. Linton	do	do	Sept. 28, 1865.
Frederick W. Lucas	do	do	Sept. 28, 1865.
Thomas A. Lyne	do	do	Sept. 28, 1865.
Richard F. Lyon	do	do	Oct. 13, 1865.
James C. Lark	do	do	Sept. 28, 1865.
James S. Latimer	do	do	Sept. 25, 1865.
A. E. Lawson	do	do	Sept. 16, 1865.
James Lynch	do	do	Sept. 16, 1865.
E. B. Loyless	do	do	Sept. 16, 1865.
James Laramore	do	do	Oct. 30, 1865.
James S. Lawton	do	do	Oct. 30, 1865.
Wm. W. Lawson	do	do	Oct. 25, 1865.
James L. Leonard	do	do	Oct. 18, 1865.
David Lockhart	do	do	Oct. 18, 1865.
Joseph Lippman	do	do	Oct. 18, 1865.
Thomas B. Lamar	do	do	Mar. 8, 1866.
O. W. Lillibridge	do	do	Aug. 25, 1865.
Benj. F. Linton	do	do	Aug. 28, 1865.
David L. Little	do	do	Apr. 11, 1866.
Wm. F. Little	do	do	July 5, 1866.
Isaac D. Laroche	do	Governor Jenkins	July 5, 1866.
S. J. Lazenby	do	do	July 5, 1866.
Mrs. Margaret Little	do	do	July 5, 1866.
Andrew J. Lamar	do	Governor Johnson	July 5, 1866.
Henry Lewis	do	do	Nov. 8, 1865.
Charles F. Lay	do	do	Nov. 8, 1865.
J. W. Lathrop	do	do	Nov. 8, 1865.
William Law	do	H. W. Birge, brevet major general, commanding	July 24, 1865.
Andrew Low	do	By order of the President	July 18, 1865.
G. B. Lamar	do	Attorney General Speed and W. M. Evarts, New York	July 19, 1865.
		Attorney General Stanbery	Oct. 22, 1866.

John W. Lewis	Member of rebel congress, and worth over $20,000.	By order of the President	July 15, 1865.
Benj. L. Lane	Worth over $20,000	Governor Johnson	Mar. 26, 1865.
Henry K. McCay	Rebel brigadier general	do	Sept. 25, 1865.
James Milner	Rebel commissioner of claims	do	July 24, 1865.
R. A. Mathews	Officer of the rebel treasury department, and mail contractor.	do	May 26, 1866.
Thomas S. Metcalf	Rebel depositary	Q. A. Gilmore, major general commanding	June 27, 1865.
J. F. McCleskey	Rebel deputy marshal	Governor Jenkins	July 5, 1866.
Andrew Mosteller	Petty civil officer	Governor Johnson	Nov. 13, 1865.
C. J. McDowell	do	do	Aug. 31, 1865.
John E. Morgan	do	do	Aug. 31, 1865.
Alexander McDuffie	Rebel mail contractor	do	Oct. 18, 1865.
A. J. Morris	do	do	Sept. 16, 1865.
E. A. Mitchell	do	do	Sept. 16, 1865.
Stephen A. Major	do	do	July 5, 1866.
William G. McAdoo	Left a loyal State, and clerk of rebel court	do	Aug. 28, 1865.
H. Marshall	Left a loyal State	Governor Jenkins	May 28, 1866.
E. B. Marshall	do	do	July 5, 1866.
L. F. M. Mills	Ex-United States and rebel route agent	Governor Johnson	Nov. 8, 1865.
J. G. W. Mills	do	do	Aug. 25, 1865.
Silas B. McGregor	Rebel postmaster, and tax collector	do	Oct. 2, 1865.
Rufus M. Meroney	Rebel tax assessor and collector	do	Nov. 8, 1865.
G. W. Mitchell	do	do	Nov. 15, 1865.
George W. McLarty	Rebel postmaster and assessor	do	Oct. 25, 1865.
William B. Marshall	Ex-U. S. and rebel postmaster; worth over $20,000	do	Sept. 23, 1865.
Felix B. Martin	Rebel tax assessor, and worth over $20,000	do	Sept. 20, 1865.
J. G. Mills	Engaged in blockade running; worth over $20,000	By order of the President	July 24, 1865.
S. P. Myrick	Member of rebel examining board, and worth over $20,000.	Governor Johnson	Sept. 2, 1865.
John F. Moreland	Rebel funding agent, and worth over $20,000	do	Aug. 31, 1865.
A. L. Maxwell	Left a loyal district, and worth over $20,000	do	Aug. 28, 1865.
William W. Merrell	Rebel tax assessor	do	Sept. 18, 1865.
Daniel B. Miller	do	do	Oct. 18, 1865.
E. G. McDuffie	do	do	Oct. 6, 1865.
Henry D. McConnell	do	do	Nov. 8, 1865.
Riley Milan	do	do	Oct. 25, 1865.
James L. Maddux	Rebel tax collector	do	Sept. 16, 1865.
A. J. Milner	do	do	July 24, 1865.
Stephen B. Marshall	do	do	Oct. 10, 1865.
John J. McKendree	do	do	Aug. 15, 1865.
W. J. Mead	do	do	Oct. 28, 1865.
James L. McEntire	do	do	Oct. 28, 1865.
James McNeal	do	do	Sept. 16, 1865.
Joel W. Mann	do	do	Sept. 11, 1865.
Delaware Morris	do	do	Sept. 4, 1865.
David W. Morgan	do	do	Aug. 31, 1865.
Rubin McCorquodale	Rebel postmaster	do	Oct. 6, 1865.
Robert Morgan	do	do	Sept. 16, 1865.
Daniel McClure	do	do	July 5, 1866.
D. F. McCrimmon	do	do	July 5, 1866.
John M. Moore	do	do	Oct. 10, 1865.
Henry L. McGehee	do	do	Oct. 2, 1865.

Georgia—Continued.

Name.	Exemption under amnesty proclamation of May 29, 1865.	By whom recommended.	Date of pardon.
John T. Manderville	Rebel postmaster	Governor Johnson	Nov. 8, 1865.
Christopher Meders	do	do	Nov. 8, 1865.
Thomas G. McFarland	do	By order of the President	Oct. 18, 1866.
James L. McCall	do	Governor Johnson	Oct. 25, 1865.
Isaac McConnel	do	do	Oct. 25, 1865.
James F. McKnight	do	do	Sept. 11, 1865.
Samuel McWhorter	do	do	Oct. 18, 1865.
Albert F. Morrison	do	do	Nov. 8, 1865.
John R. McNeel	Ex-United States and rebel postmaster	do	Oct. 18, 1865.
James McKenzie	do	do	Oct. 18, 1865.
G. R. Marcom	do	do	Oct. 18, 1865.
Archibald McLean	do	do	Oct. 18, 1865.
Harmon H. McElvy	do	do	Oct. 18, 1865.
John P. Murray	do	do	Oct. 6, 1865.
George W. F. McCay	do	do	Sept. 23, 1865.
R. W. McKee	do	Governor Jenkins	July 5, 1866.
Hugh McLean	do	Governor Johnson	Oct. 10, 1865.
John McLean	do	do	Oct. 10, 1865.
William R. McConnell	do	do	Oct. 25, 1865.
C. H. Maddox	do	do	Oct. 25, 1865.
Alfred L. Massengale	do	do	Sept. 4, 1865.
William McLean	do	do	Aug. 25, 1865.
J. L. Mustain	do	do	Aug. 25, 1865.
William C. Mitchell	Worth over $20,000	do	Sept. 4, 1865.
William J. F. Mitchell	do	do	Sept. 18, 1865.
William H. Mattox	do	do	Sept. 18, 1865.
George W. Mercier	do	do	Oct. 18, 1865.
James A. P. Metbern	do	do	Oct. 18, 1865.
Baldwin B. Miller	do	do	Oct. 10, 1865.
Rodford E. Morrow	do	do	Oct. 10, 1865.
James N. Mann	do	do	Oct. 2, 1865.
John C. More	do	do	Oct. 2, 1865.
William R. Murphey	do	do	Oct. 2, 1865.
R. J. Moses	do	do	Oct. 2, 1865.
William Montgomery	do	do	Oct. 2, 1865.
J. A. Miller	do	do	Oct. 2, 1865.
Henry B. McConnell	do	do	Oct. 2, 1865.
J. M. Middleton	do	do	Oct. 6, 1865.
D. G. McGlaun	do	do	Sept. 28, 1865.
R. H. McLead	do	do	Sept. 28, 1865.
Harriet Morris	do	do	Sept. 28, 1865.
Adam McNatt	do	do	Oct. 13, 1865.
A. W. Murphree	do	do	Oct. 13, 1865.
R. J. Morrison	do	do	Sept. 28, 1865.

Green Moore	do	do	Sept. 20, 1865.
John U. Meyer	do	do	Sept. 20, 1865.
Robert A. Murphey	do	do	Sept. 20, 1865.
George Martin	do	do	Sept. 20, 1865.
Robert Merriwether	do	do	Sept. 25, 1865.
Jesse McLendon	do	do	Sept. 16, 1865.
Thomas F. McGehee	do	do	Sept. 16, 1865.
Robert J. McClary	do	do	Sept. 16, 1865.
Richard L. Morris	do	Governor Jenkins	Mar. 19, 1866.
E. H. Martin	do	do	July 5, 1866.
Rob rt McIntire	do	Governor Johnson	July 5, 1866.
K. F. Malpass	do	do	July 5, 1866.
John B. Moore	do	Governor Jenkins	July 5, 1866.
Matthew B. McMahan	do	do	July 5, 1866.
A. N. Miller	do	do	Nov. 28, 1866.
J. McMahon	do	Hon. James M. Wayne, associate justice of the Supreme Court of the United States	July 31, 1865.
J. O. Mathewson	do	Joshua Hill	July 11, 1865.
B. N. McKnight	do	Governor Johnson	Nov. 8, 1865.
Jonathan M. Miller	do	do	Nov. 8, 1865.
Addison Maupin	do	do	Nov. 8, 1865.
Mrs. J. S. Montgomery	do	do	Nov. 17, 1865.
W. W. Montgomery	do	do	Nov. 17, 1865.
Charles H. McCall	do	do	Oct. 12, 1865.
David A. Martin	do	By order of the President	Mar. 2, 1866.
Spencer Marsh	do	Governor Johnson	Oct. 30, 1865.
Charles F. McCuy	do	do	Aug. 28, 1865.
Henry Moore	do	do	Aug. 28, 1865.
James Miller	do	do	Aug. 28, 1865.
William Markham	do	Governor Johnson and Brevet Brigadier General Winslow	Aug. 28, 1865.
Duncan McDougal	do	Governor Johnson	Oct. 12, 1865.
P. E. McDaniel	do	Governor Jenkins	Oct. 25, 1865.
Andrew McConky	do	Governor Johnson	Oct. 28, 1865.
Alexander M. Mitchell	do	do	Oct. 28, 1865.
Wiley C. McCrary	do	do	Oct. 28, 1865.
Wiley J. McClatchy	do	do	Oct. 25, 1865.
Julia Augusta St. Clair Moore	do	do	Oct. 25, 1865.
Alexander Moore	do	do	Oct. 25, 1865.
Robert McMillan	do	do	Oct. 25, 1865.
Harrison Musgrove	do	do	Oct. 25, 1865.
John M. McAfee	do	do	Oct. 25, 1865.
Rufus L. Moss	do	do	Sept. 16, 1865.
William McKinley	do	do	Sept. 16, 1865.
E. Mason	do	do	Sept. 16, 1865.
John T. Miller	do	do	Sept. 28, 1865.
M. Merritt	do	do	Sept. 11, 1865.
John McKay	do	do	Sept. 11, 1865.
William Mayes	do	do	Sept. 15, 1865.
Edwin W. Marsh	do	do	Sept. 23, 1865.
Daniel Merriwether	do	do	Sept. 2, 1865.
William Methrin, sr.	do	do	Sept. 25, 1865.
William McNaught	do	do	Sept. 4, 1865.
Thomas C. Mitchell	do	do	Sept. 4, 1865.

Georgia—Continued.

Name.	Exemption under amnesty proclamation of May 29, 1865.	By whom recommended.	Date of pardon.
David Mayer	Worth over $20,000	Governor Johnson	Sept. 4, 1865.
E. J. McGehee	do	do	Sept. 28, 1865.
Charles J. Malone	do	do	Sept. 13, 1865.
William A. Maxwell	do	do	Sept. 13, 1865.
James H. Maxwell	do	do	Aug. 25, 1865.
Alexander Means	do	do	Aug. 25, 1865.
Albert Mix	do	do	Aug. 25, 1865.
W. A. Mathews	do	do	Aug. 25, 1865.
Bright Miller	do	do	Aug. 25, 1865.
E. McDonald	do	do	Aug. 25, 1865.
James A. Mathews	do	do	Aug. 25, 1865.
A. McCallum	do	do	Aug. 22, 1865.
Robert B. Murdock	do	do	Aug. 28, 1865.
Isaac I. Moses	do	do	Aug. 28, 1865.
John C. Maund	do	do	Aug. 28, 1865.
W. S. Monghon	do	do	Aug. 30, 1865.
Robert H. May	do	do	Aug. 28, 1865.
Benjamin H. Myrick	do	do	Aug. 25, 1865.
A. T. MacIntyre	do	do	Aug. 21, 1865.
Nathan C. Munroe	do	Hon. James M. Wayne, associate justice of the Supreme Court of the United States	Aug. 4, 1865.
William N. Marks	do	do	Aug. 4, 1865.
Benjamin May	do	Governor Johnson	Aug. 25, 1865.
Walter H. Mitchell	do	do	Aug. 25, 1865.
James P. Mayne	do	do	Oct. 18, 1865.
S. R. McCarny	do	do	Nov. 17, 1865.
William A. Moore	do	do	May 1, 1866.
William Milner	do	do	July 24, 1865.
George E. W. Nelson	Superintendent of public printing under the rebel government.	do	Aug. 25, 1865.
James T. Nesbit	Petty civil officer, and under bonds to the United States military authorities.	do	Sept. 23, 1865.
Richard S. Neal	Rebel tax assessor	do	Sept. 16, 1865.
George M. Nolan	do	do	Nov. 8, 1865.
J. E. Nunnally	Rebel tax collector	do	Oct. 25, 1865.
John H. Nyly	do	do	Sept. 26, 1865.
Q. R. Nolan	do	do	Nov. 8, 1865.
Samuel D. Night	Rebel postmaster	do	Nov. 8, 1865.
Charles A. Nutting	Ex-United States and rebel postmaster	Hon. James M. Wayne, associate justice of the Supreme Court of the United States	Aug. 4, 1865.
Thomas C. Nisbet	Worth over $20,000	Governor Johnson	Sept. 19, 1865.
Mrs. Fannie C. Napier	do	Governor Jenkins	July 5, 1866.
William M. Nichols	do	Governor Johnson	July 5, 1866.
Thomas Nesbitt	do	do	Nov. 13, 1865.
Charles L. Nelson	do	do	Oct. 25, 1865.
Sterling Niel	do	do	Oct. 18, 1865.

P. M. Nightengale	do	Governor Johnson and John A. King, of New York	Oct. 12, 1865.
Solomon Newson	do	Governor Johnson	Sept. 28, 1865.
John H. Newton	do	do	Sept. 28, 1865.
T. W. Neely	do	do	Oct. 13, 1865.
John W. Nicholson	do	do	Sept. 16, 1865.
John Neal	do	do	Sept. 16, 1865.
John A. Nelson	do	do	Sept. 23, 1865.
John H. Nolan	do	do	Sept. 25, 1865.
Isaac Newell, sr.	do	do	Aug. 25, 1865.
S. Napier	do	do	Aug. 25, 1865.
Aladin T. Newsom	do	do	Aug. 25, 1865.
Leroy Napier	do	Hon. James M. Wayne, associate justice of the Supreme Court of the United States	Aug. 4, 1865.
Joseph M. Newby	do	Governor Johnson	Aug. 28, 1865.
Henry Orr	Ex-United States and rebel mail contractor	do	Sept. 16, 1865.
Silas Overstreet	Rebel tithe agent	do	Oct. 18, 1865.
John T. Owens	Rebel tax assessor	do	Oct. 18, 1865.
Gustavus J. Orr	Rebel tax collector	Governor Johnson, John Harris, John J. Floyd, Thomas S. Anderson, William D. Luckie, and J. M. Yarbrough.	Aug. 25, 1865.
John Oates	do	Governor Johnson	Oct. 2, 1865.
Samuel Orr	Ex-United States and rebel postmaster	do	Oct. 6, 1865.
Richard W. Oliver	Rebel postmaster	do	Sept. 16, 1865.
Benjamin F. O'Kelly	do	do	Oct. 2, 1865.
Richard A. Odorn	do	do	Oct. 25, 1865.
J. C. Orr	do	do	Aug. 26, 1865.
James C. Odell	do	do	Nov. 8, 1865.
Green F. Oliver	Worth over $20,000	do	Sept. 16, 1865.
Amos Opry	do	do	Sept. 16, 1865.
Richard M. Orme, sr.	do	do	Aug. 25, 1865.
William J. Owens	do	do	Aug. 25, 1865.
D. W. Orr	do	do	Aug. 28, 1865.
A. J. Orme	do	do	Aug. 28, 1865.
James S. Odorn	do	do	Sept. 28, 1865.
Alfred Oliver	do	do	Sept. 28, 1865.
Hugh H. Ogilby	do	do	Sept. 20, 1865.
W. C. O'Driscoll	do	do	Oct. 28, 1865.
H. J. Osborne	do	Lorenzo Sherwood	Jan. 25, 1866.
James Ormond	do	Governor Johnson	Nov. 8, 1865.
George S. Owens	do	Attorney General Speed	July 25, 1865.
Michael O'Dowd	do	Governor Jenkins	Mar. 19, 1866.
Shelton Oliver	do	By order of the President	Sept. 11, 1866.
Ferdinand Phinizy	Rebel agent for the purchase of cotton	Major General Humphreys	July 14, 1865.
Thomas Purse	Rebel appraiser for the port of Savannah	Governor Johnson	Oct. 2, 1865.
Wm. P. Payne	Rebel route agent	Attorney General Speed	July 24, 1865.
W. B. Perry	Member of rebel investigating board	Governor Johnson	Oct. 25, 1865.
Littleton Pitts	Ex-U. S. and rebel postmaster and tax assessor	do	Aug. 31, 1865.
Joho M. Potter	Rebel tax collector, and worth over $20,000	do	Sept. 2, 1865.
M. L. Patterson	Rebel contractor, and worth over $20,000	do	Aug. 29, 1865.
J. C. Plant	Rebel agent for sale of bonds, and worth over $20,000	do	Aug. 31, 1865.
T. N. Poullain	Ex-U. S. and rebel postmaster; worth over $20,000	do	Aug. 25, 1865.
George F. Ponder	Rebel postmaster, and worth over $20,000	do	Oct. 10, 1865.
Rev. John T. Pryse	do	do	Sept. 23, 1865.
H. M. Putnam	Rebel tax collector	do	July 5, 1866.

Georgia—Continued.

Name.	Exemption under amnesty proclamation of May 29, 1865.	By whom recommended.	Date of pardon.
Charles Powell	Rebel tax collector	Governor Johnson	Oct. 10, 1865.
Wm. H. Parker	Rebel tax assessor	do	Sept. 16, 1865.
Wm. F. S. Powell	do	do	Sept. 16, 1865.
George W. Powers	do	do	Sept. 16, 1865.
M. S. Poore	do	do	July 5, 1866.
Harvey T. Phillips	Ex-United States and rebel postmaster	do	Oct. 25, 1865.
George W. Perdue	do	do	Oct. 6, 1865.
S. C. Prudden	do	do	Oct. 2, 1865.
John D. Parker	do	do	Oct. 2, 1865.
Z. T. Phelps	do	Governor Jenkins	July 5, 1866.
Ephraim Pray	do	Governer Johnson	Nov. 8, 1865.
Joel E. Perry	Rebel postmaster	do	Oct. 25, 1865.
John N. Pate	do	do	Oct. 18, 1865.
Wm. G. Pierce	do	do	Sept. 16, 1865.
Jasper N. Pittman	do	do	Aug. 31, 1865.
Wiley D. Pope	do	Hon. James M. Wayne, associate justice of the Supreme Court of the United States	Aug. 4, 1865.
Washington Poe	do	Governor Johnson	Aug. 25, 1865.
John W. Pearce	do	do	July 5, 1866.
H. K. Phillips	do	do	Oct. 2, 1865.
Jacob T. Parker	do	do	Oct. 2, 1865.
Mrs. Mary Putnam	Rebel postmistress	do	Nov. 13, 1865.
Barton G. Payne	Rebel postmaster	do	Nov. 8, 1865.
Edwin T. Pound	do	do	Nov. 8, 1865.
Mrs. Catharine E. Poullain	Worth over $20,000	do	Oct. 25, 1865.
James A. Price	do	do	Oct. 18, 1865.
Wm. G. Ponder	do	do	Oct. 18, 1865.
Isaac Powell	do	do	Oct. 18, 1865.
William H. Pritchett	do	do	Oct. 18, 1865.
Philander P. Pease	do	do	Nov. 17, 1865.
Andrew Pless	do	do	Oct. 6, 1865.
John G. Park	do	do	Oct. 6, 1865.
Samuel Prilliam	do	do	Oct. 6, 1865.
Benier Pye	do	do	Oct. 2, 1865.
Alexander Pharr	do	do	Oct. 2, 1865.
Mary Ann Pettus	do	do	Oct. 2, 1865.
Samuel Pearson	do	do	Oct. 2, 1865.
Daniel Ponder	do	do	Oct. 2, 1865.
E. J. Plowden	do	do	Oct. 2, 1865.
S. G. Pettus	do	do	Oct. 2, 1865.
Thomas F. Parson	do	do	Sept. 28, 1865.
Henry B. Plant	do	do	Sept. 20, 1865.
Thomas Poullian, jr	do	do	Sept. 20, 1865.
Wm. R. Phillips	do	do	Sept. 16, 1865.
George W. Persons	do	do	Sept. 16, 1865.

George F. Platt	do	do	Sept. 16, 1865.
George H. Page	do	do	Sept. 16, 1865.
A. G. Peden	do	do	Sept. 11, 1865.
Wm. C. Parker	do	do	Sept. 11, 1865.
Wm. B. Pinson	do	do	Sept. 11, 1865.
James Peeler	do	Hon. K. V. Whaley and J. C. Bates, M. D	Sept. 22, 1865.
Robert Paul	do	Governor Johnson	Sept. 25, 1865.
Alfred Prescott	do	do	Sept. 25, 1865.
Jacob Printup	do	do	Sept. 2, 1865.
Lewis W. Pow	do	do	Sept. 2, 1865.
John Phinizy	do	do	Aug. 25, 1865.
Thomas B. Phinizy	do	do	Aug. 25, 1865.
Chapman Powell	do	do	Aug 25, 1865.
David Philpot	do	do	Aug. 31, 1865.
Roland R. Paramore	do	do	Aug. 25, 1865.
Job C. Patterson	do	do	Aug. 25, 1865.
S. L. Pope	do	do	Aug. 28, 1865.
Wm. Phillips	do	do	Aug. 28, 1865.
Wm. G. Peters	do	do	Aug. 28, 1865.
Edwin Payne	do	do	Aug. 28, 1865.
Virgil Powers	do	Hon. James M. Wayne, associate justice of the Supreme Court of the United States	Aug. 4, 1865.
Antoine Poullain	do	Governor Johnson	Aug. 28, 1865.
Antoine Picquet	do	do	Aug. 28, 1865.
Joshua R. Price	do	do	Aug. 25, 1865.
George R. Powell	do	do	July 5, 1866.
Wm. Peck	do	do	July 5, 1866.
M. E. Paramore	do	do	July 5, 1866.
J. J. Pinson	do	do	July 24, 1865.
Henry B. Plant	do	do	Nov. 8, 1865.
Julia A. Pace	do	do	Nov. 8, 1865.
F. L. Powers	do	do	Nov. 8, 1865.
Joseph J. Pinson	do	do	Nov. 8, 1865.
Wm. R. Pritchard	do	do	Oct. 25, 1865.
Richard Peters	do	do	June 19, 1865.
L. W. Quillian	Assayer of rebel mint	do	Aug. 25, 1865.
O. P. Quillian	Rebel mail contractor	do	Aug. 25, 1865.
B. B. Quillian	Rebel tax collector	do	July 24, 1865.
George W. Rains	Left a loyal State	do	Sept. 11, 1865.
Wm. R. Ritter	do	Governor Jenkins	July 5, 1866.
James R. Rahn	Rebel mail contractor	Governor Johnson	Sept. 28, 1865.
Robert A. Rowland	Rebel agent for collection of provisions	do	Sept. 16, 1865.
James K. Redd	Rebel agent, and worth over $20,000	do	Sept. 23, 1865.
John T. Robertson	Rebel deputy marshal	do	Sept. 28, 1865.
Roland T. Ross	Rebel tax assessor	do	Sept. 23, 1865.
Adam Ragland	do	do	Aug. 31, 1865.
Shephard Rogers	do	do	Oct. 10, 1865.
Joshua Roberts	Rebel tax collector	do	Oct. 25, 1865.
Mathew R. Rogers	do	do	Sept. 23, 1865.
Levi S. Russell	do	Brevet Major General Birge, commanding	July 24, 1865.
James T. Read	Rebel tax assessor and postmaster	Governor Johnson	Sept. 28, 1865.
W. H. C. Ramsey	Rebel enrolling officer and postmaster	do	Sept. 4, 1865.
Wm. A. Robinson	Left a loyal district, and postmaster	Hon. James M. Wayne, associate justice of the Supreme Court of the United States	Aug. 4, 1865.

Georgia—Continued.

Name.	Exemption under amnesty proclamation of May 29, 1865.	By whom recommended.	Date of pardon.
John E. Redwine	Rebel postmaster	Governor Johnson	Oct. 18, 1865.
Eucratus Rowland	do	do	Oct. 18, 1865.
Thomas Ratcliff	do	do	Oct. 18, 1865.
William Rees	do	do	Nov. 8, 1865.
Peter W. Reddick	do	do	Oct. 10, 1865.
Joel Rucker	Ex-United States and rebel postmaster	do	Nov. 8, 1865.
C. B. Robinson	do	do	Sept. 28, 1865.
Edmund Richardson	do	O. A. Lochrane	Sept. 11, 1865.
F. McRae	do	Governor Johnson	July 5, 1866.
Thomas J. Roberts	do	do	Oct. 10, 1865.
W. B. Reeves	Worth over $20,000	do	Oct. 28, 1865.
Cyrus Robinson	do	do	Oct. 25, 1865.
Roderic Rutland	do	do	Oct. 25, 1865.
Edward E. Rawson	do	do	Oct. 25, 1865.
Henry C. Rogers	do	do	Oct. 25, 1865.
W. M. Rogers	do	do	Oct. 18, 1865.
James H. Roberts	do	do	Oct. 18, 1865.
A. G. Redd	do	do	Oct. 2, 1865.
Wm. L. Rowland	do	do	Oct. 2, 1865.
M. J. Randolph	do	do	Oct. 2, 1865.
Aaron Reppard	do	do	Oct. 2, 1865.
Mrs. Francis M. Rowland	do	do	Oct. 2, 1865.
James S. Reid	do	do	Oct. 2, 1865.
Berry Rogers	do	do	Oct. 6, 1865.
James M. Reynold	do	do	Oct. 13, 1865.
Edmund Reid	do	do	Sept. 28, 1865.
Jonathan Robinson	do	do	Sept. 28, 1865.
Alexander Reid	do	do	Sept. 28, 1865.
Charles Rogers	do	do	Sept. 23, 1865.
Nathan Respess	do	do	Sept. 16, 1865.
Samuel Robison	do	do	Sept. 16, 1865.
Parmedus Reynolds	do	do	Sept. 16, 1865.
W. C. Riddle	do	do	Sept. 16, 1865.
A. A. Roff	do	do	Sept. 16, 1865.
Lewis Redwine	do	do	Sept. 16, 1865.
John E. Robinson	do	do	Sept. 16, 1865.
John R. Respess	do	do	Sept. 16, 1865.
Wm. S. Roberts	do	do	Sept. 28, 1865.
Thomas H. Roberts	do	do	Sept. 28, 1865.
John Ray	do	do	Sept. 11, 1865.
Thomas Ragland	do	do	Sept. 11, 1865.
Wm. L. Reaves	do	do	Sept. 11, 1865.
R. H. Ramsey	do	do	Sept. 11, 1865.
G. L. D. Rice	do	do	Sept. 28, 1865.

Jesse M. Roberts	do	do	Sept. 15, 1865.
Robert G. Ricks	do	do	Sept. 25, 1865.
A. S. Reid	do	do	Sept. 25, 1865.
Albert Rees	do	do	Sept. 25, 1865.
Abner P. Robertson	do	do	Sept. 4, 1865.
C. L. Ridley	do	do	Sept. 4, 1865.
Benjamin H. Rutherford	do	do	Aug. 31, 1865.
Wm. T. Respess	do	do	Sept. 4, 1865.
P. Ramsey	do	do	Aug. 25, 1865.
William Reid	do	do	Aug. 31, 1865.
Robert A. T. Ridley	do	do	Aug. 31, 1865.
John M. Randle	do	do	Aug. 25, 1865.
H. F. Russell	do	do	Aug. 28, 1865.
Wm. H. Robinson	do	do	Aug. 28, 1865.
Wm. J. Russell	do	do	Aug. 28, 1865.
Harmon Rowley	do	do	Aug. 28, 1865.
Thomas R. Rhodes	do	do	Aug. 28, 1865.
Youel G. Rust	do	do	Aug. 21, 1865.
John Richardson	do	do	Aug. 25, 1865.
B. F. Ross	do	Hon. James M. Wayne, associate justice of the Supreme Court of the United States	Aug. 4, 1865.
John B. Ross	do	do	Aug. 4, 1865.
W. H. Ross	do	do	Aug. 4, 1865.
John L. Rowland	do	Governor Johnson	July 24, 1865.
Edward Remington	do	do	Apr. 11, 1866.
Henry A. Russell	do	do	July 5, 1866.
S. L. Richardson	do	Governor Jenkins	July 5, 1866.
Wm. A. Rawson	do	Governor Johnson	July 5, 1866.
H. A. Richmond	do	do	July 5, 1866.
John A. Rosier	do	Governor Jenkins	July 5, 1866.
E. E. Rawson	do	do	Oct. 25, 1866.
Lawrence Rooney	do	do	Mar. 30, 1866.
P. Reynolds	do	By order of the President	Aug. 27, 1866.
Harriet A. Rossignol	do	Governor Jenkins	July 14, 1866.
W. W. Rhodes	do	do	June 8, 1866.
W. Remshart	do	Hon. James M. Wayne, associate justice of the Supreme Court of the United States	Aug. 5, 1865.
Elijah Roberts	do	Governor Johnson	Dec. 14, 1865.
Sion B. Robson	do	do	Sept. 16, 1865.
Sidney Root	do	Attorney General Speed	July 22, 1865.
Jacob Rockenbaugh	do	Governor Johnson	Aug. 26, 1865.
Hiram Roberts	do	Brevet Major General Birge commanding	Aug. 2, 1865.
John H. Ruckman	do	By order of the President	Oct. 5, 1865.
Charles A. Rowland	do	Governor Johnson	Nov. 8, 1865.
Benson Roberts	do	do	Nov. 8, 1865.
William Root	do	do	Oct. 2, 1865.
J. M. C. Robertson	do	do	Oct. 30, 1865.
Hardy Strickland	Member of rebel congress	By order of the President	July 24, 1865.
W. R. Symons	Paroled prisoner	Governor Johnson	July 5, 1866.
Dewitt C. Seymour	Paymaster in rebel navy	do	Aug. 25, 1865.
B. B. Simons	Ex-United States and rebel route agent	do	Nov. 8, 1865.
Silas H. Staw	Rebel postmaster and tax assessor	do	Aug. 25, 1865.
Richard T. Smith	Rebel mail contractor	Governor Jenkins	July 5, 1866.
Cicero H. Sutton	Depositary of rebel treasury	Governor Johnson	Oct. 6, 1865.

Georgia—Continued.

Name.	Exemption under amnesty proclamation of May 29, 1865.	By whom recommended.	Date of pardon.
John H. Speed	Rebel contractor, and worth over $20,000	Governor Johnson	Oct. 4 1865.
John N. Swift	Rebel tax assessor, and worth over $20,000	do	Sept. 16, 1865.
John A. Simonton	Rebel tax collector, and worth over $20,000	do	Aug. 31, 1865.
John W. Spain	Ex-United States and rebel postmaster, and worth over $20,000.	Governor Johnson and Major Hastings, commanding post	Aug. 28, 1865.
Joseph A. Shewmake	Rebel purchasing agent, and worth over $20,000	Governor Jenkins	July 5, 1866.
Burrell Sweat	Rebel tax assessor	Governor Johnson	Oct. 18, 1865.
Pitt F. D. Scarbrough	do	do	Sept. 28, 1865.
William Summerall	do	do	Nov. 13, 1865.
John H. Starr	do	do	July 24, 1865.
William F. Sears	do	do	Nov. 8, 1865.
Jackson O. Scott	Rebel tax collector	do	Oct. 18, 1865.
Mathew Sweat	do	do	Oct. 18, 1865.
E. Starnes	do	do	Oct. 6, 1865.
A. N. Simpson	do	do	Sept. 28, 1865.
R. L. Story	do	do	Sept. 16, 1865.
Thomas J. Speer	do	do	July 5, 1866.
John D. Stapleton	do	do	Oct. 10, 1865.
F. Summerour	Ex-United States and rebel postmaster	do	Oct. 2, 1865.
Dr. F. M. Smith	do	do	Oct. 25, 1865.
Raymond Sanford	do	do	Oct. 25, 1865.
Robert H. Springer	do	do	Oct. 18, 1865.
William B. Swann	do	do	Oct. 18, 1865.
James M. Smythe	do	do	Sept. 16, 1865.
J. C. Smith	do	do	Sept. 4, 1865.
John F. Smith	do	do	Aug. 25, 1865.
Robert W. Sheffield	do	do	July 5, 1866.
F. C. Stephenson	do	do	Oct. 2, 1865.
W. F. C. Smith	Rebel postmaster	do	Oct. 6, 1865.
George L. Summey	do	do	Oct. 28, 1865.
William B. Stripling	do	do	Oct. 28, 1865.
Gardner Stearns	do	do	Oct. 25, 1865.
Gilbert M. Stokes	do	do	Oct. 18, 1865.
Joshua Sutton	do	do	Sept. 28, 1865.
W. M. Sturgis	do	do	Sept. 28, 1865.
J. W. B. Summers	do	do	Sept. 28, 1865.
James D. Spence	do	do	Sept. 4, 1865.
A. H. Sneed	do	do	Sept. 4, 1865.
Calvin B. Seymour	do	do	Aug. 25, 1865.
Adam Stroup	do	do	July 5, 1866.
Ausbon Seay	do	do	July 5, 1866.
F. M. Smith	do	do	July 5, 1866.
Josiah C. Spurlin	do	do	July 5, 1866.
Henry H. Swatts	do	do	Oct. 10, 1865.

Charles S. Sorrells	do	do	Oct. 10, 1865.
Henry E. Smith	do	do	Oct. 10, 1865.
Virgil R. Smith	do	do	Nov. 13, 1865.
Martin W. Stamper	Worth over $20,000	do	Sept. 25, 1865.
William Strong	do	do	July 5, 1866.
Thomas Steele	do	do	July 5, 1866.
Mrs. T. C. T. Slack	do	do	July 5, 1866.
James C. Sproull	do	Governor Jenkins	July 5, 1866.
Charles Spalding	do	do	July 5, 1866.
William Smith	do	do	July 5, 1866.
J. G. Strupper	do	Governor Johnson	Sept. 16, 1865.
John Smith	do	do	Sept. 16, 1865.
A. K. Seago	do	do	Sept. 16, 1865.
George R. Sims	do	do	Sept. 16, 1865.
G. H. Slappy	do	do	Sept. 16, 1865.
William Solomon	do	do	Sept. 16, 1865.
William S. Stokes	do	do	Sept. 20, 1865.
Thomas P. Saffold	do	Governor Johnson and Joshua Hill	Sept. 20, 1865.
William A. Saffold	do	do	Sept. 20, 1865.
James P. Smith	do	do	Sept. 20, 1865.
Davis Smith	do	Governor Johnson	Oct. 2, 1865.
C. F. Stubbs	do	do	Oct. 2, 1865.
James A. Spivey	do	do	Oct. 2, 1865.
Garrett Smith	do	do	Oct. 2, 1865.
Albert Sears	do	do	Oct. 2, 1865.
Charles D. Stewart	do	do	Oct. 2, 1865.
L. S. Salmens	do	do	Oct. 2, 1865.
Thomas L. Smith	do	do	Oct. 2, 1865.
Dilson F. Sapp	do	do	Oct. 2, 1865.
Mrs. Mary A. Stark	do	do	Oct. 2, 1865.
John A. Smith	do	do	Oct. 2, 1865.
Ira E. Smith	do	do	Oct. 2, 1865.
David W. Spence	do	do	Oct. 2, 1865.
Alvis Stafford	do	do	Oct. 2, 1865.
William Searcy	do	do	Oct. 2, 1865.
Joseph Smith	do	do	Sept. 4, 1865.
Harrison Summerour	do	do	Sept. 4, 1865.
James S. Sims	do	do	Sept. 4, 1865.
John P. Sykes	do	do	Sept. 4, 1865.
William W. Simpson	do	do	Sept. 4, 1865.
Thomas J. Smith	do	do	Sept. 4, 1865.
David Solomon	do	do	Sept. 4, 1865.
George W. Sapp	do	do	Oct. 13, 1865.
William Sapp	do	do	Oct. 13, 1865.
James Sutlive	do	do	Sept. 23, 1865.
Theophilus Sapp	do	do	Sept. 23, 1865.
John D. Stewart	do	do	Sept. 23, 1865.
Edward T. Shepherd	do	do	Sept. 23, 1865.
Ware Shoderick	do	do	Sept. 28, 1865.
McAlvin H. Spence	do	do	Sept. 28, 1865.
Oliver Shelton	do	do	Sept. 28, 1865.
Berry W. Sanford	do	do	Sept. 28, 1865.

Georgia—Continued.

Name.	Exemption under amnesty proclamation of May 29, 1865.	By whom recommended.	Date of pardon.
Caleb Spivey	Worth over $20,000	Governor Johnson	Sept. 28, 1865.
B. G. Smith	do	do	Sept. 28, 1865.
Lewis Scofield	do	Governor Johnson and J. G. Parkhurst, colonel and provost marshal general	Sept. 13, 1865.
Andrew A. Spitzcomb	do	Governor Johnson	Oct. 18, 1865.
Henry Sumerlin	do	do	Oct. 18, 1865.
Ezekiel B. Smith	do	do	Oct. 18, 1885.
John S. Scofield	do	do	Oct. 6, 1865.
James Story	do	do	Oct. 6, 1865.
James Seymour	do	do	Oct. 30, 1865.
Gilbert M. Stokes	do	do	Oct. 30, 1865.
Hedges L. Spencer	do	do	Oct. 28, 1865.
James Steward	do	do	Oct. 28, 1865.
William Smith	do	do	Oct. 28, 1865.
Benjamin R. Smith	do	do	Oct. 28, 1865.
S. H. Sibley	do	do	Oct. 28, 1865.
William Slade	do	do	Oct. 28, 1865.
William J. Sans	do	do	Aug. 28, 1865.
Henry H. Steiner	do	do	Aug. 28, 1865.
Thomas P. Stovall	do	do	Aug. 28, 1865.
Benjamin G. Smith	do	do	Aug. 28, 1865.
William W. Shipp	do	do	Aug. 28, 1865.
M. P. Stovall	do	do	Aug. 28, 1865.
W. L. Salisbury	do	do	Aug. 28, 1865.
T. J. Smith	do	do	Aug. 25, 1865.
Isaac W. Stokes	do	do	Aug. 25, 1865.
John D. Snelling	do	do	Aug. 25, 1865.
William Sims	do	do	Aug. 25, 1865.
Thomas Scutchen	do	do	Aug. 25, 1865.
D. W. Shine	do	do	Sept. 25, 1865.
Josiah P. Stevens	do	do	Sept. 25, 1865.
John A. Strother	do	do	Sept. 11, 1865.
Josiah Sibley	do	do	Sept. 11, 1865.
S. W. Swanson	do	do	Aug. 31, 1865.
Robert R. Slappey	do	Hon. James M. Wayne, associate justice of the Supreme Court of the United States	Aug. 4, 1865.
John Smith	do	do	Aug. 4, 1865.
Peter Solomon	do	do	Aug. 4, 1865.
Charles Strong	do	Governor Johnson	Nov. 8, 1865.
Jordan R. Smith	do	do	Nov. 8, 1865.
John Small	do	do	Nov. 8, 1865.
Henry J. Schley	do	do	Nov. 13, 1865.
William G. Salter	do	Governor Johnson and Herschel V. Johnson	Nov. 13, 1865.
James L. Seward	do	By order of the President	June 19, 1865.
A. M. Sloan	do	Governor Johnson	Aug. 26, 1865.
William J. Sasnett	do	do	Sept. 19, 1865.

Mrs. Mary E. Shorter	do	do	Mar. 3, 1865.
Albert Sears	do	do	May 28, 1866.
Sarah A. Stephens	do	do	May 12, 1866.
Enoch Steadman	do	do	Apr. 11, 1866.
E. L. Strohecker	do	Hon. John Erskine, United States judge for Georgia	Aug. 21, 1865.
George P. Screven	do	Hon. James M. Wayne, associate justice of the Supreme Court of the United States	July 19, 1865.
John Sherlock	do	do	July 24, 1865.
Thomas L. Salter	do	Governor Johnson	Oct. 12, 1865.
Charles M. Smith	do	do	Oct. 12, 1865.
Isaac Scott	do	do	Aug. 29, 1865.
John Screven	do	Hon. James M. Wayne, associate justice of the Supreme Court of the United States	July 19, 1865.
Thomas F. Screven	do	do	July 19, 1865.
Alfred Shorter	do	Governor Johnson	Aug. 26, 1865.
Linton Stephens	do	do	Sept. 2, 1865.
W. C. Sibley	do	Joshua Hill	July 5, 1865.
James N. Simmons	do	Governor Johnson, J. C. McDaniel, and R. A. Pittman	Sept. 28 1865
E. R. Sasseen	do	Governor Johnson	Oct. 6, 1865.
Noah Smith	do	do	Mar. 26, 1866.
C. G. Trammell	Proceedings commenced for confiscation	do	Nov. 8, 1865.
William H. Tucker	Rebel deputy marshal	do	Oct. 2, 1865.
Calvin Till	Rebel mail contractor	do	Sept. 28, 1865.
Dosier Thornton	Rebel agent for purchasing supplies	do	Oct. 10, 1865.
John J. Thrasher	Member of rebel State legislature, and worth over $20,000.	do	Oct. 28, 1865.
Nelson Tift	Rebel agent for the construction of vessels, and worth over $20,000.	Hon. James S. Wayne, associate justice of the Supreme Court of the United States	July 20, 1865.
A. F. Tift	Rebel agent for the construction of vessels, &c	do	July 20, 1865.
Ansbon J. Taylor	Rebel tax assessor	Governor Johnson	Oct. 25, 1865.
William Tharp	do	do	Sept. 4, 1865.
James Tillman	do	Governor Jenkins	July 5, 1866.
John C. Talbert	Rebel tax collector	Governor Johnson	Sept. 16, 1865.
Richard S. Taylor	do	do	Sept. 4, 1865.
Horton S. Turner	do	do	Aug. 31, 1865.
Thomas J. Threlkeld	do	do	Aug. 28, 1865.
K. Tyner	do	do	Nov. 8, 1865.
Jack Tompkins	Ex-United States and rebel postmaster	do	Nov. 15, 1865.
James M. Triplett	do	Governor Jenkins	July 5, 1866.
J. D. Trammell	Rebel postmaster, and worth over $20,000	Governor Johnson	Sept. 25, 1865.
Sanford M. Tufts	Rebel postmaster	do	Oct. 18, 1865.
Robert S. Tomms	do	do	July 5, 1866.
Willis Twiggs	do	do	July 5, 1866.
William Turk	do	do	Oct. 2, 1865.
Smith Turner	do	Governor Jenkins	July 5, 1866.
Nat. Teagle	do	Governor Johnson	Nov. 8, 1865.
Thomas P. F. Threewits	Worth over $20,000	do	Sept. 11, 1865.
William A. Thomas	do	do	Sept. 11, 1865.
Dexter B. Thompson	do	do	Sept. 11, 1865.
Hugh D. Treanor	do	do	Aug. 25, 1865.
Daniel R. Tucker	do	do	Aug. 25, 1865.
John S. Thomas	do	do	Aug. 25, 1865.
Stephen Thomas	do	do	Aug. 25, 1865.
George M. Thew	do	do	Aug. 25, 1865.

Georgia—Continued.

Name.	Exemption under amnesty proclamation of May 29, 1865.	By whom recommended.	Date of pardon.
S. P. Thurmond	Worth over $20,000	Governor Johnson	Aug. 25, 1865.
Gabriel Toombs	do	do	Aug. 25, 1865.
Robert Thomas	do	do	Aug. 25, 1865.
John Thomas	do	do	Aug. 31, 1865.
James M. Truitt	do	do	Aug. 31, 1865.
A. E. Tarver	do	do	Nov. 13, 1865.
William D. Tinsley	do	do	Oct. 18, 1865.
Charles E. Taylor	do	do	Sept. 23, 1865.
Seth K. Taylor	do	do	Sept. 25, 1865.
George W. Thomas	do	do	Sept. 25, 1865.
George H. Tuttle	do	do	Sept. 25, 1865.
W. H. Turpin	do	do	Sept. 4, 1865.
Uriah O. Tate	do	do	Sept. 4, 1865.
Thomas M. Turner	do	do	Sept. 4, 1865.
W. H. Tutt	do	do	Sept. 4, 1865.
John M. Thomas	do	do	Sept. 4, 1865.
Barton Thrasher	do	do	Sept. 16, 1865.
Joseph Thompson	do	do	Sept. 16, 1865.
James Trice	do	do	Sept. 16, 1865.
W. B. Tarver	do	do	Sept. 13, 1865.
Jared Tomlinson	do	do	Oct. 6, 1865.
John R. Tucker	do	do	Oct. 28, 1865.
Samuel Tate	do	do	Oct. 28, 1865.
Henry Toomer	do	do	Sept. 28, 1865.
Mrs. W. Eliza Terrell	do	do	Sept. 28, 1865.
John T. B. Turner	do	do	Oct. 2, 1865.
Nathan Tucker	do	do	Oct. 2, 1865.
Augustus Trimble	do	do	Oct. 2, 1865.
James Thomas	do	do	Oct. 2, 1865.
H. F. Thigpen	do	Will. A. Adams, colonel commanding	Oct. 2, 1865.
P. R. Thomason	do	Governor Johnson	Oct. 2, 1865.
John Thompson	do	do	Oct. 2, 1865.
Ephraim Tweedy	do	do	Aug. 28, 1865.
John F. Troutman	do	do	Aug. 28, 1865.
M. L. Troutman	do	do	Aug. 28, 1865.
Lewis Tumlin	do	do	Aug. 28, 1865.
John Thompson	do	do	Oct. 25, 1865.
Joseph Tooke	do	do	Oct. 25, 1865.
Owen Thomas	do	do	Sept. 20, 1865.
M. S. Thompson	do	do	Sept. 20, 1865.
Early W. Thrasher	do	do	Sept. 20, 1865.
Henry A. Tarver	do	Hon. James M. Wayne, associate justice of the Supreme Court of the United States	Aug. 4, 1865.
James Thervatt	do	do	Aug. 4, 1865.
M. H. Tucker	do	Governor Jenkins	July 5, 1866.

John Treanor	do	Governor Johnson	July 5, 1866.
James Theatt	do	do	July 5, 1866.
James F. Taliaferro	do	Governor Jenkins	July 5, 1866.
W. H. Tibbs	do	Governor Jenkins and William W. Boyce	July 5, 1866.
Allen W. Turner	do	Governor Johnson	Nov. 8, 1865.
J. P. Thomas	do	do	Nov. 8, 1865.
Z. B. Trice	do	do	Nov. 8, 1865.
Henry A. Tarver	do	do	Nov. 8, 1865.
Joshua Taylor	do	Governor Jenkins and Joseph O'Neil, brevet major United States army	Dec. 3, 1866.
H. H. Tucker	do	Major General Steedman, Judge King, and N. B. Browne	Jan. 17, 1866.
L. L. Thomasson	do	By order of the President	May 19, 1866.
Henry Tayloe	do	do	Sept. 27, 1866.
W. H. Tison	do	do	July 24, 1865.
Jefferson Thomas	Rebel postmaster	Governor Johnson	Oct. 25, 1865.
William R. Utter	do	do	July 5, 1866.
F. L. Upson	Worth over $20,000	do	Oct. 2, 1865.
James C. Venable	Refugee	Alexander Henry, mayor of Philadelphia	July 5, 1865.
David A. Vason	Rebel funding agent, and worth over $20,000	Hon. James M. Wayne, associate justice of the Supreme Court of the United States	Aug. 4, 1865.
D. B. Verdel	Worth over $20,000	Governor Johnson	Oct. 18, 1865.
Joseph Vason	do	do	Sept. 20, 1865.
R. H. Vickers	do	do	Sept. 28, 1865.
J. A. Van Winkle	do	do	Aug. 28, 1865.
John L. Villalonga	do	do	Aug. 28, 1865.
Thomas Vaughan	do	do	Aug. 31, 1865.
A. E. Vickers	do	Hon. James M. Wayne, associate justice of the Supreme Court of the United States	Aug. 4, 1865.
*William T. Wofford	Rebel brigadier general	George H. Thomas, major general United States army	July 24, 1865.
E. B. Walker	Rebel master of transportation	Governor Johnson	Sept. 4 1865.
C. C. Winn	Rebel deputy marshal	do	Sept. 28, 1865.
Henry Williams	Rebel district attorney	do	Sept. 11, 1865.
Rufus P. Wood	Rebel commissary agent	do	Aug. 31, 1865.
James M. Woodruff	Member of rebel "investigating board"	do	Oct. 6, 1865.
Lewis N. Whittle	Commissioner to receive subscriptions to rebel bonds	Hon. James M. Wayne, associate justice of the Supreme Court of the United States	Aug. 4, 1865.
Young Wood	Petty civil officer	Governor Johnson	Aug. 31, 1865.
Thomas H. Wells	Left a loyal State	Governor Jenkins	July 5, 1866.
Bryant A. Wood	Rebel purchasing agent	Governor Johnson	Aug. 28, 1865.
Joseph Williams	Rebel mail contractor	do	Oct. 7, 1865.
Aaron B. Wright	do	do	July 5, 1866.
John C. Warwick	Rebel route agent	do	Oct. 2, 1865.
J. R. S. Wilson	do	do	Aug. 25, 1865.
Mitchell G. Willcox	Rebel tax assessor	do	Oct. 25, 1865.
M. D. Willcox	do	do	Oct. 18, 1865.
Thomas Watts	do	do	Aug. 31, 1865.
A. M. Wood	do	do	Aug. 31, 1865.
John Whidby	Rebel tax collector	do	Oct. 25, 1865.
William F. Williams	do	do	Oct. 6, 1865.
Larkin D. Watson	do	do	Oct. 2, 1865.
B. F. Willis	do	do	Sept. 16, 1865.
Josiah L. Warren	do	do	Sept. 28, 1865.
Thomas F. Willis	do	do	Oct. 10, 1865.
Charles L. Williams	Ex-United States and rebel postmaster	do	Oct. 25, 1865.
Thomas White	do	do	Oct. 18, 1865.
Robert E. Wylly	do	do	Oct. 18, 1865.

Georgia—Continued.

Name.	Exemption under amnesty proclamation of May 29, 1865.	By whom recommended.	Date of pardon.
Elijah Wells	Ex-United States and rebel postmaster	Governor Johnson	Oct. 6, 1865.
William G. Way	do	do	Oct. 2, 1865.
William Wood	do	do	Sept. 20, 1865.
William R. Willborn	do	do	Sept. 16, 1865.
James Whittle	do	do	Sept. 25, 1865.
William M. K. Watts	do	do	Aug. 31, 1865.
John Wall	do	do	Nov. 8, 1865.
John H. Walker	Rebel postmaster and tax assessor	do	July 5, 1866.
Western R. Welch	Rebel postmaster	do	Oct. 18, 1865.
Ladson Worley	do	do	Oct. 18, 1865.
James M. Watson	do	do	Oct. 18, 1865.
William J. Williams	do	do	Oct. 6, 1865.
Samuel A. Walkup	do	do	Oct. 2, 1865.
C. C. Willis	do	do	Sept. 11, 1865.
William S. Williams	do	do	Sept. 4, 1865.
Green M. White	do	do	Aug. 31, 1865.
J. L. Wikle	do	do	Oct. 10, 1865.
William Whitten	do	do	Oct. 10, 1865.
Luana Watson	do	do	Nov. 8, 1865.
N. K. Williams	do	do	Nov. 8, 1865.
U. B. Wilkinson	Rebel depositary, and worth over $20,000	do	Sept. 4, 1865.
George H. Winston	Rebel tax assessor, and worth over $20,000	do	Aug. 31, 1865.
George W. Woodruff	Rebel contractor, and worth over $20,000	do	Oct. 12, 1865.
W. H. Wiltberger	Paroled prisoner, and worth over $20,000	Hon. James M. Wayne, associate justice of the Supreme Court of the United States	June 30, 1865.
Campbell Wallace	Worth over $20,000	Governor Johnson and M. C. Fulton	Oct. 2, 1865.
Walter H. Weems	do	By order of the President	May 11, 1866.
J. F. Waring	do	do	June 19, 1865.
John R. Wilder	do	Hon. James M. Wayne, associate justice of the Supreme Court of the United States	July 25, 1865.
James J. Waring	do	By order of the President	July 18, 1865.
Hiram Warner	do	Hon. James M. Wayne, associate justice of the Supreme Court of the United States	Aug. 11, 1865.
LeRoy M. Wiley	do	Hon. E. D. Morgan, Alex. T. Stewart, John J. Cisco, John A. Stewart, John Sturges, John Slade & Co., and Tweed, Butterfield & Co., of New York.	July 20, 1865.
Arthur P. Wright	do	Governor Jenkins	Apr. 11, 1866.
Lucinda Williams	do	do	Apr. 11, 1866.
Andrew W. Walker	do	Governor Johnson	Nov. 13, 1865.
George W. Wylly	do	Governor Johnson, C. H. Hopkins, and A. S. Hartridge	Nov. 15, 1865.
Nicholas Wylie	do	Governor Johnson	May 19, 1866.
John L. Woodward	do	do	Sept. 20, 1865.
William G. Woolfork	do	do	Sept. 23, 1865.
Austin M. Walker	do	do	Sept. 23, 1865.
John P. C. Whitehead	do	do	Nov. 8, 1865.
J. W. Warrin	do	do	Nov. 8, 1865.
John B. Wright	do	do	Nov. 8, 1865.
John D. Watkins	do	do	Oct. 30, 1865.

John W. Wallace	do	do	Oct. 28, 1865.
Ruben S. Williams	do	do	Oct. 28, 1865.
J. Washburn	do	do	Oct. 28, 1865.
Isaac S. Whitton	do	do	Oct. 28, 1865.
P. L. Wade	do	do	Oct. 25, 1865.
Samuel B. Wright	do	do	Oct. 25, 1865.
Jesse S. Walton	do	do	Oct. 25, 1865.
J. M. Williams	do	do	Oct. 25, 1865.
Robert M. Williams	do	do	Oct. 25, 1865.
George Walker, jr	do	do	Aug. 31, 1865.
Irwin H. Woodward	do	do	Aug. 31, 1865.
Henry West	do	do	Aug. 31, 1865.
P. H. Whittaker	do	do	Aug. 31, 1865.
H. S. Wimbish	do	do	Aug. 31, 1865.
Daniel Ware	do	do	Aug. 31, 1865.
Augustus C. Ware	do	do	Aug. 31, 1865.
Rowan H. Ward	do	do	Oct. 18, 1865.
Edmund J. Walton	do	do	Oct. 18, 1865.
Joseph M. White	do	do	Oct. 18, 1865.
Bud C. Wall	do	do	Oct. 18, 1865.
John B. Whitehead	do	do	Oct. 18, 1865.
Matthew Whitfield	do	do	Oct. 10, 1865.
Philip West	do	do	Oct. 6, 1865.
William H. Whitehead	do	do	Oct. 6, 1865.
Andrew J. Ward	do	do	Oct. 6, 1865.
Joseph C. White	do	do	Oct. 6, 1865.
N. F. Walker	do	do	Oct. 6, 1865.
Charles P. West	do	do	Oct. 6, 1865.
Judith W. Winfrey	do	do	Oct. 2, 1865.
Ewell Webb	do	do	Oct. 2, 1865.
Thomas Whitsell	do	do	Oct. 2, 1865.
Jeremiah Walter	do	do	Oct. 2, 1865.
Thomas F. Wills	do	do	Oct. 2, 1865.
Benjamin V. Willingham	do	do	Oct. 2, 1865.
Lucinda H. Wright	do	do	Oct. 2, 1865.
Samuel W. Wynn	do	do	Oct. 2, 1865.
P. L. Wade	do	do	Oct. 2, 1865.
John R. Whitehead	do	do	Oct. 2, 1865.
John L. Wynn	do	do	Oct. 2, 1865.
James A. Wade	do	do	Oct. 2, 1865.
Edmund Walker	do	do	Oct. 2, 1865.
Maurice Wilkinson	do	do	Aug. 28, 1865.
Benjamin H. Warren	do	do	Aug. 28, 1865.
Ezekiel Williams	do	do	Aug. 28, 1865.
John B. Walker	do	do	Aug. 28, 1865.
William West	do	do	Aug. 28, 1865.
Robert R. Wimberly	do	do	Aug. 28, 1865.
Basil A. Wise	do	do	Aug. 28, 1865.
James A. Wright	do	do	Aug. 28, 1865.
Josiah Whitehurst	do	do	Aug. 28, 1865.
A. E. Ward	do	do	Aug. 28, 1865.
John N. Webb	do	do	Aug. 28, 1865.

Georgia—Continued.

Name.	Exemption under amnesty proclamation of May 29, 1865.	By whom recommended.	Date of pardon.
Jacob Waldburg	Worth over $20,000	Governor Johnson	Aug. 28, 1865.
Michael Wartzfelder	do	do	Aug. 25, 1865.
William G. Woodfin	do	do	Aug. 25, 1865.
Samuel G. White	do	do	Aug. 25, 1865.
Samuel E. Whitaker	do	do	Aug. 25, 1865.
Robert A. Ware	do	do	Aug. 25, 1865.
Ezekiel Wartzfelder	do	do	Aug. 25, 1865.
Benjamin A. White	do	do	Aug. 25, 1865.
William S. Whaley	do	do	Aug. 25, 1865.
Mrs. Eliza C. Woodward	do	do	Aug. 25, 1865.
John West	do	do	Aug. 25, 1865.
Bedford S. Worrill	do	do	Aug. 25, 1865.
Benjamin L. Willingham	do	do	Aug. 21, 1865.
Thomas H. Willingham	do	do	Aug. 21, 1865.
Thomas Willingham	do	do	Aug. 21, 1865.
Francis R. Wright	do	do	Aug. 21, 1865.
Andrew J. White	do	Hon. James M. Wayne, associate justice of the Supreme Court of the United States	Aug. 4, 1865.
James C. Whitaker	do	do	Aug. 4, 1865.
Moses Walker	do	Governor Johnson	Sept. 28, 1865.
James B. Wade	do	do	Sept. 28, 1865.
John W. Woolfolk	do	do	Sept. 28, 1865.
William Wells	do	do	Sept. 25, 1865.
Charles A. Walker	do	do	Sept. 25, 1865.
Henry J. Walker	do	do	Sept. 25, 1865.
James P. West	do	do	Sept. 25, 1865.
H. S. Wimberly	do	do	Sept. 25, 1865.
W. H. Wakefield	do	do	Sept. 25, 1865.
Joseph Wood	do	do	Sept. 13, 1865.
F. D. Wimberly	do	do	Sept. 13, 1865.
William Watkins	do	do	Sept. 13, 1865.
John W. Walker	do	do	Sept. 19, 1865.
James B. Walker	do	do	Sept. 19, 1865.
L. C. Warren	do	do	Sept. 19, 1865.
Willis Willingham	do	do	Sept. 16, 1865.
John R. Wallace	do	do	Sept. 16, 1865.
Alexander C. Walker	do	do	Sept. 16, 1865.
Edward R. Ware	do	do	Sept. 16, 1865.
Travis A. D. Weaver	do	do	Sept. 16, 1865.
John White	do	do	Sept. 16, 1865.
J. P. Williams	do	do	Sept. 16, 1865.
Marshal H. Wellburn	do	do	Sept. 15, 1865.
James M. Wellburn	do	do	Sept. 15, 1865.
John H. Walton	do	do	Sept. 11, 1865.
Robert Weldon	do	do	Sept. 11, 1865.

James T. Whitehead	do	do	Sept. 11, 1865.
Jeremiah Walters	do	Governor Jenkins	July 5, 1866.
Augustus P. Wetter	do	do	July 5, 1866.
C. S. Winn	do	Governor Johnson	July 5, 1866.
Mrs. E. L. Wyatt	do	do	July 5, 1866.
Samuel B. Warnock	do	do	July 5, 1866.
William J. Weeks	do	Governor Jenkins	July 5, 1866.
James Watson	do	Governor Johnson	Sept. 4, 1865.
Thomas Whaly	do	do	Sept. 4, 1865.
K. J. Willis	do	do	Sept. 4, 1865.
Joseph Winship	do	do	Sept. 4, 1865.
George W. Watkins	do	do	Sept. 4, 1865.
James H. Woolfolk	do	do	Sept. 4, 1865.
J. B. Willcoxen	do	do	Sept. 4, 1865.
W. P. Yates	Rebel postmaster	do	Oct. 2, 1865.
L. E. R. Young	Ex-United States and rebel postmaster	do	Oct. 28, 1865.
William H. Young	Rebel depositary and worth over $20,000	do	Aug. 28, 1865.
Pickens Yarbrough	Worth over $20,000	do	Oct. 28, 1865.
R. M. Young	do	do	July 5, 1866.
R. M. Young	do	do	Nov. 8, 1865.
Benjamin C. Yancey	do	do	Aug. 28, 1865.
Lewis Zachry	Rebel tax assessor	Governor Jenkins	July 5, 1866.

O